WHISPER OF COSMIC LAW

WHISPER OF COSMIC LAW

BY
LAMONT H. COLE

INKWELL PRODUCTIONS

Copyright January 2005
by Lamont H. Cole

Printed in the United States of America.
All rights reserved.
First printing February 2005.

No part of this book may be reproduced or transmitted in any form or by any means, electronic or mechanical, photocopying, recording, or by any information storage and retrieval system, without the written permission of the publisher, except where permitted by law.

ISBN: 0-9766340-1-5

Library of Congress Control Number: 2001012345

Published by
Inkwell Productions
6962 E. First Avenue, Ste.102
Scottsdale, AZ 85251
Phone (480) 481-6036
Fax (480) 481-6042
Toll Free 888-324-BOOK (2665)
Email: info@inkwellproductions.com
Web site: www.inkwellproductions.com

TABLE OF CONTENTS

IN THE BEGINNING	1
SECRET	23
LOWER MIND	53
HEAD POUNDING	110
GATHERING OF TOOLS	149
FUTURE BUILDING	195
NEVER ENDING JOURNEY	229
FASTING	239
MIND PUZZLE	266
THE POWER OF TRUTH	276
WHEN THE WIND BLOWS	292
GATHERING OF MALE HORMONES	302
DREAM READINESS	318

Introduction

Come with me on a voyage filled with secrets of the inner mind that will change your way ot thinking forever. Walk through doors that will lead you to an awakening of the powers of your mind. Feel the changes rush through you and see them change you as a person. You will become a stronger more powerful person than you ever thought possible. You will see things through a looking glass that was constructed on cosmic law, not man-made law.

These stories, dreams and daydreams are true. Oh, how many times I wish that they were not! I have wished that my spiritual guide, Koz, had chosen somebody else. But on the other hand, I have lived a life like no other. As my life unfolds, you are brought along on this cosmic trip. This trip is headed, not for a place, but for a higher level of thinking. Those who take this trip will be changed and will change those whom they touch. I only wish that I could reach everybody at the same time. I have benefited greatly from the guidance of Koz.

Let this trip of the mind flow in without judgment. Your judgment may not be your own, but the collection of the best intentions of men who wish to lead you to what they believe to be true. Every day they are eating their words as the truth becomes known. The world is not flat. The earth is not the center of the universe, not even the center of the solar system. Even the law that, "all things that go up must come down," has gone by the wayside.

Come now and join with me on a cosmic journey that will change forever how you think about things. Feel the feelings of change and how it builds power in you. Come along now with a fresh, open mind, as if it were seeing things for the first time. Let us now start this journey into the Giving Greater Known.

If you dare, the journey begins.
Lamont H. Cole

In The Beginning

In the beginning I was alone. There was only me. There were times when I thought I was in tune with the whole world and beyond. I knew that this was a special gift, I knew because nobody else was talking about his or her link with a higher knowledge source. I can tap into a very vast amount of knowledge. It has taken many years of life experiences to acquire this way of thought. My mind has linked into Cosmic Law. These ideas and actions have pushed me through a world wind of an adventure.

Cosmic Law was there first, before there were words, numbers, and man-made rules or laws. An ancient spirit adopted me. I named him Koz, short for the Knowledge from A to Z. I, at times, would go into a daydream. I would feel that I was not fully awake; things seemed hazy. During these hazy times I would have daydreams and see visions.

Come join this adventure of life experiences, dreams, daydreams and knowledge from cosmic law. Let this knowledge source that I call the Giving Greater Known work magic in your life. Let the journey begin.

I believe my journey into the Giving Greater Know started when I was a young child. During a near death illness, spinal meningitis and polio, I was infused with a healing energy. I was in a Hawaiian hospital. I had little chance of living. There was a great calling for help. This calling was of a very ancient source with deep roots in the Hawaiian way of thought. There was a family member of the Giving Greater Known (Cosmic Law) who needed help. This calling must be answered. The elders from many villages gathered together. Through a dream state they sent an energy surge. Energy flooded the hospital room. This energy was not meant for me, but for a Hawaiian boy in the bed next to me, but the Hawaiian boy was already dead before the healing energy arrived. There was no other choice; the energy was there and it would be used. I was very lucky to be in the bed next to this Hawaiian boy and receive this healing energy. KOZ (a healing force, a pure knowledge) went to work on me. It looked like a hopeless case, but after a rough three days of high temperature and sweats, I would have a full recovery with outstanding health. Many years later, through a process of arranging many thoughts and basic natural laws, things started to click. There was not a starting point. There was a pulling together of past thoughts and present actions. Come along with me on this journey that jumps from the past to the present and propels us into the future. These stories will, at times, seem disconnected. Follow the underlying message and structure to receive this message from the great beyond; the Giving Greater Known (Cosmic Law).

* * *

People Needing Help

It was a cold autumn. I was sitting in Bitch'n' Bobs Bar in Watford City, North Dakota. In came a man who was looking for help. His truck had broken down. I immediately was in the haze. There was a link of some sort between people needing help and me going into the state of no self-control, which I call the "haze." I told the man that I would do whatever it took to get him back on the road. It was dark, I suggested he stay at my place and we would tackle the problem in the morning. I ended up towing his pickup truck some 15 miles down into the Little Missouri River breaks south of Watford City, North Dakota. He thanked me and wanted to pay me, but I said no. Then he invited me to dinner.

* * *

A few days later, I entered a bar to find a lady crying. She explained that her husband was in jail for a non-sufficient check and that she only had $100 of the $250 bail. I was in the Haze. I went to my savings account, pulled out $150 and she and I went and bailed her husband out. They assured me that they would pay me back as soon as their social security check caught up with them. I never saw them again.

* * *

A while later, after helping the man with his truck, I was headed home. I was going through my regular routine. I would fill up two five-gallon containers with water, (I didn't have running water yet.) then I would stop off at the rural electric to see if there were any pallets that the transformers came on. I did this as long as the weather was good. The pallets are made of oak hard wood; they burned like coal, slow all night long. This was the only heat that I had besides my construction LP heater. This day was different. Leaning up against the back wall of the office were two used but nice doublepaned thermal windows. I went inside. It was a Friday about 4:30. There were just a few people left, one was the manager. I asked about the windows; he said that they were all spoken for by members of the board of directors. When I got home to my twenty-foot by twenty-foot shack that had no windows my phone was ringing. The man that I helped with the truck was asking if I would like to come down to eat and play some games tomorrow. After eating, the conversation got around to that I was building a house. I told him about the windows I missed out on, how I could have used them, and how the board members beat me to them.

The man, started to explain to me that it was the customers of the rural electric who had first rights to any of the materials that were left over from the remodeling of the business office, not the employees or the board members. He said he knew this to be a fact because his father was the director of the board of the Rural Electric Association. He gave his dad a call, explained what I had said, then handed the phone to me. His dad told me that I should have first choice and that I should go talk to the unit manager first thing Monday mourning. When I got there the unit manager said to follow him. He took me to a large metal building. Inside were all the remains of an extensive remodel job. There was a hot water heater, a 200 amp electrical panel with all the breakers in it, nine small windows and three medium, and a large plate glass window, doors, paneling, toilet, nine electric baseboard heaters with two automatic set back thermostats, and much more.

He asked me what my bid was. I said $500, he said sold. I was in the Haze, it was all too automatic. What had I done? I had no means to transport all that I had and no place to store it. When I got home I was in a bewilderment about how was I able to pick up $4,000 worth of building materials for $500. I asked the "why me?" question when things went right. This was different, I usually only asked this question when things were going wrong. I was still in the haze when Koz reverberated in my head: THINGS COME TO THOSE WHO GIVE!   I understood it; it was not something to be questioned. The message was pure intellect, known from the timeless cosmic knowledge bank.

From that day on I was a different person. I looked at how I conducted myself and what I had possibly done to have this universal law of giving and receiving unload on me and send my life into a whirlwind of an adventure. I could only think of the man whom I had helped with the truck. Oh, also the man I had bailed out of jail. And the time that I baby-sat for a lady free of charge for two weeks. Was that all that it was going to take to have good luck kick in?

Then KOZ boomed in: BE MINDFUL OF YOUR TAKING: THOUGHTS, WORDS, AND BODY LANGUAGE SO AS NOT TO TAKE FROM OTHERS!

I was on a search for any kind of link to this giving and receiving universal cosmic law. This was different, it was an area of thought I had never worked in before. It had no edges, no guidelines. It was a mental structure that was held together with strings of thought. I became a student of myself. What had I done in the past, and what was I doing in the present that might ruin this cosmic stew that had brought such good things my way? My past was easy, with a few apologies, and no hard feelings expressed in a few phone calls, I mended fences. KOZ tuned in: FORGIVENESS FREES THE MIND SO IT CAN FOCUS ON YOUR DESIRED GOALS.

After forgiving everybody for what I had perceived in my mind as being unfair to me, I set out to make sure that the individual was free from any thought of any animosity that they thought I held against them. I went back as far as I could think, looking at my past.

I was looking for any signs of this giving law. I wanted to relive them, to squeeze out the feelings and make them part of my present understanding. I wanted to build a bridge between the past and the present. I was doing this to see if I could see any patterns or correlations that I could use as guidelines for my future actions.

* * *

Ten Feet Tall

I was in Biloxi, Mississippi and of the age that I was able to make myself useful and pick up some pocket change; I was big into raking and mowing lawns. It was a very hot, sticky day in the summer of the late 1950s. I was walking down the road of Mugtown Trailer Court in Biloxi, Mississippi with my dad. He saw a lady mowing her lawn. He said that she should not be doing that and that his son would do it for her. I was in the haze; I jumped the fence and started mowing the lawn.

When I was done, it was dark. I had mowed, raked and bagged the trimmings. I was offered money, but I said that I could not take it. When I got home my father said, "You made me feel ten feet tall."

I got my new bike that summer. I remember that day as if it were only last week. The feelings come rushing forward and somehow give support to this process.

KOZ: YOU CAN'T GIVE WITHOUT RECEIVING, DEED, WORD, THOUGHT OR EXPRESSION. YOUR THOUGHTS ARE WHAT DRIVE EVERYTHING FROM THE EMPTY TO THE FULL.

* * *

Another time that I was in the haze was when I was a boy in Germany. It was my father's second three-year hitch there for the military. I was in the Boy Scouts and was at an International Jamboree when I was picked as an interpreter. One evening we went to visit a group of German scouts. There I was all of a sudden, a ten-year-old boy, the leader of the meeting. The German Boy Scouts were much older than the American Boy Scouts. Their ages were from nineteen to twenty-two.

We were invited into their tent. It was like an American Indian tent. There were three German Scouts and three of us in the tent. I found out that they shared the hauling of the tent. One would carry the poles, another the fabric, and another the pot and chain. They were slowly fueling a fire under the pot with pinecones. The pot was hanging from a chain off of the poles that met at the top of the tent. We were all sitting, leaning on our elbows to keep our heads below the smoke line. They dipped a tin cup into the pot, took a sip and passed it to the person next to them. When the cup came to me I took a sip. In the cup was a red semi-sweet wine, Glue Wine (German). The talk was flowing and the cup was the director of the conversation. The person with the cup had the floor. This night was a special night for there were new people to listen to. The wine, smoke, fire, body-touching- body environment was of a separate reality within a reality.

    I had learned that it was not what you knew that counted, it was what other people thought you knew that really counted. The feeling is like being stuck in a whirlwind of interactions, a dream state, like a mass of floating atoms that is not grounded anywhere but in touch with everything. It is something that is felt within oneself, a feeling that nothing could go wrong. I sure hoped my translations were accurate. I hope I did not take too much license. I have thought of this moment in time where minds were melding together in a collective thought process.

    Collective thought can structure the future in ways that are just now being brought to light for the masses. Gandhi, Martin Luther King, and Billy Graham, knew this to be true. If you get enough people to focus their thoughts in the same direction you can shape the future. People in power have used whatever means on hand to mold the thought patterns of the many. At first it was done by word of mouth, then by group meetings. When writing was invented it was used as the means to shift public thought. This process was enhanced with the printing press and movable type. The advent of the pony express, the car, the train and the airplane aided in the time factor of assimilation.

    Where people meet in small groups for conversation, there is a direct linkage into the cosmic knowledge source, the Giving Greater Known (Cosmic Law). The hard part was to reconfigure the group selection process. Present structure selects cookie cutter copies that run in circles based on the same teachers and textbooks. Cognitive Thinking Pools, work in a different mode than most think tanks. It's the adverse relationship that stretches the thinking patterns of minds. Throw a farmer, an engineer, a salesperson, a computer assisted draftsman, a mechanic, and a chiropractor together and see what kind of pick-up that would come off the drawing board. How will another person push you off center into another thought pattern that you would not have reached by yourself?

The key person to find is the observer, coach, and referee. This person is the overseer of the group. If thoughts are not kept in check they will go into an "I know what I know and you can't tell me anything different" mode. The mind is very protective of what it thinks to be right. It will try intimidating other minds, brow beating them into silence. It would like to change the other minds to its way of thought and in doing so receive a shot of a pleasure endorphin directly into the control function of the brain. This is why quiet people are so well liked: they are the catalyst for a self-centered recognition boost to one's own ego. All paths of informational flow must be left open. When a person has been identified as a dominant control force, he must be replaced as soon as possible. He may do well in another group. He should not be allowed to force his way of thinking on to someone else only to express his thoughts. There are some people who just won't adjust, a time factor demands their removal.

* * *

Speck Of Pepper

One speck of pepper in a stew will not make any difference in perceivable taste. But if you were to put it into your eye it surely would change your point of view. When we work with the nature of the giving and receiving area of our intellects we must be very careful. What your mind has become impressed with will upset the process. There are not any set guidelines. A speck of pepper is huge, it's off the scale, and in fact it is not even in the same realm or dimension as the workings of the mind. At this level we must think on a scale that has no perceptible weight, size, or shape for what we are dealing with is the electrochemical impulse that jumps from the dendrite across the synapse to the ganglion in a nerve string.

* * *

What I Have Quit Doing

It has not been what I'm doing that has dominated my new way of life but what I have quit doing that has brought me into alignment with the giving and receiving natural law of the Giving Greater Known. What small act done in the large realm of the physical will take this wonderful gift away from me? I have quit taking things that I have found. I turn them over to someone nearby whom I feel would have the chance to return them to their owner. Whatever their value it cannot hold a candle to the value of the natural giving and receiving law.

I find myself doing things like putting found pennies in gumball return slots or pony rides. The penny was not mine so I put it somewhere a young finger might find it. All those rubber bands, paperclips and pencils are now passed by. Today I found a pair of gloves on the grass near a shopping mall construction site. I picked them up and took them over to a worker. He thanked me. These seemingly small acts could have immense ramifications on the whole scheme of the giving process, they are not judged by the weight of their importance, but on a scale that is perceived by your mind. A big problem is that a person could be taking even when he perceives that he is giving, for example, you buy someone their fourth drink in an hour and they go out and kill themselves in a car wreck. I see so many people short-circuiting the whole process by cheating, lying, stealing, and scamming, always looking for the angle, the short cut. If they could control their beast within they would join the realm of the wonderment of life.

* * *

Thinking Bad Or Negative Thoughts

The area that I am working on now is to not think bad or negative thoughts about somebody else, because somehow this is perceivable by that person. I have been using my bottomless cavern system to stop this negative internal thinking. In my mind I write the thought down on a piece of paper, wad it up and throw it into one of those glacial crevasses that seem bottomless.

KOZ: NEGATIVITY DEPLETES VITAL FORCE, THE ENERGY NEEDED FOR THE BRAIN TO WORK.

* * *

Putting Yourself Last

As a young man I didn't have a father in my life. He was a military man and was gone a lot and when he was there, there seemed to be a wall of aloofness. I can remember that I qualified for the Big Brother mentor program one summer when my father was around. One day they took about ten of us boys to a creamery in Santa Rosa, California, in the mid-60s. I felt out of place. I had a father, what was I doing in this group? At the end of the tour, a box of ice cream bars were given to us. I was holding the box open, and I stood there in the Haze as the other boys grabbed the bars like a pack of wild dogs. The bars were all gone; I said I didn't need one, but they rounded one up for me. I was treated differently and talked to with a real sense of wanting to get to know me better. One of the Big Brothers said that my actions were commendable, the way I had not grabbed, in fact, putting myself last. The Big Brothers came by several times that summer, I had a good time.

KOZ: THOSE WHO PUT THEMSELVES LAST SHALL PUT THEMSELVES FIRST.

* * *

The Wrong Bus

I was standing outside Soto Conto Air Force Base trying to catch a bus to Laseba on the north shore of Honduras. The Haze was leading me; I had never been there before. With my son in tow, I got on the first bus that came along, but it was the wrong bus. It was a local going in circles around Cogmiwana. The bus driver said that the through bus to Laseba was right behind us. He let us out and we got on the bus behind us. My son said, "You did it again. Things always seem to work out for you." We got on the wrong bus, which turned out to be the right bus, because that was the only way to get on the right bus, which was a through bus that would not have stopped.

KOZ: A WELL-PROGRAMMED MIND WILL FIND THE SHORTEST PATH.

* * *

Copan

After La Ceiba, Honduras, we went to Copan, an ancient Mayan city. We got there late, found a hotel and went for a walk. I had stepped back in time thousands of years. I came across an ESL (English as a second language) school. I stopped to ask for directions to the Mayan ruins. One of the teachers said that her husband owned a local bar and he was a Mayan anthropologist who gave tours of Copan. I explained to her that I was on a tight schedule and that I would have to do the tour in the morning and be back at the Soto Conto Air Force Base that afternoon. She said that was no problem that her husband knew of some local drivers. I gave her my hotel name and room number. We continued our walk. A young man approached us with a flyer about the location of a rooftop reggae bar. My son gave me that look of disbelief as if to say, "You did it again. How did he know that we were looking for a place to eat and drink?"

It was a nice place. We ate a couple of chicken dinners, drank a few beers, and stared up into the ancient Mayan star-filled sky. When we got back to the hotel there was a note for me, "The tour would start at nine a.m., end at eleven, cost $35, and an air-conditioned mini bus would have us back to the air base by four p.m. Cost: two hundred dollars for a two hundred-plus mile trip." I got that look from my son again as he shook his head in disbelief.

* * *

Melding Of Ideas

There I was, fulfilling a lifelong dream, I was among the ancient Mayan ruins, but this was better than my dream, my son was with me and we had a personal guide, a Mayan anthropologist. He was able to read the ancient inscriptions and tell us the stories and history behind what we were looking at.

I stepped back to take a few pictures of my son and the guide. The whole experience was more than just the parts.

There was something else going on that I wanted to capture. Somehow the melding of what my ideas were and my son's expectations were and the Giving Greater Known had fused together and produced a surreal manifestation. KOZ: MINDS OF LIKE PATHS JOIN TOGETHER TO DEVELOP AN OUTPUT GREATER THAN ONE ALONE.

* * *

Fishing Trip

My son and I went on a fishing trip to Canada. A couple of weeks prior to going I started to look for a small outboard motor, five horsepower or less. I wanted it for my Sea Nymph canoe that had a flat backend to it. I found nothing and I told my son that I would find something on the way up or when we got there.

We were headed for Lac La Rouge. It was a two-day drive. The first day we paddled, no luck fishing. Second day I rented a motor, forty dollars a day, still no luck fishing.

We hit the bar, started talking to some locals. They invited us to their table. I told them of our luck, and they said that the lake had been commercially fished with nets and that it would be better if we went up to Stanley Mission, ten miles north.

I said what I really needed was a motor. A young man with the group said he had one for sale for $200.

"Let's go look at it." I said. I heard it start and said sold. I started to count out the money and he said that some cushions, a gas tank and a set of oars went with it, and since I was paying in U.S. dollars it would only be $180.

When I got back to the bar and told my son that we got our motor he just shook his head. I saw another group of people playing darts. I approached them, asked them if I could play and they said sure. They also told us that we should go up to

Stanley Mission to fish. One man said that I should tell the worker at the Northern Lights Supply store that he had sent me, and to let me use the empty faculty house. Another man asked how long we were going to stay and said that if we were still around in a week he would show us where to fish. The next day when we arrived at the Northern Lights store I used the wrong person's name, but he still let us use the fully furnished house. My son asked me if I was Jesus Christ or what, people were coming out of nowhere to help me. KOZ: WHEN ON THE PATH OF GIVING GREATER KNOWN, THINGS WILL COME WITHOUT WORDS.

Take this path with me, but I have been told that if you are not ready to have your life changed forever that you should stop this journey. For the brave souls who join me, wonders will abound and make of you a family member of the Giving Greater Known.

*** * * ***

The Giving

I called the man whom we met in the bar who said that he would show us where to fish. He came, towing a 30-foot boat that had a thirty-horsepower motor, and asked us if we were ready. We went a long way down two small rapids that my canoe wouldn't have made. He showed us his favorite fishing hole. He was using a jigging method of fishing that neither my son nor me were familiar with. We caught nothing, he caught five nice walleyes.

I was in a high state of awareness. I was looking for a feeling not a thing. I saw it in his eyes. I asked him why he was doing so much for my son and me. He said, "That he knew that I would, in turn, help someone else." On the way back, we stopped off at a small church that was a boat ride away from the reservation village. He filleted the Walleyes for us, and said, "Have a good stay, goodbye." My son and I looked at each other in awe and disbelief. KOZ: THOSE WHO ARE ON THE PATH OF THE GIVING GREATER KNOWN SEND OUT A MENTAL AURA THAT ALERTS OTHERS ON THE PATH.

* * *

Stopping

In the years prior to my military hitch I did not smoke very heavily, but then came the order, if you got them smoke them. It seemed the thing to do. The military supported the habit. They had smoke breaks, smoking areas, sold cheap cigarettes and all the cool paraphernalia from lighters (Zippos), to flints, and even little Velcro strap-on pouches for around your ankle to hold a pack of cigarettes.

If you did not smoke it was perceived that you did not need a break and you were given something to do. You were the oddball, not part of the group, somehow non-patriotic. It was the late sixties, a time of turmoil. When I decided to quit smoking, I was able to use some tricks that I got from KOZ. One thing that I did was I told myself that if I did not stop smoking by my thirty-third cigarette that a chunk of my head was going to blow out of the side. I used the film of the Kennedy assassination as a visual, the part where Jackie is trying to catch the chunk of scull from JFK as it bounced off the trunk of their car. After it happened to me it was going to happen to everybody else who smoked. I was on a crusade to save the smokers of the world, not just myself. I kept my quitting a secret; I did not need anybody telling me that I couldn't quit. The ridiculous (a chunk of skull blowing out of the side of my head) has a way of impressing the Lower Mind (a level of your brain that holds memories) that can help focus its energy in a multiplying force. It can be used on its own but has greater powers when used in conjunction with seriousness. KOZ: MANY TOOLS OF THE MIND ARE BETTER USED WHEN USED IN A MULTIPLE.

* * *

Word

The Lower Mind is impressed with the written word, more so when the words are written personally. The mind thinks this must be very important, the mind must go to work on it right away. Always keep a list of things to be done, written down in order of importance. This list should be read as soon as you get up in the morning every day. Every Monday morning, the list should be rewritten. Keep a pad of paper next to your bed, one in your car, and one on your person. Be ready for the next message from your Lower Mind that it has gathered from the Giving Greater Known.

After writing down a problem, always give the Lower Mind forty-eight hours to draw the answer from the Giving Greater Known. KOZ: TO PUSH THE LOWER MIND INTO FULL ACTION ONE MUST BUILD A MENTAL STACK TO BUILD UP PRESSURE TO FORCE THE LOWER MIND INTO ACTION, MANY TOOLS MUST BE USED AT THE SAME TIME. It took me many years of studying this process to see it working in my life. It has gotten me away from wishful thinking to actually building a working foundation for action in my mind. I see these tools that push the mind as part of a recipe for action that pushes me to greater and greater accomplishments.

* * *

Not Alone

The Lower Mind is very watchful of everything that is going on in its environment. This environment has a structure of four levels from which it draws. First the normal environment, the common day inputs, conversations, television, reading, theater, and all the visual information that is your ongoing multi-billion bite-receiving function. Second, the internal dialogue, which are your wants and desires, no matter how grandiose or inconsequential. Third, the pulling in from the Giving Greater Known that will give the linkage with other minds that builds a cosmic shortcut. Forth is input at a level not yet perceivable, which has been called intuition. KOZ: THE MIND MUST BE LED LIKE A CHILD THROUGH THE WILDERNESS OF THE COLLECTIVE THOUGHT. THESE TOOLS TO PUSH THE LOWER MIND ARE OF THE MOST IMPORTANCE.

I along with you, have a hard time following this way of thought. I see this work of impressing the Lower Mind into action as one of my most cherished secrets. The Lower Mind is the go-between me and my Higher Mind, which can tap into the Giving Greater Known. Stay with me as we learn more of how this works and builds power within us.

* * *

Yes-No Rebound

I coined the Yes-No Rebound. It was like bouncing a black basketball off of the backboard and getting a white one back, then a black one back. There seemed to be a direct link between yes and no. To understand this process, I thought about the idea that these two neural pathways lie side by side, the only thing separating them is the two submicroscopic thicknesses of the myelin sheeting. As in electrical wiring, there is bleeding between them. Whenever the yes is thought, it bleeds over into the no. Whenever the no is thought, it bleeds over into the yes. This is an inescapable function in the thought process. If you are not aware of it, you will find yourself in a mind knot that will make spur of moment decisions that may be detrimental to your direction in life. Advanced breakdown of the myelin sheeting will bring on MS and Alzheimer's. You must think of the yes-no rebound as an automatic function of the brain. It is how your brain is wired, it is not you. Knowing this, you will be able to sidestep bleed-over and re-think a choice between yes or no. KOZ: BRAINWAVE MIXING IS NECESSARY TO THE HIGHER BRAIN PROCESSES.

* * *

Have No Conflicts

Now I am ready to start a new adventure. Every day from now on will be a joy to see what may come my way. I will have my eyes peeled looking for something to do for somebody else. KOZ: HAVE NO CONFLICTS BETWEEN YOUR PERCEIVED MORES AND YOUR ACTIONS. This was hard for me to grasp. It would take me many years of inner mind looking to really know my deep-rooted set of values. I learned that these conflicts could undermine everything else that a person has tried to put together. While your thoughts are stuck on a conflict it can't tap into the Giving Greater Known. I would not be able to even imagine not being tuned into this knowledge and healing power. The mind will go into a fixed action pattern, doing things that are rooted in a protection mode. It takes a higher level of thinking to keep those automatic patterns in check. I wonder if I will ever be fully free of the beast inside my psyche. I often find myself revaluating past actions and things that I have said. This is an on-going work in progress for me, not really knowing in what direction it's going in. I will always be on the lookout for new tools given to me from the Giving Greater Known that will help me resolve my inner conflicts.

* * *

Scared

My son and I had just left Kadena Air Force Base Okinawa. We were standing waiting for the traffic light to change. It was sunset and the light was dim. All of a sudden my son was startled. Off to his left, just in his peripheral vision down in the gutter, something had moved. It could have been anything; we were already at a state of high awareness. In a foreign country a very long way from home, where every ten steps brings something new or different, the senses go on high alert. A second look revealed that it was a little old lady begging for money. To this very day his eyes will get big and he will shake all over when I remind him of it. Scary has a unique way of impressing the mind into a quickened set of actions that is related to survival. This tool is best used along with the ridiculous. KOZ: TO BE SO MOTIVATED IS A GOOD TOOL TO USE BUT DO NOT HOLD TOO MANY BAD THOUGHTS, THEY DRAIN YOU OF ENERGY. If I can see that my mind has slowed in working on a problem, I can scare it into action. All I have to do is bring scary feelings to the forefront at the same time giving it instructions of what needs to be done. Letting the mind know who's Boss. More on this subject later.

* * *

Guardian At The Gate

A brain looping sequence is when your thinking of your past fills your present and it becomes your future again. Everything that you supply the brain will become part of your future. The Guardian At The Gate is there to make sure that mind polluting inputs that disrupt or replace the hard-fought-for self-made deep implants into your Lower Mind are not allowed in. Be very mindful of what you read, watch on television or what shows you go to. Be very careful of whom you bring into your circle of close friends. Be aware that your work environment is not adversely affecting the rest of your life. There are people who are paid to insert all kinds of secret agendas into what would be passed off as entertainment. KOZ: DON'T LET THOSE THAT DON'T KNOW THAT THEY DON'T KNOW POLLUTE YOUR BRAIN. I find myself leaving movies after only five or ten minutes. I will stay clear of negative people. I will let people know that I will not put up with illegal actions. I let them know from the onset and this filters a lot of bad inputs away from me.

***

Inward Looking Eye

This technique is done at night as you fall to sleep. Put a slight amount of pressure on one eye and start looking for pictures stored in your brain. The brain stores memories in pictures, not words and numbers. We don't read a dream, we see it in our minds eye. At first you will only see lines or bright spots; watch these carefully and they will turn into pictures and stories. This is looking at the contents of the Lower Mind, which creates your future through the Giving Greater Known.

At this point you can shape your future: if you see things that are not part of your plan you can change them. This is done by replacement; using repetitive new overriding thoughts in a session of meditation. Your work can be checked the next night and adjusted as necessary. If there are not any pictures forming after a few minutes go into Future Building. More on this later.

* * *

Cosmic Shortcut

Tapping into the Lower Mind of others is a Cosmic Shortcut. Not only will they bestow upon you their collective knowledge of many years, they will be happy to do so. It will make them feel good. The real bonus is when they tap into the Giving Greater Known, and the next day call you up with a suggestion. Quit trying to think with your Middle Mind for new ideas, it is only a gatherer. When you have a problem, tap into the Cosmic Shortcut. Add this information to your Lower Mind. Let it incubate, when it comes to you, you will know it. Write it down to impress the Lower Mind. Stay on this path developing a Cosmic Stack of Lower Minds and the Giving Greater Known. When you have done this process many times, you will feel the power within you, with which you can at any time tap into the Giving Greater Known. KOZ: THE GIVING GREATER KNOWN CAN ONLY BE TAPPED INTO BY THE LOWER MIND THRU THE HIGHER MIND WHEN THERE HAS BEEN A CHALLENGE THROWN DOWN THAT THE LOWER MIND IS UNABLE TO WALK AWAY FROM. I see this as an area that I can do a lot of work on. The more time I spend on enlisting the help of others in impacting my mind, the more often things will fall into place for me. I have been using this system for many years and it always amazes me how well it works.

***

Challenge

The Challenge is a tool that can focus the mind in an all-consuming, driving force. There are three facets to the Challenge. You can Challenge somebody else's Lower Mind either in a positive or negative way. "I bet you won't amount to much: You are a loser" or, "I know you can do it, go for it, don't let them get you down." You can Challenge somebody else's Lower Mind to Challenge somebody's Lower Mind like an instigator but in a positive mode. The facet that has the best effect is when you Challenge yourself. The self-challenge is totally under your control; it should be used every day. Start off with a very small challenge such as reading ten minutes a day. Build on your success and feel the newfound inner control. KOZ: THE SELF-CHALLENGE IS MADE MORE POTENT WHEN IT IS KEPT FULLY INTERNAL, LINKED WITH THE SECRET. At first I didn't think to much of this inward challenge. As time goes on you will find how important this internal self-challenge is. The starting point of an inner challenge is the hardest part. Your brain will see this as change and rebel. I make sure that I always let it be part of the process that the challenge is only a temporary experiment. I use an egg timer telling myself that when the bell dings I'm done. The starting is easier when the finish line has been drawn.

***

Secret

The word secret seems to have its own special pull on the mind. When talking of a secret we seem to shift our voice volume to a whisper. The only true way to tell a secret is to whisper it to a person. The whisper is so linked with a secret that the mind thinks of them like smoke and fire. The saying is "where there is smoke there is fire". When the brain detects a whisper it perceives that there must be a secret lurking about. This mind bending can be captured and be a useful tool of the mind. When the mind holds onto a bit of information that it believes that it is a secret it feels a position of power. This feeling of power is at our command. Linking the secret to a challenge or a change in our lives will make the process flow. Keeping it a secret will guard it from attack.

*＊＊

Internal Brain Shift

There I was at the bottom rung of all job assignments, snowplow control, night shift. Who were they kidding? I controlled nothing. This was one of those jobs that the military dished out that never hits your record. They knew I was a married man, that I was highly trained. This was pure punishment. All I was doing was supplying things for the snowplow drivers. They would check them out and return them after their shift was done. Tire chains for 20" wheels, shovels, safety kits, flashlights, and sleeping bags. I could have let all this get the best of me. I was in the Haze. I did an internal brain shift out of my left-brain into my right. Koz had never let me down. There had to be something that I was being pushed into. I found it. I was able to study for my SAT and get accepted to Great Falls College. I took only one class, freshman English composition. I got a C. It was enough to make me a transfer student when I applied to South Dakota State University.

Everything that I had done wrong was the right thing to do one more time. The only way that I could have had a night shift was by them thinking that it was the worst thing going. If they knew that I was glad to have the time to study and to be away from the day shift and all of its back stabbing ladder-climbers, they would have surely moved me. I was in my own universe there was not a chance that they could even grasp the endless grand voyage that I was on. All they could see was that I was bucking the system and that would get me absolutely nowhere. Oh! if they knew what powers I had they would have stood in awe. They were not my powers they were everybody's that would just tap into the Giving Greater Known. KOZ: LET THE INTERNAL MIND SHIFT; PUSH YOUR LOWER MIND INTO THE MENTORSHIP OF THE GIVING GREATER KNOWN. The personal stories that I tell are meant to build pictures in your mind. This will flood your Lower Mind with a mass infusion of energy that it can use to link into the Giving Greater Known.

* * *

Mind Energy

The ability to tap into the Giving Greater Known takes large amounts of cosmic energy, Mind Energy. You must always be looking for ways to increase your storage of mind energy. If you are down the proverbial dead end alley, depressed, non-communicative, isolated, suicidal, take action. Get on the phone. Find a place to volunteer your time; this will build up your Mind energy. The minute you touch the phone with this intent in mind the process begins. As you meet new people, tap into their Lower Minds. Tell people your dreams; what you are looking for, a job, a car, a mate… Use the secret of the cosmic short cut, tapping into others people's minds. If you don't quit, it won't fail you, it can't, it is a cosmic universal law. If at first it seems that you are not getting anywhere, remember the 48hr rule about the Lower Mind being able to retrieve feedback from the Giving Greater Known. Some people you talk with may have lost this link, so look for others. There is a lag time from when the Lower Mind receives enlightenment from the Giving Greater Known to the time the Middle Mind will adopt it as a truth. Then there is another lag of time until the Middle Mind can conceive the gravity of the enlightenment and express it in words. Then there is yet another lag of time to find the use and application to one's own life. At this point you must assimilate this information into your Lower Mind and give it 48hrs to tap into the Giving Greater Known. Be patient with this process; there is no other. Be kind to yourself give yourself a chance to build a new path to travel. Work the system over and over again. Do not, give up. You are working for the future that is rightfully yours. This is your right under the cosmic universal law. Your life is going to change, be ready to accept change. KOZ: STEP FORWARD. WALK INTO THE FAMILY OF THE COLLECTIVE LOWER MIND. IT IS YOUR BIRTH RIGHT. DON'T THROW IT TO THE WINDS. Don't give up. Stay the course. Powers unimaginable will be at your command.

* * *

Self-Asking Question

The Self-Asking Question is a short cut to your Lower Mind. It should be asked not expecting an answer at that moment. Give the Lower Mind a period of time that is open-ended, so that it may tap into what is already at hand. Give it time to tap into the Lower Minds of others. Give it time to seek help from the Giving Greater Known. Be even-handed. Ask why this is happening when things are going well or badly. This should be done daily in a meditation mode, sitting with eyes closed. This is a very important extension of your nightly Inward-Looking; many people have found out that they fall asleep very readily in this mode. Falling asleep is the natural flow of this process; it is what happens when we shift into the Giving Greater Known. KOZ: THE GIVING GREATER KNOWN HAS ALWAYS BEEN THERE WAITING TO HELP ANYONE WHO IS WILLING TO SEEK IT OUT. MANY DO NOT REACH THE NEXT LEVEL OF THOUGHT BECAUSE THEY CONTINUALLY TRY TO SEARCH THEIR MIDDLE MIND FOR GUIDANCE.

* * *

Preaching And Teaching

The Lower Mind feels that it is working at its fullest extent when it is preaching or teaching. In this mode if it is really connecting with the students, it has the ability to receive Mind Energy from each student. You know when you are in this mode of mind fluxing when you finish teaching, and the students want to shake your hand as they leave and say thank you. I have volunteered over 150 hours to Lutheran Social Services teaching English as a second language. These students are very eager to learn. They can sense when you are really there to help. I like working with the new students. It takes a lot of patience. I learn something every time I teach. KOZ: TEACHING IS A PURE FORM OF GIVING AND WHEN DONE TO MANY AT ONE TIME IT IS THE BEST WAY TO BUILD UP MIND ENERGY. I along with you am going through this transformation. The format of this book is like nothing I have ever read before. For me I'm going to follow this path as written, trying not to let my preconceived ideas of how things should go get in the way of receiving this message from the great beyond. The more out of the man made norm, the more I feel that I have found something worth trying.

* * *

Dream Within A Dream-Mind Energy Stacking

A dream is pure mind energy coming from the Lower Mind. Be sure you write down every bit and piece of a dream, for this is a window to what the Lower Mind has been impressed with. When your dream is inside of another person's dream, the fluxing of Lower Minds has a multiplying effect. Bring your dream with you and show it around. It will find another Lower Mind to flux with. Don't give up. If you have found a person with a dream and you are now inside of their dream, you must take care not to try to change or control that person's dream. They have put a lot of mind energy into their dream at great cost. They have taken energy away from their ability to tap into the Giving Greater Known. They have used up energy that would have been in reserve for healing. They have used up the energy that is needed for the working of the four brains. They have calculated their expenditures of energy very closely. Keep in check your wants and desires and focus on giving them as much of your mind energy as you can without running yourself short. When the dream holder feels that you are giving him some of your mind energy freely he will give some back to you. He will also take obstacles out of your way so that you may concentrate on sending him more mind energy. He will pay or give you more of whatever you need to stay focused on his dream. If it is money, a place to live, or a car, if this will free up some of your mind energy they will do it. Mind energy is more valuable than any of these things. There is just so much mind energy a person can generate. He must rely on others for more if his dream is so big that he alone will not be able to supply enough mind energy. Mind energy, it is not for sale. It must come to you freely from other people. If you start taking too much energy from the dream holder you will find yourself outside of the dream looking for another. KOZ: STACKING LOWER MINDS WILL GIVE YOU THE POWER TO DRAW IN LARGE AMOUNTS OF MIND ENERGY. THIS STORAGE OF ENERGY IS WHAT MAKES THE DIFFERENCE BETWEEN THOSE WHO PULL OUT OF A GREAT ILLNESS AND THOSE WHO DON'T. I feel that someone is finally telling me the truth and really giving me some concrete step-by-step instructions that I can follow. I'm going to stay the course. Stay with me on this mind and thought-provoking journey from the great beyond.

* * *

Power Of Oneness

The power of Oneness is the knowledge that I myself have great powers to change things. Change starts with the changing of the instructions and inputs to the Lower Mind. The power of Oneness also is the use of the Guardian at the Gate to keep other people from sabotaging your hard-fought Lower Mind programming. When you keep your actions a secret, there are not any targets set up for others to take potshots at. The Lower Mind is very impressionable; it, like a young child, must be protected from those who would like to steal a portion of your mind, no matter how small. These three things, (change in the instructions to the Lower Mind to be more of a precise direction), (keeping your plan a secret to protect it), and the use of the (Guardian at the Gate to keep detrimental thoughts out), can be put into action. This is the Power of Oneness. Governments, corporations, institutions, clubs, gangs, would like you to give this internal birthright, power given to you by the universal cosmic law, to them. They want the control of your mind for their agenda. Anything that even hints of self-control must be outlawed and snuffed out.

I heard of a judge that wanted to step down and return to his private practice and spend more time with his family. The workload of being a judge was getting more and more and he was not being compensated for his time. The Federal Court System would not let him step down. In fact if he even tried to quit they would slap him with some heavy fines and challenge his right to practice law. This very smart man was able to sidestep all these problems. He went to a local food store and stole a package of meat. Now he was a kleptomaniac and could not be a judge. How this would ruin his life. His was the last laugh; all his lawyer friends, clients and family knew what the real story was. This wise man used the system against its self to solve his problem.

KOZ: DON'T WASTE YOUR MIND ENERGY ON CHASING, CHALLENGING, REPLACING OR CHANGING. USE IT FOR GETTING AROUND IT. SYSTEMS LIKE THESE ARE PUT TOGETHER BY THE WEAK-MINDED TO PROTECT THEMSELVES. I feel that I must continue this path of transformation for those that may follow. This process has become bigger than me alone.

*　*　*

Champions

The Lower Mind knows what it knows and goes into an automatic search pattern to find what you have impressed on it what you want. It will come up with the best answer to your wants with what information it has. This answer may not be correct or the best way to do it. One's first step is to be aware of one's own Lower Mind's limitations. This is where the Middle

Mind plays a very important role. It must choose whether the Lower Mind should handle the problem alone or in combination with the Giving Greater Known. If there is a time factor that will not give this process enough time to follow the natural course, then you must find an external Lower Mind, a Champion. This must be done at the moment of the earliest detection of one's own Lower Mind's limitations. The thing to key off of is the feeling of frustration. Frustration is your Lower Mind telling you to back off, that it needs more time to tap into the Giving Greater Known or that we need a Champion on this one. KOZ: CHAMPIONS ARE BEST USED IN A STACKING MODE IN DIFFERENT FIELDS OF EXPERTISE.

* * *

Left Brain-Right Brain Shift

When you are being confronted, analyze that person's mindset. Is this person in his right-brain where all the pictures and creativity are, or is he in his left-brain, where all the words and numbers are. You must know which brain you are talking to or your time will be wasted.

One time I was being chewed-out by one of my employers. I could see that he was in his left-brain where all the words and numbers were. I said that if the work on my desk got any higher I would have to grow a neck like a giraffe to see over it. I would have to grow arms like an octopus to shuffle paper, and another set of arms like a gorilla to move the stacks around. I was thinking of getting a scooter to do my running around with. This has shifted him into his right brain. He would have to picture me with a giraffe's neck, octopus arms, gorilla arms, and running around the hallways on a scooter. Now the shift to the left-brain: but I will get on your project right now, you will have it by 3:00.

He was stuck in his right brain, unable to shift back to his left-brain, to find the words and numbers to continue to chew me out. So he turned away as he said "good", shaking his head, still looking at that mythical beast riding a scooter down the hall, having no idea he had been mind shifted. When used in conjunction with a challenge it can be a formidable tool.

I needed some time off work. I approached my supervisor. He was stuck in his left-brain and his showing of emotions let me know that the beast was about. I said I would get back to him later in the day; I had something important to ask him. This also used the secret tool; he will be wondering all day long what I might have that was important. Later that day he was more receptive. In fact He was anxious to see me, wanting to hear my question to get rid of that nagging sense of something that he did not know: what was the (Secret) that was so important? I said that I was going to have to quit or have myself cloned. I need two of me running around in circles to get everything done. That put him into his right brain. Now the (Challenge). I don't know if you can help me or not? (Back to the left-brain.) I have to take my son to a new day-care. He would throw a fit and do a lot of crying if my wife takes him, and I need to get tags for my truck. I know the workload around here is heavy but if you could give me just a half-day off it would help. (Restate the Challenge,) I sure hope you can be able to do this; if you can't I will understand. His answer was. Why sure you can have the time off. Take whatever time you need. That solves that. I thought you had a real problem. Brain shifted one more time, not knowing what hit him; he was still in his right brain seeing my two selves walking the halls. KOZ: INTERNAL BRAIN SHIFTING WILL GIVE YOU POWERS TO MOLD YOUR REALITY, TO SHAPE YOUR FUTURE.

* * *

Laughter

There are ways to build short duration bursts of mind energy internally. Laughter is one of these tools; the best is laughing out loud, from the gut until your jaws and sides ache. Even if you only hear someone laugh this will transfer mind energy to you. Just seeing somebody else laugh and not hearing him or her also works. Not only does this gain energy, it also impresses the Lower Mind that things are in order. It feels that it can get on to the work of tapping into the Giving Greater Known. The laughter covers over any internal conflicts between your Lower Mind and your Middle Mind. This is an internal cosmic universal law inside all of us to be able to push forward even in the direst circumstances. People will break out laughing even at the point of death. People will laugh when given a sentence of life in prison. They will laugh after crying in heartache to the point of tears and start crying again and then laughing again. This tool is the key to the safety net of the fragile physiological and emotional frailties that must be continually managed to subvert mental breakdowns. People that have little or no laughter in their lives must learn to fabricate some in any way that they can without seeming to be off balance. Even though we have internal systems to supply all the laughter needed, an outburst out of the blue will put you in a straight jacket. So to keep the laughter legitimate we will go to the movies, the opera, tell a joke, watch a funny TV show or listen to funny songs, and do anything to give pretext to why we are laughing. Any laughter without any supporting pretext is questioned? They want to make sure that they are not missing out, or that you are not laughing at them. And the answer, "Oh, it's nothing," just won't cut it. It will be met with, "Oh, come on, you can tell me. KOZ: PEOPLE MUST REMOVE THEMSELVES FROM ANY CONTROL THAT DOES NOT PROMOTE LAUGHTER, HOME, FRIENDS OR WORK. If you have been putting the force of Koz into your life or seeing more and more things that key into and relate to his message, you have become a family member of the collective Giving Greater Known. This process will take some time to become part of your Lower Mind. I have been in this cosmic whirlwind for years and still find more powers and universal knowledge through short bursts of what Koz has told me than anything else out there has to offer.

***

Music

As a young man, things were not the best. Between my father taking an isolated no dependent tour of duty to Pakistan and my mother seeing another man while she was still married to him, I was just not in the plans. One night when the sheriff was called because I had come home late, I was hauled away to juvenile hall. The trumped up charge was "uncontrollable." After three 89 day maximum stays before they had to give you a court date, I was sent to Fout Springs Boys Ranch. On Christmas of that year a counselor thought it would be nice if the boys would put a choir together. I think the only thing I had ever memorized in my life to that time was "Chestnuts Roasting On An Open Fire". Song, singing, chanting, and (story-telling) were the tools of early man to instill into the Lower Mind information that was passed down from generation to generation. Most of the western world has turned this valuable tool into a plaything used for entertainment. These tools should be picked back up, dusted off, the rust scrapped off and well oiled. Do you remember when you learned your ABCs it was a song? "ABCDEFGeee... Now I know My ABCs. Aren't you proud of me?" We still find ourselves running through this song when we are trying to remember someone's name. KOZ: THE

LOWER MIND IS A CHILD THAT IS LAZY, THESE TOOLS TRICK IT INTO HOLDING ONTO INFORMATION WHETHER IT WANTS TO OR NOT. YOU ARE NOT YOUR MIND IT IS A TOOL TO WORK WITH. To re-establish these tools so that they become part of you, will give you control. Until you have these firmly cemented into your Lower Mind, keep this transformation a secret. This is a very vulnerable stage when all sorts of people wouldn't like to see you in control, and their Lower Mind is too lazy to go through this transformation. It will not be possible to get everyone to give up his or her established mental security blankets.

* * *

Movies

Movies have been with us for a long time. They are the Lower Minds way of transferring vast amounts of information from the Giving Greater Known. All the wants and desires of the Middle Mind are transformed from words to internal mind movies that are presented to the Higher Mind. Inside of each one of us that still has a fresh brain, there is a vastly superior mode of transferring information. This brain of ours is a true gift from the cosmic communication network. The caveman knew of this when he drew on the wall. Those images were some of the first stages of transferring large segments of information in an instant. Looking at the American Indian and the fire dance you can see the movie story, hear, smell, and feel the change of the fire's heat as the dancers pass in front of you. They had it down to a science, on how to instill into the Lower Mind messages of hunting, of war, or the need for rain. They along with the aborigines of Australia had cosmic powers that we beat out of them in various physical and mental ways. The scientific thought patterns of many island peoples have been outlawed so as to be able to replace their vastly superior established Lower Mind with a set of rules to control them. In America we ripped young children from their mothers' arms and sent them off to white mans' school. This was the only way that we could break the chain of Lower Mind to Lower Mind transferring of information from their elders. This was done again when the one room schoolhouse was centralized. There were no more reports of who didn't show up to school by the children. These reports were Lower Mind to Lower Mind communications between family units, which made them strong. "Oh Billy didn't show up I will take a ride over to their farm to see if there's a problem." Each and every time that Koz wishes to interject his cosmic knowledge I have various indications through body feelings. I have left these out in the past and will in the future to facilitate writing. But I want you to know that they are still there and even more intense. I have felt a sense of urgency so I have extended my writing sessions. KOZ: ALL THINGS WILL HAVE TO BE LOOKED AT WITH SUSPICION USING THE RULES OF COSMIC UNIVERSAL LAWS. I have the feeling that I am walking around in a crowd of unknowing brain-fried zombies. The shame of it all is what we could be doing together as a collective thought force, not having the powers-that-be, pitting us against each other. I think it was Martin Luther Kings' point of view, he had a movie story: "I Have A Dream." At this point a rush went through my body. I got goose bumps, a message from Koz that I am on the right path.

* * *

State Of Nothingness

The Lower Mind is lulled into a state of nothingness that it must be pushed out of. When it hits its self-realized point of "I have arrived, this is where I'm going to stay" it is called homeostasis.

    I was needed. My Aunt Roe was a small lady who needed my help. Art, her husband, was a 240+ pound man and was wheelchair-bound. He had contracted cancer of the brain and liver. He was too much to handle on a good day. When he was feeling the effects of his radiation and chemotherapy he would fall. There was no way that she could move him. She would have to call 911 and the Para-medics would come and get things back in order. This is where I could help and so I came in my camper and stayed until he passed on and I felt that my Auntie Roe was in good hands in making this transition in her life. Art my Uncle was told that he should stop smoking, stop drinking, that it did not help with the medication. There, they said it. The doctors had spoken. This was the end of it. No more need be said. He was stuck in the Nothing State. His deeply implanted Lower Brain habit patterns were left intact, even the fear of death would not budge them, and there was not a support system to make this transition. When he didn't quit smoking and drinking they blamed all his problems on him. The news came back from the doctor, nothing more to do; we only give you six weeks. I felt that this was a very cold and cruel way of saying that it was your entire fault and we are giving up on you. I could do only what was needed to make life more bearable for Aunt Roe.

    It is all of our jobs to be able to realize and know when we have entered into the state of nothingness. Then take out the cosmic tools given to us by Koz to push the Lower Mind into change. I told my son that, although I do not consider that I'm killing myself in getting things done by any means; I do something towards my goals every day. This makes it look like I'm getting a lot done compared to someone stuck in the Nothing State. He came out with a profound statement that made my heart sing: "A person should do more than nothing." Wow, I had been getting through to his Lower Mind. KOZ: DON'T

BE JUDGMENTAL. LOWER MINDS NOT TAPPED INTO THE GIVING GREATER KNOWN ARE BUT WANDERING SOULS THAT ARE YET TO BE HARVESTED AND TO BE ALIGNED WITH THE COLLECTIVE FAMILY OF THE LOWER MIND. I have learned to be kind to myself and not to drain too much of my Mind energy off helping others. After draining energy I go to places to recharge, for what would I be able to give if I were empty? Join with me; you also have the energy to give. This will build power in you that will draw in larger and larger amounts of Mind energy.

* * *

Judgment

No matter how many times you put air in a tire that has a slow leak, in the morning you will have a flat tire. There are things that people do that are slow leaks of their Mind Energy. One of these is the judgment mode of life. They are the people who will not shut up at the theater; they have something to criticize every two minutes. Out come the shushes and awe- shut ups. Don't they realize that it is just a movie? We are in just a movie, this life of ours. We play just a small part, just a stand in, an extra; we are just a ticket holder. It is not our job to police everything that is said or done. Some people never seem to be satisfied; no matter what you say or do there are always things that are wrong. I remember this feeling of being on the receiving end of such a person as that. It made me feel that, that person was very unfair and mean spirited and got some kind of joy out of my dilemma.

This was our free time, the time between when we were done being chewed on about everything by the drill instructors and time to go to bed. This was a time and space to shine your shoes to a spit shine polish, to fold your underwear so it was the width of the length of a dollar bill, a time and place to learn the code of conduct that had to be memorized. Finally there was no one yelling in your ear about the latest thing that you had done wrong. Your mind, body and beat up spirit were set free of this spin cycle called Basic Training. Oh to be able to just lie down and take the weight off your sore, aching feet. In they came, the drill instructors. They made a beeline for the mop closet. Three mad men in action. There was no rhyme or reason behind their actions. They could have said, "This closet needs some cleaning up" and it would have been done. No, they had to yell like deranged mad men at everything they thought was wrong. One was pulling things out, yelling what was wrong, handing something to one of the other two drill instructors. He in turn threw the item down the hall in one direction and then the other direction. "Look at this can of cleanser. There's cleanser on the top of it." He handed it off, one of them came out with a knife, cut the top off, and threw it down the hall, spewing cleanser all over the other things they had thrown in the hall. There we were, taking our turns peeking down the hallway and turning back into the room covering our mouths to hold in the laughter so as not to be heard. We just stood there shaking our heads at the antics of these three men who wanted us to respect them enough that we would do anything for them, even go into battle. All they did was lose respect. Who would follow such childish actions anywhere? Their last words as they were leaving were, "OK ladies inspection in 30 minutes. Lets get this F- mess cleaned up." We were all thinking how much we hated them and how they should clean it up, they did it. After an assignment as a drill instructor I wonder how their lives turned out, after draining off so much Mind Energy for hours day in and day out. What was their retention rate in the military? Or were they just, tools of the system? What was their divorce rate, suicide rate? I really already have a good idea. A person cannot take and take without things taken from them, and all I can do is pray for these men assigned the task of taking. I forgive them for their trespasses. KOZ: INTERNAL JUDGMENT CAN BE EVEN MORE DRAINING THAN THE EXTERNAL. TURNING INWARD CAN DECAY THE LOWER MIND'S FOCUS ON TAPPING INTO THE GIVING GREATER KNOWN. After hearing my picture movie story about taking, using this as a short cut to your Lower Mind, I want you to think of your own story that has happened to you along these same lines. The images that you store inside of you will be the true self-sensitized short cuts to impress your Lower Mind. These stories will push your Lower Mind into the understanding of the collective family of the Giving Greater Known.

* * *

Internal Body Knowledge

All of us have an Internal Body Knowledge that surpasses our brain knowledge by a huge margin. We are just scratching the surface of the frontier of what our bodies know. The best minds in the world have been studying the human body from the beginning of man's first footsteps in the sand and we still do not have all the answers to how it works. I am now talking only of the physical body functions. On the mental and the emotional side we are still in the cave man days as far as our understanding of how things work.

I had smelled the money. I was going to drop out of college and go to work. While I was headed to class one day I saw a man at work on the school's heating system. His name was Mike Steabell. We talked for a while, and he said with my knowledge of pneumatic controls I could get a job working for Johnson Controls. So I did, and about three months into it I contracted a virus in my left arm. One day at work I told Mike that my arm was hurting so badly that I was going to have to quit work and seek medical help. The doctors gave me some antibiotics and sent me home. My arm just got worse. There was a hole in my forearm the size of a quarter, about two inches down from the bend of the elbow on the inside of my arm. At it's worst I could start at the base of my wrist and push with my thumb towards the quarter size hole and push a mass of pus and lymph out. This bug was eating me up from the inside out. This was the early 1970's and there was nothing that they could do. When the doctor raised the dosage of antibiotics and said that if this did not work that they would have to take it off at the elbow, I went into action. This was not a bug, this was my body sending me a message: "Get back to school!" I made peace with my Lower Mind, telling it that I was going to quit work and go back to school and asking if it would please help me with my arm. I was in the Haze. I took a vacuum pump used in air conditioning work to evacuate systems, and preceded to suck out of my arm as much as I could. Then I made a paste of water and baking soda. I would pile this on the open sore, let it dry, push it off and do it again, about five times, in the morning, at noon and in the evening before I went to bed. About three days of this and I was cured. I went back to work and another sore opened up. This time in my right arm just below the wrist on the little finger side. I went into the office and told them I was going back to college, and I did. You can't fool your Lower Mind. Don't even try you will really have a mess on your hands. Where but from the Giving Greater Known was I able to come up with the actions that saved my arms? The internal system worked on its own level of knowledge. Once impressed by the Lower Mind to heal itself, it did. This system of body knowledge has been given to all of us. We must relearn as a human race to recapture this gift of being able to consciously push our Lower Mind into the action needed to impress the Body Knowledge into the action of healing. KOZ: THE

LOWER MIND CAN TURN AGAINST YOU IF YOU TRY TO DECEIVE IT. IT CAN BE VERY STUBBORN AND VINDICTIVE. These tools from the great beyond will take time to be integrated into your daily actions. Take your time be kind to yourself. Don't give up, the best is yet to come. With these tools you will be able to build your castle in the neighborhood of the cosmic collective of the Giving Greater Known.

* * *

Cosmic Lookout

As a traveler in the cosmic realm you should always be on the lookout for the next link in your programmed instructions to your Lower Mind. What you find may not make sense at the time but it may be only the first pearl on the string that leads you to the next pearl that may bring you to the fulfillment of instructions to the Lower Mind.

I was in Escondido, CA., visiting my sister. I had left the bar at closing time 2 A.M. I grabbed something to eat, then, on the way home; I stopped off at a 7-11 gas station for gas. It was about 3 A.M. I was standing in line waiting to pay. In front of me in line were two men asking the teller where there was a camping site. The teller was of Mexican background with limited English skills and I could hear the German accent of the two men. I said in German that I did not know where there was a campground but they could put their tent up at my sister's house. They said, "great we will follow you." I was driving my 70' Chevelle with a bored out 60-thousands 454 cubic inch big block. They had a time keeping up with me in their 4-cylinder rental car. I had told them that it was not too far, about 4 or 5 miles. It was more like 15 or 20 miles. The lights of the city were being left behind; the streetlights were becoming fewer and fewer. The road had gone from a four lane to a two-lane asphalt, to a two-lane gravel, then to a one-lane dirt. I pulled into the back entrance of my sister's property. They pulled in behind me. I could tell that they were a bit nervous. We stood and talked until 5:30 A.M., We talked about things as far reaching as men from outer space and Mars, down to how I knew German. The next morning I had them up to the house for coffee and breakfast. It was in December. They helped decorate the Christmas tree. As they left they said that I would have to come to Germany to visit. I said that I would be there the 28th of Sept. the next year on my birthday. I'm sure they were thinking that I was just kidding.

I was there the date that I said I would be. Tommy one of the German men, picked me up at the Regensberg train station. He had to wait a while, because the train that I said I was on was an earlier one. I'm glad he waited for the next one; I would have been lost. I was treated like an old lost friend. We went to his parents' house; his mother was home and his father was off on a business trip. The next day the three of us went to Muchen to the Oktoberfest. I had a great time.

How could I weigh this on what type of scale, what was my return on a camping spot and breakfast? And there was much more to come, this was only the first pearl on the string of this cosmic chain. KOZ: THE LOWER MIND WILL NOT FAIL. THE TRICK IS THAT YOU HAVE TO LOOK FOR SITUATION PICTURES. THIS IS HOW YOUR LOWER MIND COMMUNICATES WITH YOUR MIDDLE MIND. If you have adopted the ways of Koz every day from now on will be an adventure, knowing that you are on a controllable, ever-expanding, life-enriching journey. Stay with me, for without you being a witness, all is for naught.

* * *

Body Language

The protective system, the fight or flight mode, has in it the first circle of defense, called by Koz (Lower Mind Body Posturing). This is a remote sensing; at a distance, one can first interpret anything that may be an indication of what the Lower Mind of this person or animal has programmed into it. The body knows what the Lower Mind is up to. It wants to be ready at a moment's notice. It pre- postures itself; this is an inward looking window into the Lower Mind. Just last night when I took my girlfriend out to eat, I saw a good example. The man was in his late forties, long blonde hair with a ponytail. When my girlfriend and I came into the restaurant he did a normal scan and I did one in return, then we went on with our respective paths. Settling into our meals and drinks, I did another scan, of this man, out of the corner of my eye. I saw that he was scanning somebody else. There was a young man working there clearing off tables. His gait, his rhythm, is different, there was a bobbing, dancing motion in his step. The blonde-haired man was transfixed on his scanning subject. There are not the normal perimeters, this is different and he wonders what to make of it. As the employee was sweeping the floor with one of those roll around sweepers, a waitress needed to get by. The young man's body language was saying, "sorry, I got in your way. Can't you see I'm working here?" The blonde-haired man was totally focused on his antics. He couldn't get a fix on this guy, friend or foe. His primitive caveman system of remote scanning had to have an answer before relaxing. I knew what the problem was, this was a refugee from perhaps Uganda. This could very well be his first job in the U.S. He was moving to a different drummer and was no threat to me.

* * *

I was visiting Tommy, one of the men that I gave a campsite to five years earlier. He had graduated from college, and was working for BMW as an engineer. He had been transferred to Oxford, Eng. When he was at work I would do day trips. I was sitting in an open-air courtyard talking to a lady who was there visiting her son. She was sitting on the bench with me. She was to my right. There was a man sitting to my left who was a stranger. In turning to talk to the lady I was turning my back to the man to my left. I turned to him and said that I was not doing it out of disrespect and that I hoped he was not offended. He said not at all and that if he had such a beautiful lady to talk to his back would be turned. We started exchanging information. He was from Morocco, working as a cook in Oxford. After talking for a while, the lady had to go see if her son was at the meeting place out front of a McDonald's out on the main drag not too far away, she would be back.

There I was in the haze talking to what could be the next pearl on the cosmic string. I have always wanted to visit Morocco; I would like to visit the Berbers of the Atlas Mountains. "Hey", he said "you will have to come and visit. Would you and your lady friend and her son come to my house? I will cook for you." The lady returned with her son. They said that they had a planned evening together. I accepted. We jumped into his car and after stopping at a food store, off to his house we went. After two hours of good food and wine he dropped me off where my German friend and his co-workers were meeting for a beer. All of this for a campsite. KOZ: THE ALERT MIDDLE MIND WILL BE ABLE TO FOLLOW THE COSMIC PATH SPREAD OUT BEFORE US BY THE GIVING GREATER KNOWN.

These two examples of reading body language were given so that you in the future will not miss your next cosmic connection.

Lamont H. Cole

* * *

Pure Question

There are times when you need the answer to be right. You need that yes or no response to your question. There is a way to transfix the brain to steer the thoughts, and get the answer. There are two paths of thought in the brain that lie side by side. I want you to think in mind pictures seeing these two paths. They are cutting through a grassy field, so close together that at times they merge as one. There are trees and large boulders that make the traveler weave from path to path. There are snakes and wild dogs that have to be avoided, that will make the path not so straight. There are people along these two paths who would sway you in their direction. These present obstacles and past experiences of traveling these paths influence the traveler. There are constant bleed-overs from path to path. Now think of these paths transforming into two wires. These wires are then merged with a bundle of wires that are so numerous that they cannot be counted. There are all ranges of colors and disrepair. Many of these wires have bad places on them where the insulation is missing. This allows voltage to bleed from wire to wire. There is also the rough voltage running between the wires, that builds a leakage soup. This leakage soup is a natural function of the brain. Now I want you to think of these wires as so small that you could put a million of them through a hole the size of a pencil lead. Now transform them into neural pathways in the brain. Look at this bundle of leaking mush. There are many possibilities of what the outcome may be.

This is what you are working with when you are a traveler in other people's minds. You must bring with you a good supply of insulation tape to seal up these leakages. You must build walls and fences to keep the traveler on the right path.

The traveler that I'm now talking about is the thought or the answer. You are one of the people standing along these thought paths. With your guidance you will be able to wring out of all the leakage the answer you are looking for.

Your first step is to know this person's mind very well. Probe with the FORM system of asking questions. F: ask about how his family is doing. O: ask about his occupation and how is it doing. R: talk about recreation the things that he enjoys doing. M: ask him if he is being paid what he is worth. This is drawing him out of the mind cave, so that you can plant the steering seed. These questions are Pure Questions; questions that you know that they can answer. Now ask five questions that you know will come up with a yes answer. In doing so you are fencing the thought in the yes-neural pathway. It will have a hard time jumping over to the (No) neural pathway. As you are reading this your mind is not ready to except this as true. Your mind at this point sees both sides of this system and wants to reject that it could possibly be so easily steered. This is normal, it is the mind's protective system kicking in. It's saying that would not happen to me, I would see right through all that posturing. But how many times have we bought something from a salesman only to ask ourselves the next day why did I buy that stupid thing? I don't even have a use for it , I'll never use it. Think about the law called buyers' remorse, that gives anybody 72 hours to pull out of a sales contract no question asked or at least without any reason necessary. These mind fixing techniques are well known and governments have made laws to protect the public from them. KOZ: MIND FIXING MUST BE DONE IN A NON-TAKING MODE. THIS IS NOT A TOOL TO BE USED FOR STEALING MIND ENERGY. IF YOU USE IT IN THAT WAY YOU ARE THE ONE WHO WILL HAVE THE LOSS OF MIND ENERGY. The messages that KOZ has brought forward to you are tools of the mind. People who would like to see you stay a cog in one of their power seeking machines have hidden them from you. These tools of the mind are very rusty. You must use them over and over again, until they become part of your normal operating procedures. This will take some time. You will not be able to pick up tools and use them to their greatest use if you do not work with them on a regular basis. These mind tools have been brainwashed from you by the controllers of people. Now is the time to reclaim them and put them to use in your own success mental toolbox.

* * *

Choice Directing

I have a hobby: I fold dollar bill origami. Over the years I have picked up quite a few different ones to fold. I have for many years given them as tips or made them up for people as gifts. I have found out they can work wonders in breaking the ice in a strange bar. I can go back to a bar many years later and have someone say, "You are the guy who folds the dollar bills, aren't you?" as they are handing me a dollar bill asking me to fold them a bird. I have also learned how to make roses out of bar napkins, leaves and all. The women really like them. They will take them home and keep them for many years. They have told me so: "Those flowers you folded last time? I still have them at home on my dresser right next to the boot, bird, and whale the one where you used the eye of the pyramid and its shadow as its eye and mouth." These small, hand held three dimensional mind pictures are surely short cuts to their Lower Minds. When I am at a place for the first time I do Choice Directing skill practices. I look at the waitress and try to think of what she would choose if she had a choice of one of three things. Would she pick a bird, a boot, or a whale for me to fold out of a dollar bill? I fold let's say the bird. I call the waitress over. I tell her of my hobby, and that she is to pick two out of the choices of a bird, a boot, or a whale. Now if she picks the boot and the whale I ask what is left over, she says the bird. I say as I'm handing it to her, here is your bird. She asks how did you know I was going to pick the bird? If she had picked the bird and whale I would have asked her to choose one of those. If she said the whale I would have said and what's left over she would say the bird and I would say here's your bird and she would say how did you know I was going to choose the bird. This is Choice Direction; the person feels that they are in control choosing, that their choices are somehow transformed into a long established thought pattern of their Lower Mind, that somehow I was able to read their mind in what they were going to choose. Using Choice Direction along with the Seed Planting is a very formidable tool, when used in a picture mode being presented to the right brain. This stacking of tools can put an idea into a persons Lower Mind, while it is thinking that it had installed this prized deep implant. KOZ: THE TRUE MASTER OF THE LOWER MIND FIRST MASTERS HIS OWN. WHEN TOOL STACKING BECOMES THE RULE THEN YOU BECOME THE RULER OF YOURSELF AND THE MANY. Now come the higher-level stages of this transformation, the stacking of tools to synthesize Lower Mind deep implants. If you have not been doing some re-reading this is a transition place where you may get lost and left behind. If you are feeling this way and want to continue this voyage then I suggest that you re-read what KOZ has said until you are up to speed. For those who are still with me and are comfortable with their newly rediscovered tools, let us now go into the next level of cosmic law. Keep your tools sharpened, you will need all of them.

* * *

Leakage Soup

There are times that ideas come out of nowhere, after a period of rest or just after waking in the morning. These are the clumping of thoughts, thought blending. This happens in the Neural Leakage Soup. These conglomerations of thoughts are not restrained to a fixed set of rules. The Lower Mind looking for answers will mix and match at will anything that is in the Neural Leakage Soup. There are three cooks that are throwing ingredients into your Neural Leakage Soup. The Middle Mind, (the awakened you), is out gathering. It is pulling in vast amounts of information from the 360deg. Field of Influence. The sought after by the Lower Mind tapings into the (Giving Greater Known) are added to the Neural Leakage Soup. Information is also brought in by other visiting Lower Minds (champions) that infuse Mind Energy and their tappings from the Giving Greater Known. This is a triad, a power of three, which must be kept in balance. Once you can picture the Neural Leakage Soup in your mind's eye then you become the master chef of THE COSMIC NEURAL LEAKAGE SOUP. Now in your movie picture mind I want you to see a mixing bowl. This mixing bowl is made out of a material from the class of etheric materials, called Super-Stretchers. This material will stretch to the size needed. You never have to worry about having enough volume; this bowl will never overflow. Look into this bowl, What do you see in your bowl. Does it look like a well-rounded soup or is it just neural meat and potatoes? What is the size of your bowl? Think of yourself as walking into the Master Chef's office. See yourself standing in front of a large filing cabinet, one of those four draw legal size ones that stands five feet tall and two feet deep. Look at the sign on the front: TOP SECRET FOR THE MASTER CHEF'S EYES ONLY. Don't stop. You are the Master Chef. You have been on the job, oh well, let's say, ah ,ah, gee, how old are you? That's how many years you have been adding to this COSMIC NEURAL LEAKAGE SOUP mixing bowl. Open the top draw of your filing cabinet. What do you see? Are there many folders all neat and labeled or is there just a small stack of paper recipes in the bottom of the drawer. Reach out, pull something out of this drawer and look at it. What's there? Just another order for more meat and potatoes? What are you thinking as you are looking in this drawer? Are you shaking your head in disgust at the shabby record keeping and the lack of variety? Maybe you are ready to send in your recipes to Betty Crooker or IBM.

How your cosmic journey is going is in a direct ratio to what is in your COSMIC NEURAL LEAKAGE SOUP. You, yes you, have been given a soup strainer. It is a gift to you by the Cosmic Collective Giving Greater Known. Your Middle Mind needs only to pick it up and use it. Now go back to your movie picture mind. See yourself walking over to the wall. You are taking down a strainer. This strainer is also made out of an etheric material called Super-Stretchers. No matter what the size of the strainer when it is on the wall, it always fits the bowl of COSMIC NEURAL LEAKAGE SOUP. The strainer and bowl become as one, there are no dividing lines, and there is no leakage past the strainer. Now look out the side of your eye, first to the right. As far as you can see there are strainers on the wall. They are all yours. Now look to the left. As far as you can see there are strainers on the wall. They are all yours. I want you to look at the mesh on the strainer; there is none. The mesh is a super-conducting force field that you can calibrate by your thoughts alone. Now put your selected strainer into the bowl, see how it fits perfectly; wow it has fused together. Go to the second drawer down in the filing cabinet. Don't let go of the strainer, just tilt your head to one side, and think the drawer open. In this drawer are your future building sessions that you do at night. Take one out by levitating it to a position in front of your eyes. The optical neural link will transmit your future building session through a neural flux filter then on to the super-conducting force field of the strainer mesh. It will be automatically be calibrated to seek out the components that are needed to fill the order of the future building session. This finely tuned strainer can be dipped into billions of impluses that make up the neural thought soup and it will find just the ones needed to fit your order.

Now that you know the marvels that no amount of money could buy, gifts that you have been given by the order of the Cosmic Universal Law, it is your job to put them to work for YOU!!! Look into your movie picture mind. How are the ingredients being added to your COSMIC NEURAL LEAKAGE SOUP BOWL? Is the input that you are trying to forge a good life out of coming in from many sources? Look past your hair on your head; go beneath the skull. See a picture of doors- (thousands of them) all over your brain. There are also windows and electric sockets. Stand looking, observing what's going on. Are there bicycles or trucks going in and out of the doors, or are they locked down with a big padlock on them? Can you see through the windows or are they covered with drapes and have not been washed for years? What's plugged into those electric outlets and where are the cords going? You are the shipping and receiving dock boss. What you say goes. It's the law. Pull out your clipboard. Start writing down what you want to be changed. See this clipboard change into a gun that shoots seeds. Not garden seeds but idea brain planting seeds. Now aim it at the Lower Mind. I want you to see it as a group of construction workers chomping at the bit, waiting for your instructions. See them picking up their tools and jumping into neural portholes at light speed or faster; your wish is their command. Also shoot a brain seed to the Middle Mind. Let it know that you are not happy with what you are seeing or keep up the good work. If you are not happy, tell it to get in gear: that you need truckloads of new information of all sorts so that the strainers will have what they need. Do not be concerned so much about contents but veriety and huge amounts. I want to see a convoy of trucks streaming in the doors on the surface of your brain. You may have to unplug some of the cords, re-route some, and plug some new ones in. KOZ: OTHER LOWER MINDS CAN SENSE THE SIZE OF YOUR COSMIC NEURAL LEAKAGE SOUP BOWL. THESE OTHER LOWER MINDS ARE LAZY. THEY ARE LOOKING FOR COSMIC SHORTCUTS. THEY WILL EITHER DRAW YOU CLOSER OR PUSH YOU AWAY BY WHAT THEY THINK YOU MAY HAVE THAT WILL MAKE THEIR COSMIC JOURNEY INTO THE COLLECTIVE GIVING GREATER KNOWN COME TO FRUITION. I have been told by KOZ that there are many more tools to be reclaimed but first we will have to build a mental toolbox for these tools. They will work at a level that we have not even touched on yet. Some of these tools you are ready now but they will have to wait for sequential alignment so they are more readily adopted. I hope you will stay with me on this transition, I don't want to leave anyone behind. Sometimes I feel that I am getting things from KOZ that are mixed messages and that I am not presenting them in their best light. I know what he is saying and what it means; but how do I take million bite picture movie transmissions and express them into words that will do them justice? I feel at times that this is an impossible task and I am messing things up. I would rather not say or write anything than to mislead anyone. Even though I feel this way at times KOZ has assured me that he would not let me go astray.

* * *

Lower Mind

Slow Lower Mind Shifting

There is a safety blowout or an anti-overload control circuit within us. It protects us from information overload. Koz called it the Unwilling Lazy Lower Mind. To know about this process is to know the secret of the inner change sequence. The brain will skip over large amounts of gathered information and focus on the task at hand. It will not count all the telephone poles as you are driving, or the white dash lines in the middle of the road. The Lower Mind can be shaped very easily if it is done slowly enough. The Lower Mind has worked hard for its own self-recognizing truisms that are deep implants, which it does not want to give up. In fact it will set up a defense program to protect them whenever they are attacked. In knowing this there is a level of change that will sneak under this protective radar. This can be used to change the deep unwanted implanted habits of the Lower Mind. When I quit chewing snuff I used this technique. I did not let the Lower Mind know that I wanted it to give up this bad habit by letting it know that I was quitting. The quitting word never passed over my lips. I went about the task of looking at all the aspects of chewing snuff. First of all there were the over swollen buds in my bottom lip that were begging for another hit of nicotine. Then there were the places that I went into that sold snuff and the whole ritual of choosing the right brand. Taking a sniff of the bottom of the can, which was like inspecting a cantaloupe, it was a check for freshness. Reading the date stamped on the bottom of the box was important to make sure that it was not too old. There was the use of one's fingernail to open the can. The buying of a juice drink not for the juice but to have something to spit into while I was driving. Mine was pink grapefruit. This was the cleaning of the pallet and the appetizer for the main course, the snus or snuff. I tore into every little step of the process finding the smallest change that I could do. The first new rule was that I could buy anything and as much as I wanted in a place that I usually bought snuff if I did not buy snuff. I went through a lot of teriakki beef jerky, licorice, and chocolate. I learned that these chemically keyed into the taste buds in my lip and fooled it into being satisfied, it not knowing; (my body) that I was quitting. In the short run it was costing me more and I would also have picked up some more habits that I would deal with when the time was right using the same process. If I went a month without snuff I got to buy a western shirt of my choice no matter the cost. This was used to push the Lower Mind into a challenge, and used an already established desire of the Lower Mind (a shirt) to make it make a choice, one or the other. Small change after small change, I am now snuff free. KOZ: THE PUSHING OF ONES OWN LOWER MIND PUTS THE POWER OF SELF CHANGE INTO YOUR EVER EXPANDING TOOLS FROM THE COSMIC COLLECTIVE GIVING GREATER KNOWN. Even though I have been told by Koz to write this book, I some times think it is a waste of time. Koz has for many years spoon-fed me these messages coming at the right time and the right sequence. How was I to convey this process in a condensed version of a book? He told me not to underestimate the written word and that the ones who are ready to change will and those that won't are the ones who will not tolerate change and have resigned themselves to the fact that they are what they are.

***

Lower Mind To Lower Mind Communication

I had noticed that my wife had two warts on the top of her head. She said that she was going to have them burned off. I was in the Haze, "I'll get rid of them for you, I said." "Oh, that's OK," she said. I'm sure she had visions of me using a soldering gun or a red-hot poker. Then out of the blue I said that I would think them away, that all I would have to do was lay my finger on the spot and think about it. She said "OK", probably out of appeasement to me, not thinking that it would work. I put my finger on her warts and talked out loud what I was thinking. "Wow, we have some nice carrots here. Calling all bunnies. Come and have some carrots. I can see them coming from all over your body. I'm going to pick a large brown one as the boss rabbit. He will know when a rabbit has had its fill and replace it with a new one. They are going to eat these carrots from the bottom up." I told my wife that I wanted her to think about this little story three or more times a day. The story will kick in whenever you are eating or going to sleep. I will also think about the story mind movie at the same times. The stacking of our Lower Minds would have a multiplying effect. Three weeks passed and the warts were gone. I have done this on some people who did not know that I was doing it and they also had good results. This let me know that there was a sub level communication system between Lower Minds. Those eerie feelings and chills or goose bumps, are all messages from your Lower Mind to be on guard. Don't brush them off as just something that happens. Use them, tune into them like you would any other input in your 360 degree circle of information gathering. These are messages that are by passing the Middle Mind of the sender: Lower Mind to Lower Mind flow of information that is not twisted by the Middle Mind to embellish it for its own enhancement. Every day we are receiving these Lower Mind messages. They come in as feelings that pushes a mind movie across our mental screen. All Lower Mind messages are sent in movie format. They should be recognized as a right brain function first, then a left-brain analyzing function. Holding these messages in your right brain for a moment as if in a trance or dream state, this will give the time lag needed to receive the full message. The sending Lower Mind will not waste its time if you are not tuned in. KOZ: THE TOUCH THAT HEALS IS A CONDUIT TO PASS MIND ENERGY FROM LOWER MIND TO LOWER MIND. MIND ENERGY CAN ALSO BE STOLEN FROM YOU THIS WAY, BE MINDFUL WHO YOU TOUCH OR ARE BEING TOUCHED BY. The amount of change that it will take in one's thinking patterns seems overwhelming at times. There seem to be gaps and holes and bits and pieces that are not falling together in a coherent flow. Koz has told me that this is the normal feeling of the unlinked Lower Mind not tuned into the Giving Greater Known, and to stay the course. What wonders and powers lie at hand to be unfolded to those who continue this transformation!

* * *

Lower Mind Transfusion

I want to teach you how to become a person within a person. I want you to walk with me down a neural path that has no direction or edges. I want you to learn how to use an etheric cosmic joining, to do a Mind Energy transfusion. Think of yourself as a mass of atoms that you can transform into any configuration. I want you to find someone who could use your help. I want you to stop being yourself. I want you to think of yourself as a spirit extension of this person that you are going to help, that they have complete control of you, as if you were a string-guided puppet. You will turn on an inner messaging system that will put you in a no time factor link with this person's Lower Mind. Not only will you do as asked, but also you will anticipate at a higher level their needs. You will fill in the gaps and add an aura of confidence and mental support.

    I want you to go into your movie picture mind and see things that only your Lower Mind will be able to grasp. See yourself standing in front of a mirror. Look into this mirror and see your reflection. Watch your reflection turn into a bookcase. There are many books on the shelves. The titles are a blur except for one. On the third shelf down from the top there is a book that you can read the title of. The title reads; THE MIDDLE MIND (ALSO KNOWN AS THE WALK AROUND EVERY DAY SELF). See yourself taking this book off the shelf and putting it into a lockbox, a large lockbox like the ones you see on stagecoaches. Open the lockbox and place the book in it with its title face down. Pull from your pocket a key and lock it. Look to your right and see a large chain and padlock. Wrap the lockbox with this chain and lock it with the padlock. Look to your left. There is a hole dug in the ground. Drag the lockbox over to the hole and bury it. Stand next to this Middle Mind grave and say out loud, "I will not let my Middle Mind interfere and will not dig it back up until this walk is over. I know that my Middle Mind gets in the way and I must do this to impress my Lower Mind that it is in control." Walk away now knowing that you are now walking with me, our two Lower Minds stirred together Lower Mind within Lower Mind. This bond that you have made with me is so you may come along with me on this cosmic path. As we approach the person we are going to help I want you to feel my feelings. I am feeling myself flow into this person's body. I flow in and out the other side. I want you to think of how they depict a person in a movie who is doing something at a super speed. I think of

Superman or the Tasmanian Devil. My flowing into this person is going to make him feel like a super human being, that he has twenty hands and twenty eyes and twenty brains all working as a partnership as one unit. I want you to do some eye reading. Look but don't look, see but don't be seen, looking. At a fast glance look into the eyes and read the WOW. This Wow feeling that they are feeling will infuse you with large amounts of MIND ENERGY. This energy will give you super staying power. There will be no amount of mental or physical pressure that will make you unravel. Whatever needs to be done that you can do, you will do, without question or comment. If they attempt to take their time to show you how to do something that you already know how to do, you say I have it under control, I will take care of it. You want them to feel that they have full control even if they in reality are ready to fall apart. You will say to them things that they need to hear. Read every negative self putdown as a sign that you must turn around to the positive.

Come with me now and join a joining of Lower Minds. His name is James Horton, he is a young man in his middle twenties. The stage that he is in is the hunting, looking, finding oneself stage of life. I have known him for two years and like him a lot because I see myself in him when I was young and afraid and unsure of myself. He had told me he had contracted with the volunteer Fire Department to cater their Christmas party. I could sense a bit of anxiety in his voice. I fell into the Haze; I asked him if he needed any volunteer help. I told him that I would do anything that he may need help with. He took me up on my offer and asked if I would meet him at one o'clock to check out the kitchen and the serving line where I would be working. We met and I started my Lower Mind to Lower Mind transfusion. "Looks great, I see there is a good triple sink to do dishes in, that's a plus. Look at that stove that's a nice one. Looks good we shouldn't have any problems and in fact everything will be fine, I'm sure of it". Looking, but not looking into his eyes for any doubt. I was there ten minutes early so as not to build up any amount of anxiety in him of me not showing up. I let him get his doubts and fears out of the way, running them past me, all along switching all negative things to the positive. The meat was going to have to be taken to a restaurant across the road to an oven. I had my pick-up. I said that he was going to need some partially cooked meat and that it will be just right for those that like it rare and by the time half the line is through it will be just right; and it was. We ran out of strawberry preserves for the desserts; but that was OK because some people will like their chocolate mousse without; and they did and it worked out fine. He was hoping that we had enough food and I assured him that we had more than enough and we did. I stuck with it looking but not looking into his eyes, looking for cracks to be filled. I packed the frosting pastry bag with strawberry preserves and started making desserts. I read his eyes, he was pleased that I would take the majority of this task off his hands. I saw him starting to do it and acted as if he was handing it to me to do. Then on to the chocolate mousse, then whipped topping, layered in a desert glass. At the end we got a round of applause. I was not done, I got the dish washer started and put a plate of food together for my housebound aunt and took it to her house. I knew that I had done something and had left something behind in that brief moment of time that brought a piece of Cosmic Law to light that touched everyone there. And doing so will bring to me ongoing Mind Energy from those that I touched and flowed over with the power of the GIVING GREATER KNOWN. I could see the light in their eyes as they looked at me. They wanted to know who I was and what I did; trying to get a handle to hold onto this ride, a feeling that they did not want to let go. Many of them personally came to touch me and say thank you. I could sense that it was far more than what I had done but for just being myself. KOZ: YOUR REALITY WILL SHIFT AT WILL AS YOU REACH OUT TO HELP OTHERS TO SEE THE PATH OF THE GIVING GREATER KNOWN. THESE SMALL JOURNEYS INTO THE REALM OF JOINING LOWER MINDS WILL BRING IN LARGE AMOUNTS OF MIND ENERGY THAT WILL FUEL LONGER TRIPS DOWN THIS COSMIC PATH. I want you to think in your past of such a giving of yourself and recapture those feelings. Let the remembering of those feelings push you into action down that path again. Bring with you all that you have to give and reap more than you brought in by your leaving but not leaving. These actions will weave a blanket that will take you on a magic carpet ride through a cosmic other world realm that will tie you to the GIVING GREATER KNOWN.

***

Lower Mind Focusing

The Lower Mind is a child at play and must be kept focused. The Lower Mind must be continually surveyed to make sure that it has not wandered off into a brain looping sequence. This can happen often to the person who has become a modern day self-medicating chemist. Mood swings are a natural function of the body, telling you that it is in transition and that you will have to wait for a stabilized functioning format before you can expect the Lower Mind to focus on anything. The problem and the challenge are to structure a stabilized format that the Lower Mind can stay functioning in. The Lower Mind does not like change and must be warned of major changes or it will rebel. Most people have never reached anything close to a stabilized format that is Lower Mind compatible. Even the smallest changes in one's environment or diet or drinking or drug taking can make a huge impact on the Lower Mind. Your brain is an electro-chemical process that is directly influenced by your body chemical make up and balance or unbalance. The accounting of one's own actions in the laboratory of life is a task that most will not undertake. The problem is the Middle Mind's way of looking at problems. The Middle Mind likes to see the whole problem so big that it is unsolvable. It needs to be trained to change, to seeing the small. The weight control or healthy diet is a common set of ideas readily accepted because of their betterment to the living body. The brain is also part of that same body; it must function on whatever crosses over your lips. We must start looking at the brain-diet connection if we are ever going to build a stabilized working platform for the Lower Mind. The constant shifting of one's diet will keep the Lower Mind searching for stability and build up anxiety and frustration to a point of the feeling of no self-control and depression. This vicious circle that people are trapped into is very hard for the untrained mind to break free of. People are not willing to accept that they are the problem; that the problems and the challenges are within.

 I want you to go into your movie picture mind function. See yourself standing in front of a file cabinet. Open the top drawer. You will see all the folders that are the blueprint of who you are. There are hundreds of folders but I want you to only focus on the first one. The tab reads DRINK. In there is a record of everything that you have ever drunk in your whole life, from the sipping of placenta fluid to the first shot of whiskey. Check this list , comb it with a fine tooth comb. Put a check mark by the drinks that you have consumed in the last week that are not found in a natural state in this world. This would include highly processed natural drinks. These drinks would include milk, water (chlorine, fluoride) and store bought fruit juices. What does your list of checked items look like? If you are like most people who have been mind-beaten into submission, all of them have been checked. There are two things that most people can see where the critical performance of a liquid is of the utmost importance. The first is the steam iron that must only be filled with distilled water. If you use tap water you will risk the chance of rust staining your new garment. This is a no-brain-er, you use distilled water in the steam iron every time. Something like a cola drink would be out of the question. What are you, nuts? The other thing is the water in your car battery. This critical functioning part of your car gets only the best water distilled. You would not even think of putting anything else but distilled water in it. Even the sacred cow of all liquids, milk, would be out of the question. Now I want to introduce you to a piece of equipment that is thousands of times more sensitive to what type of liquid that you supply it with than the crude steam iron or the car battery. You have such a piece of equipment inside your head: it is called a brain. This brain is yours, you are its caretaker. Go back to the file marked DRINK. I want you to look at this file as a maintenance record of what type of liquid has been supplied for the brain to function on. Keep in mind that you are the boss who has hire and fire capabilities over the caretaker. How did you rate the job that the caretaker has done? Were there plenty of plant liquids and good pure distilled water on the list or a bunch of bullshit liquids that you would not even put in a steam iron? Do you see what the problem is? The problem is you can't fire yourself. No matter how bad a mess you have made of things you are stuck with what you have.

  The fight begins, the inner fight for control. This is a fight that you must win if you ever expect to be a family member of the GIVING GREATER KNOWN. This must be a well-structured battle plan with a lot of contingency planning. You are going to have to fight your own brain to take control. Your efforts are coming from the Middle Mind, which is vastly inferior to the power of the Lower Mind. There are the tools that Koz has given us that will show us the gaps in the protective wall of the Lower Mind. These tools are very powerful if used properly. They must be used to slowly shape the Lower Mind, so slowly it does not perceive the change and call out the guard. The next folder is labeled BATTLE PLAN DRINK. This folder is where you are going to keep track of how you are going to attack and your progress. Written on the front of the folder is TOP SECRET NO ACCESS FOR THE LOWER Mind. Step one of the battle plan reads drink one large glass of distilled water every day upon rising. This is a big step in taking back control of your mental and physical self. Do this until it becomes a habit that your Lower Mind will adopt. When you find yourself doing it automatically without thought it has become part of your new Lower Mind. This will be a great milestone in your life and should not be taken lightly. The Middle Mind doesn't have the capability to grasp at this time the magnitude of this seemingly small step. This small accomplishment will put you into an elite group of people that is a very small number indeed. Let yourself know how proud you are of its accomplishments with a reward. Tell yourself of your new-found power and the great things to come and how much you like this new powerful self. Feel the power of self-change at this first step into self-control. Be sure you recognize this power and give it its proper distinction. Guard it well for it is a gift of true value that you cannot buy at the hardware store for any amount of money. Keep this powerful tool of change always plugged in and working for you at a slow steady pace. When it has conquered one goal, put it to work on the next without delay. Your life will become an adventure of self-change and bring wonders into your life that you will find hard to believe that you brought about. You will feel such a rush of power within you that you will be steadily looking for something that you can change with the idea that there is nothing so big that the power of your mind cannot handle. KOZ: THE POWER TO SHIFT ONES OWN LOWER MIND OPENS THE DOOR TO THE CONTROL OF YOUR ACCESS TO THE COSMIC LAW OF THE GIVING GREATER KNOWN.

* * *

Dislodging An Entrenched Lower Mind

I could feel a mistrust, even hatred toward me from this person. He was my elder with some twenty-five years plus on the job. I was going to need all the help I could get from him; he knew the workings of this hellhole of a work place better than any of them. I was going to have to pull out all the stops, use every tool given to me by Koz to reshape this man's Lower Mind. I could see him scanning me. I wanted to make sure that I was not sending any body language that would put him on the defensive. Watching for the first sign from him that he was at ease with my presence, reading the amount of time that he had scanned me before turning to talk to somebody else or to glance away to look in a different direction.

Then I planted the seed that would be the turning point of his Lower Mind. Making sure that he was listening, I said that I was so new around here that I squeaked when I walked. That I was going to have to hire a guide to find my way around this packinghouse. That I did not know the difference between the front and the back end of a pig, let alone how to process one. And that there were machines that I was scared of just looking at them, let alone working on them, and how I would never learn all of their names and where they were located. I feel like a one legged man in a butt kicking contest. Can you pick out the tools that I was using? The moment I saw the smile and then chuckle, then I shifted him to his left-brain by saying, so if it seems that I don't know my ass from a hole in the ground when I come to you asking for help, I don't.

Not too much time had passed when I made sure to approach him with a plea for help. It was a big vacuum pump on the 8th floor. It was seized up and I did not know how to take it apart any more than I had already. He did not seem surprised that I had come to him. He took it as a challenge to his knowledge. He said "I'll be right up and take a look at it." When he got there he took control. "First thing, put the #$%$#$ pump back together. What your problem is someone let it run low on oil and the bearings are shellacked up. That is why it is not moving. Get yourself a case of carburetor cleaner and soak those bearings down. Go down to the tool room and check out the 36" pipe wrench, stop by the plumbing shop and pick up a 10 foot length of pipe that will fit over the handle of the pipe wrench and make sure that it is black iron. We are going to use it as a cheater." After many cans of carburetor cleaner and pulling on the pipe wrench with cheater attached to the flywheel we got it fixed.

A month had passed, Ron and I crossed paths again. We were paired up together to handle the night shift maintenance and tear down for two weeks. After the two weeks were over Ron took me out to a steak dinner saying that I was the best worker that he had ever worked with. He and I no longer work for John Morrells, and we have carried forward our friendship to this day. Well-planted seeds in the Lower Mind can work wonders. KOZ: WHEN DOING A LOWER MIND SEEDING BE SURE NOT TO EVER TELL THE PERSON OF

THE PROCESS. THEY WILL FEEL MANIPULATED AND TURN ON YOU. I am reaching out to you hoping that you too will join the family of the Cosmic Giving Greater Known. I would wish that you would do your own experimenting with the messages from Koz. Build on your own experiences and your own tappings into the Giving Greater Known. For some day I hope Koz will talk to you directly, he has told me that he talks to many people besides me. Maybe you will become the next conduit to receive messages and enlighten others and me. This will come to pass if you stay on the path of the Giving Greater Known.

* * *

Collective Lower Mind Pressure

I was sitting in the Harbor bar in Nice, California. I had come to get something to eat. I peeked my head into the kitchen to see if they were still cooking. The cook asked if I was looking for something to eat. I settled for a ham sandwich, some potato salad and a Seven-up to drink. The inside of the bar had a decor that made me feel like I was aboard a ship. There was a ship's horn that was hand powered. A swift down pull on the handle and it would blast out a deep horn sound. There was a tall standing table set back from the bar that had a ship's compass imbedded in it. There were all types of ship-like things on the walls and ceiling. The one that caught my eye and transfixed it was a porthole on the back bar. The porthole had a mirror fitted in it and it was mounted on a mirrored wall. The mirrored wall was built in bits and pieces; each section of mirror gave you a different view. Looking into the mirror I could see my friend James. As I looked into the next mirror over I saw the person he was talking to. This was odd, it looked like he was talking to a blonde when I looked in the mirror. But when I looked directly at him I saw that he was showing the man next to him how to fold a rose out of a bar paper napkin. My eye shifted over to the porthole mirror on the mirror.

 I had fallen into the Haze. I was daydreaming. I was standing on a catwalk above a group of people who seemed to be looking at a ball hanging from a string. The ball was the size of a basketball and it was mirrored. The ball would move side to side in a straight line and the people would follow. As the ball rotated the person would rotate with it. They were so intent at watching their ball that they saw nothing else going on around them. I saw them bump into one another and went on their way starring at their ball without saying I'm sorry or even looking at the other person. I was having a hard time figuring out what this was trying to tell me when KOZ boomed in. THE LOOKER AND THE NOT SEEN ARE SO TRANSFIXED THAT THEY DON'T SEE THEMSELVES. THEY DON'T SEE THEMSELVES AS THE LOOKERS SEE THEM. THEY ARE SO INTENT IN SLIPPING THROUGH REALITY AS AN ENJOYMENT THAT THEY CAN'T SEE THEMSELVES STRUCTURING THEIR OWN FUTURE. I stood there long enough to see a clash of balls and two people looking at each other in a state of rage. They turned away and went looking for another ball. I also saw at one time that after bumping into some other person that that person would lose their reality ball and wander from ball to ball trying to find theirs. They would go from ball to ball until a ball without a person looking at it came their way and they then adopted this new ball as their own. Off to the right I could see a line of people with their ball tucked under their arm. I walked over that direction without my feet moving. They were lined up in front of a window and above it was written the words, REALITY EXCHANGE. They were turning their balls in and they were given a card that read "Go to Door Two." I saw them looking at the card and looking for Door Two. They were looking at each other's cards and saw that it also had "Go to Door Two" written on it. They were standing in little groups looking at each other's cards and looking around for Door Two. Off to my left I could see a large door with a large number "two" written on it. I went over to one of the small groups and pointed out to them this large door with the number two written on it. They looked over that direction but shook their heads and looked back at their card and shook their heads again. I said, "The door that you are looking for is right over there." I headed for the door and gave them the follow me wave. They were entrenched. They were not coming my way. I got to the door and written on it were the words, ONLY FOR THOSE WHO CAN SEE THEMSELVES. I walked through the door and a rush flowed over my body. It was like walking through an air curtain, but you did not feel it on the outside, you felt it on the inside. I was floating along a long line of people. These people had a clipboard strapped to one side of their head and a traffic light sticking out of the top of their head. I could see wires coming out of their heads and going to the clipboards and to the traffic light. They would turn to each other and I could see them plugging an extension cord from their ear into the person's head next to them. The traffic lights were going from red to yellow to green in a blur.

  I was brought back to the bar scene reality. It was my friend James asking me to buy him a drink. I said, "Sure I would." I did a brain shift on him and got him thinking that he should buy me a drink. I said I could buy you a drink or I could loan you twenty dollars. I slipped him twenty dollars and with his newfound wealth he bought a man he just met a drink and asked me if I wanted one. I had to leave, I could see that the twenty dollars was not going to last long at that rate. I slipped out the front door and was gone. They were all staring at their own reality balls and did not see me leave. KOZ: THOSE WHO CAN'T SEE THEMSELVES CAN'T SEE THEIR FUTURE. BECOME A LOOKER WITH OTHER PEOPLE'S EYES TO SEE THEIR SEEINGS. THE COLLECTIVE LOWER MIND PRESSURE WILL PULL YOU IN A COSMIC LAW DIRECTION. TO CONTROL THE LOWER MIND PRESSURE IS TO CONTROL YOUR OWN FUTURE. I will from now on be very self watchful and take the driver's seat on this bus trip through reality. I have used this tool to shape and blow my future through a long string of cosmic reality and non- reality. Which way is your reality being blown? Do you feel in control or are you just along for the ride? If you have come this far you are ready for the driver's seat. I want to tell you my dreams and daydreams. I have been told by Koz that is where vast amounts of cosmic law will be coming from. That I should not try to understand these messages with my middle mind that I should just let them flow into my Lower Mind.

***

Lower Mind Pumping

From the beginning man has used hiding as a defense. The best places were caves. We were able to have our backs up against a wall and make the intruder approach the black hole of the unknown. Coming in from the light was a disadvantage; your eyes took time to adjust to the low light conditions. During that transition the man already in the cave could see quite well. He had the advantage of home turf, knowing ever nook and cranny, every mound and hole. The man in the cave had such an advantage that there was no going in after him. At the outset there would be too many unknowns, too big a risk. What was in that black hole waiting for you? The best action was just to wait them out. They would have to come out some time for food or water. This could be a long time, not knowing how much food they had, and some caves had water in them. When the mastery of fire came about there was a different approach. Let's smoke them out! This would displace the clean fresh air with toxic smoke. They would have to come out for fresh air. Now the tide had turned and the man on the outside of the cave had the advantage. His eyes were adjusted to the light; they were not burning because of the smoke. The cave was on its way out. The castle was the next hiding place.

In every mind there is this black hole of the unknown that is used for defense. When a person is silent and secretive this gives him the advantage. He knows what he knows and those on the outside know not. How does one read a person like that? The only thing to do is to mentally smoke them out. As soon as you have determined that this person is not on your side and is not working on your behalf, then the protective stance changes. This becomes a double smoke out job: as they are trying to smoke out your thoughts you should be smoking out their thoughts. You don't want to give up your advantage. It could lose you your job or freedom or even your money or your life. The best way to handle probing questions is with another question.

In the work place there are all types of challenges that a person may mess up on. I remember one such exchange between my senior ranking duty sergeant and myself. "Was it you that used the oxygen and acetylene cutting rig last night and did not return them to the tool cage and chain them down?" My reply was, "If a person did admit to doing that what would be the repercussions of such actions?" "Well since it was against shop policies and was a gross neglect of safety guidelines that may have endangered other people's lives, I'm sure that there would be some strips taken, a reduction in rank and pay." "Well if that's the case I might have had something to do with it but I'm not going to admit to anything. With the way that this has been blown out of proportion who would admit to something like that? You would be putting your head on the chopping block. You would be offering yourself up as the sacrificial lamb. Who would stick their head in that bear trap?" Without a full-blown investigation there was no course of action, so it blew over. These are some good questions to put in your mental toolbox. How do you mean that? I don't understand what you are trying to get at? Do you think I had something to do with that? Who else have you asked this question and what did they say? Why are you asking me this question? KOZ: GIVING OUT YOUR HARD FOUGHT FOR THOUGHTS AND PLANS OPENS THE DOOR FOR OTHER LOWER MINDS TO STEAL OR DESTROY. THIS IS A BIG DRAIN ON YOUR MIND ENERGY. KEEP YOUR THOUGHTS WELL GUARDED. GIVE THEM ONLY TO OTHERS WHO ARE ON THE PATH OF THE GIVING GREATER KNOWN. The best way to keep yourself out of troubles is to be able to sidestep them in the first place. There are programs set up by the government to have other people report on you. Don't make yourself an easy target. Be very careful of who you let into your cave.

***

Triad: The Power Of Three

I was in a steak house trying to explain to the manager about enlisting the help of a Champion. I said that what she needed was a good attorney. She laughed and said not those crooks, as she walked away. I did not get a chance to explain about stacking of Lower Minds. The key to real performance is doing a stacking of Lower Minds in threes. If you know what type of champion you are looking for to solve your problem, do not go to them directly. I want you to think of putting two other people in the stack of Lower Minds. Find someone that you and other people think highly of. Ask their opinion as to whom they would go to with a problem. Take their advice and go talk to that person. Ask that person whom they would recommend as an attorney in your problems. When you talk to the attorney mention your team that is helping you with your problem at the onset. Mayor Joe Smith led me to Jim Larson, the head mechanic at the Ford dealership. He said that if any body knew something about car problems it would be you and that you are a fair man. This puts the attorney on notice that he has more to lose than you as a client if he does not treat you fairly. He can see that you are not acting on your own but you have put a team of champions to work on this problem. Say to the attorney that you respect these men's opinions very highly and that you will be using their guidance along the way, that they are good sources of information and that you will be bouncing your questions or problem off of them. This is how to structure a Lower Mind Stacking. Do this whenever you are having problems.

    I was sitting at the bar in the Outback restaurant in Sioux Falls, South Dakota. The man sitting next to me was commenting how long it was taking to get something to drink. I felt that he was a bit impatient. Thirty seconds had gone by and he said, "What does it take to get a drink around here?" The bartender asks the people to my left what they would like. These people had come in after me and the impatient man was there before me. He said, "Hey, what about this end of the bar?" The bartender then asked me what I wanted to drink. I said to her that the impatient man to my right was there first. He said, "Thank you".

I was thinking that there might be some kind of insight on this man in his showing of impatience. I was thinking that he had a job that had a lot of structure to it. Something like a police officer or fireman or doctor. Well let's see. I asked him what his occupation was; he was in the army and was just home on leave. Wow! I was right, a very structured lifestyle. His impatience had given me a window into his Lower Mind. I told him that he has just given me something to write in my book. He asked me what kind of a book was it. I did not know what to tell him, I have not seen a book like this one before. I told him it was a metaphysical guidebook, the best that I could describe it at that time. The man to my left said that he heard that I was writing a book and asked how long had I been a writer and if I knew of a publisher that could help him get his motivational book printed? I told him that I had not been published yet. The thing to do is to contact one of the local colleges and ask them if there is a writers' club in town. I did not get the man's name or phone number. I feel that I may have passed up a pearl on the cosmic string. I would have liked to of read his book. Who knows? It could have been giving to him and adding to my Mind Energy. I need to be more careful in the future so I do not pass up any more cosmic pearls. I need to go back in this book and reread, dream within a dream and Lower Minds on similar paths. I really feel a loss. Don't let it happen to you. Try to pick up on these connections that are short cuts in our journey through this cosmic cloud called life. Never go out in public and turn your back to someone, especially if you are sitting at the bar. If you do not want to talk to people and make new contacts please stay at home. When a person turns his back on somebody so close to him as the next bar stool this is a real show of social ignorance. The person who is receiving the back turn feels that you think that he is a non-identity, not part of the human race that is in this collective push to say "I too was here." Don't take from someone what might be their only reason for being here their statement I am here. Please just stay at home for you do not know how much you are taking from somebody and what you may be missing. KOZ: STAY AT HOME IN YOUR SHELL UNTIL YOU REALLY WANT TO JOIN THE COLLECTIVE HUMAN MOVEMENT TO THE GIVING GREATER KNOWN. I feel that if I can just change one person away from the taking life style to the giving life style that my writings have been worthwhile, if I could somehow let them see how much it hurts someone when they are taking. The person you are taking from may have had a background of mental problems and what you say or do in your takings may not seem like much to you, but they could be devastating to that person. I would like to take the backtuners to the side and let them know that their actions are not acceptable that they are not helping with the collective goal, that each and every person they meet is very special. I think that we as people are very rare and should be treated with the utmost respect. We have reached out to the heavens millions of miles and have not even found a fly; this makes the human a very special highly stationed being. Please direct any of your taking at me if you think that you must for I have enough Mind Energy to be able to absorb your taking and still respect you as something very special and precious.

***

ROCK THE ROCK

There are times when you should push softly: the first swing ride when the young child is more afraid than anything else. It will take time for them to enjoy this new swinging motion, and be saying higher, higher. Their first pull in a wagon, their small arms and smaller hands holding on for dear life. Things going by so fast that they don't know what to look at. Then the first bicycle learning session with the slow tender touches and soft encouragements. You can do it, if you don't give up.

You are so nervous; your life is in somebody else's hands. You try not to let on because you know they are also nervous, it's their first driving lesson. We have all at some time leaped forward into a new realm of physical and mental interactions. We first had to let the teacher know that we were ready.

There are times when you should push hard. You are off the bus first you have a plan. If I can get the jump on that bully I can outrun him and be home safe. If I can move fast enough I will make it to the safety of my car, before that dog catches me. I have to pass this test. I will study all night long, get the grade and it will be over. We all had to push hard at times. We had to become very single-minded to get past one thing after another.

It had been all set up. It was a go: white water rafting in Austria. After donning our cold-water gear we were put into teams of eight. This was a well-mixed team, women, men, German, Turkish, Greek, and I the only American. We all stood in silence; we wanted to hear every word that the instructor had to say. Then the order was in a loud voice "Hoch." Which in German meant high. All together in one smooth movement we had lifted the raft over our heads and were headed to the river. I was thinking that this just might work. We worked as a team and got the boat this far. "Unter" this meant under in German, and the raft was set down. All we had to do was to pick it up, run into the water, and jump in. (Hop ghea)which ment in German, let's go. All made it into the raft but a young German lady in her twenties and me. I took her by the hand and jumped in the river. The current was swift. We were not going to catch the raft. It was pulling away from us we were being left behind. Then the instructor had every one in the raft row upstream. This slowed them down and we were able to catch up. We were at the front of the raft. The young gal was going to be pulled under the boat by the force of the water. I held onto the raft with my right hand and pushed her to the side of the raft where three people pulled her and then me in. One of the men in the raft was Jorg. He was one of the German men that I gave a camping spot to at my sister's house. Tommy, the other man I gave a camping spot to was in the raft coming behind us. The young German lady and I were given a hand of applause; Jorg gave me a thumbs up and said gutte (good). Then the silence hit again. Several times he asked me if I had understood the instructions. I assured him that I did and repeated what he had said in German and said. Ich verstehe alles. I understand all. I could see that there was a show of confidence in the gestures of the rest of the crew. Off we were on the ride of our lives, with our lives depending on the collective efforts of this spaceship's crew. After a few rough rapids and some rock dogging we were feeling pretty good about ourselves.

    We were in a stretch of calm water but it was still running swift. We were having small talk about who almost fell out and how if someone had not grabbed onto me that he or she would have gone overboard. Then we heard it, the other raft was under full paddle, their instructor calling out the cadences "lauf, lauf. Row; row". Our instructor did the same but they had the jump on us and caught up with us and passed us by. On the way past they gave us a good splashing with their paddles.

Further down the river after some more rapids the other raft had come to a rest mode. It was our turn. We instinctively knew what was happening when we did not go into the rest mode after the rapids. It was time to push hard. We had the jump on them and we were as one. We hunted them down and the splashing and yelling and laughing were only stopped by the order of the captain. "Let's go. We have a long way to go yet."

It was over. We were back on dry land getting our land legs back in working order. There was an eerie, short pause not only in the talking but also in the movement. Our minds were transfixed on what had just happened. I did not want it to stop. I felt as though I was leaving a newly formed family. I wanted the team effort of empowerment to stay with me forever. This is surely what team sport players feel after winning a game, after astronauts return home from space, and when men come home from war. This is why I have pulled my son very close to me so we can work as a team. What a let down was the ride back to Feuerbauch, where I was staying at Jorg's apartment. I thought of how great it was to pull together a mixture of many people and make things happen. Why can't we do this as one people on this rock we call earth?

***

REUNION

An alien was controlling me. This was not an outer space alien; this was Tommy, one of the campers from California. We're going to see the Befenkshalle. The what? In my mind it meant after trying to translate, the thinking place. He told me that I was close, it meant "remembering place." There it was off on a far away hilltop. It looked like a large cupcake or second layer of a wedding cake. It still took forty-five minutes of driving to get there, through several small towns then up a road heavily wooded on both sides. There would have been no way that I would have found it on my own. It seemed to be placed so that people would not come there by accident on the way to someplace else. When you get there that's where the road ends. There was paid parking, they had you. There was no where else to park for eight miles. I saw that we still had a long way to walk, seeing a toilet; I decided to relieve my call of nature. Who knew when I'd reach the next one? It was a pay toilet. They had me again, I felt that I had been in a maze of "gotchas". As we started walking toward this place I had an eerie feeling that this was a place that KOZ wanted me to see and experience. There were three steps going up the side of this structure, then columns all around, then smaller columns higher up. I was in the haze, I was dream walking. I found myself being led around like a person on a mental ward that had been drugged up so that they were subdued and easier to handle. I could not take my eyes off of it. It just kept getting bigger and bigger. I felt that I was being sucked in, that I was going there to be transformed, soon I would be washed over with a rush of transfused Mind Energy. I was touching it. Those steps I saw in the distance were huge. I stand 6' 8" tall and the first step was higher than my head by a least two feet. I could see people high up they were pigeon size. That second row of columns was a walkway around the top. I was shown the entrance. There was a charge to get in, about five dollars each. They had me again. I walked inside. It was a dome, the largest dome that I had ever been under. All around were fourteen-foot high angels with their hands extended. I walked to the center. The rush of Mind Energy over me was so great that it took less than a minute for all four of my turnings. Looking up and turning I got vertigo and had to walk over to the side and hold on until I got my balance back. I was standing there and a flood of pictures; places and feelings flowed together into a pure synthesized thought that pulled my past into focus. The first time I was in the Haze I was in a tree, a natural dome shape. The second time I was in a tee-pee shaped tent that was a modified dome structure. Then came other times and they were under dome structures. I had been instructed by KOZ to build my own dome structure.

All these locations that were dome related were not by chance places where I was in the Haze. I put this in the back of my mind on a slow simmering burner in a pot made of super stretcher material. I tied a string on one of the handles of the pot and tied the other end of the string to a strainer on the wall. I then took another string out of my pocket; this was a special string. This string was a silver string infused with Mind Energy. This string I tied to the strainer on the wall and to the next pillow that my head was going to rest on just before going to sleep. As soon as my head hit this pillow I would follow these strings back to what I needed to do. I was going to strain that pot of neural thought soup to establish a new guideline about domes and the Haze connection. This was all done in a few seconds. My friend Tommy did not know that I had left to go to the kitchen in my mind and had returned. I wanted to make this dome a part of me. I left a coin wedged on the outside of the upper walk way. I wasted no time saying anything about it; I just really thanked him for bringing me there and said that he would never know how much that it meant to me. Thank you so very much, just think all of this for a camping spot. We both thought about that and knew that it was not about a camping spot it was much bigger than that. I did not know what he was thinking. I was thinking about like Lower Minds on the same path, one reaching out giving the other a boost of Mind Energy, (life force), the most precious gift that could be given to anyone. It crosses all space and mindsets. It is pure universal giving. Maybe Tommy will some day understand how much I really appreciate all he has done and given to me, and most of all the gift of unquestioning trust. But the highest gift even if he does not realize it is his gift of joining me on this journey and giving me Mind Energy to continue my task of passing KOZ'S message forward. I hope that this writing will become a book some day and he will read and understand. This would fill my heart with joy and make me cry with a feeling of inner accomplishment that I did not let KOZ down.

KOZ: IT IS YOU AND MANY OTHERS THAT GIVE ME LIFE. WITHOUT YOU I WOULD HAVE NO PLACE TO SPEND MY MIND ENERGY AND IN RETURN RECEIVE YOURS.

There are things to come that you must not think about with your old establishment brain. You must stay on the path of the Giving Greater Known in your thought processes to receive these higher level gifts. Let them flow into your Lower Mind without your Middle Mind getting in the way. You will have time to pull down your strainer and synthesize for yourself what feels right and weigh it against all other inputs that are running you and me in circles.

***

Sycophant Looping

There I was sitting in Shelly's Pub Sioux Falls S.D. partaking of the sandwich bar and drinking iced tea. I was celebrating. I had broken the 30,000 word count in writing this book. There seemed to be no end. I felt at times that the book was my master, I was just a pawn in a long line of pawns. After visiting a large national bookstore chain, I wondered why I thought there was a need for another book. How would I feel when my book hit the $3.98 clearance table? It reminded me of the time I was in a dollar store and could not believe my eyes. There it was, the best selling book of all times, The Bible $1.00. I wished I had the money to buy them all and donate them to a church; they could have given them to the bible school.

    The men sitting to my left must have been from a different country. No, from a different planet. I had been sitting there listening looking for a place to butt in but I had no clue as to what they were talking about. I wondered what had happened that they were so well versed and I was totally lost. I started out by saying I have a question for you. I could see in his eyes that he thought that I was going to test his knowledge, a challenge. How old were you when you first got interested in sports? He said at a young age about 7 or 8. Well that might explain it. I was in Germany in those years of my life. I asked if their fathers were sport fans. Oh! Yes and his team was… they were off; there was no stopping them, they had shifted into talking about their dads and their choice of teams and players. They even talked about some of the players and coaches and said they don't make'em that way anymore, they were the greatest. They talked through their whole lunch. One man said that his son was a big sports fan, he said it in a way that made it sound like, yeah I brought him up right. He told me that his son was in college. I asked what was he taking, he said philosophy. I said that's great he will be able to tap into many ways of thought that will enhance whatever he does in life. I could see that he was disappointed, that his son was in engineering but then went into philosophy and he wondered why. In the back of my mind I was thinking that if he would of learned how to communicate and listen to his son instead of mind looping on sports that he would better understand him.

    Just the other day I was looking up a totally different word when I ran across this one; sycophant: (sik'\a\fant) n. flatterer, or one who fawns on the rich or famous; parasite… I was not the only one thinking that there was something wrong. These people had been infected by a brain-looping virus and did not even know it. Even before they had learned about the direction and the political view of their country, they were turned into non-caring mush brains. This was Oct. 25, 2000 eight days from the presidential election and not a word was said about the race. I go hacking my way through life with a double-edged sword. At times I think of what a waste of good brain cells and how they are frozen in the past. But then I also think how much easier it makes it for me to be leaps and bounds ahead of such poor creatures. It reminded me of the Romans. When the populous got out of control they ordered up more lions and Christians. Let the GAMES distract these feeble minds. Oh! How well it worked back then no one was minding the store, and how well it is working now; the shop keeper's head is into everything but getting off this rock. There has to come an awakening and a freeing of the mind that has never in the past been addressed. The stealing of one's mind should be a crime even more than of any material thing, like a car. There should be a second calling of the outcry, "LET MY PEOPLE GO" not only in body but also in mind. I think of the TRILLIONS 1,000,000,000,000,000,000 a million, million of lost hours and dollars, and of lives. I think of this as the biggest crime perpetrated on the human race. This will come to light some day and make the lawsuits against the tobacco companies seem like small peanuts. I could just imagine what the prosecuting attorney questions would be. I understand that you have a pool of psychologists, sociologists, and psychiatrists numbering in the hundreds in your employment? Answer; yes. And is it not true that they are employed to get something into a person's mind, something without them realizing it, or even wanting it in there? And you did not even ask permission for this trespass of this person's mind? Is it not true that you used repetitive exposure on a non-scheduled interval in a brain washing technique that you adopted from military research? You have played around with and off of some of a person's most intimate and emotional feelings to get your product sold. You used sex and the loss of loved ones and their love, which are all very deep-seated emotional mindsets to make a dollar. You have used all these covert methods to lure people into great debt and weakened the stability of our country.

I contend that they are guilty as charged and they will pay as sure as the sun will shine for millions of years to come, mark my words. Is there not precedent for has not the government already stepped forward and said no beer drinking on TV beer advertisements? And just lately ordered, the tobacco companies to stop using animals to entice children into thinking that smoking is cool? They already know that these processes are detrimental to us all and some day the people will matter, not the purse strings of the corporate PAC packers. KOZ: THERE HAS ALWAYS BEEN THE MIND PLAYING STAGE IN THE COSMIC EVOLUTION. THIS IS PART OF THE COSMIC GENE POOL TEST. THOSE WHO DON'T PASS WILL NOT MAKE THE JOURNEY HOME TO THE COLLECTIVE GIVING GREATER KNOWN. I can only hope that my writings will not be forgotten and that people in my lifetime will be given back their mind freedom. We together can do much more than just one voice in the wilderness. Come stand by me and pull your megaphone out of your back pocket too, and together we will yell, "Does anybody know where we are going?

**

THE FUTURE REUNION

One day as I was sitting at my favorite gravitational

anomaly, Koz came to me and asked me to go into my movie picture mind. He was going to take me on a trip in my mind to see the future. He said that he was doing it because it would give me the push to keep me writing. So come along with me and see what I saw in the Hase. I want you to go into your movie picture mind. Think about holding a round piece of glass in front of you. As you let your hand down this piece of glass stretches and flows around you in a football shape. Around this shape is a ring within a ring with many football or eye shaped holes in the inner ring. These eyes rotate around slowly in the inner ring. The outer ring does not move in a circle, it flops forward and backwards as we near a mother ring. This mother ring is not visible until the much larger football shaped eyes turn on. Just as you get close enough to see a circle in the football shaped holes in the mother ring they turn off and disappear. This happens so fast that all you see when you first start out is a blur of light that makes you feel like you are traveling through a tube of light. Only after you have traveled for what seems like ten minutes or so do the mother rings seem to slow down or become further apart. Then about another ten minutes pass before you can see the eye shaped holes on the mother rings. These were called energy rings. They were built to move matter at great speeds through space. As you neared the mother ring the shape of the glass football stretched out long like a cigar, and then regained its shape. Looking at a distance you only could see stars as they were falling behind. Then all of a sudden there was a yellow snowball glowing in front of my face on the other side of the glass. I jerked back. What was that? I was told that was what was called a Look-Look or Lo-Lo. They had been with us in space from the beginning of our leap into space. They seemed to be some kind of remote sensing device or maybe an inquisitive advanced life form, they know that we are coming. Coming up to the next energy ring I could see a large ball of smaller balls. I was told that this was a collection point for asteroids or anything that may be of use. The next phase was that the energy rings were coming on sooner and staying on. Either we were going slower or the energy rings were getting further apart. The energy rings had gone into reverse, slowing us down. As I looked around me there were about twenty other people along for the ride. I wondered if these were some of the other people that Koz was talking to and if there were so many of us why had I not run into any other reports of them on earth. Now the outer ring on the glass football pitched to one side and we plunged into a pool of blue-green liquid. This brought us to a stand-still as far as our perceptions could read. The glass football shrank down to that piece of glass you put in front of your face. We were standing in this liquid for only a moment when I noticed the top of my head felt warm and as this liquid drained away down past my eyes I could see a large door. When all the liquid had flowed out of holes in the floor the door opened. We were moved forward on a floor of wheels within wheels they were called Ezekiel wheels. The door behind us shut and another door in front of us opened. We were approached by people with backpack vacuum cleaners who gave us a good going over. We were then striped of our clothes and furnished jump suits, some green, some blue, some tan. Mine was green and I was led to a green door along with five others. I was told that when I reached a higher level of awareness that I would come back and progress through twelve levels, and that green was level one. We were handed dark glasses and hard hats and gloves made out of a finely woven metallic material. A very large center pivot wall swung and we walked forward. In my hard hat I could hear a computer-like voice say "Welcome to Reach One." There was no one to meet us. We just wandered around at first in a group and then we drifted apart and I was alone.

Everything was covered with a grass moss highbred, even the walking paths. The walking paths were made out of a Plexiglas grate that the grass stuff grew up through. The grate protected the plant from being trampled down to the roots. I came to a standard door thirty inches wide by seven feet tall. There was no door handle I pushed on it, it did not budge. I tried several other doors until I found out only the green doors would open. The first door that I went into led to a park, I was filled with the feelings of childhood. Off to my right was a group of people playing a game it was half way between bingo and battleship. I asked how to play but they did not hear me. I was just a witness I was not able to interact with anyone. I moved towards a small shrine-like structure. I looked inside there was a stack of fruit on a platter. I picked up one piece that looked like an apple. A curtain opened and a little lady looked out. I stepped forward and looked past the curtain inside was what I would call the smallest living quarters I had ever seen. I left. I walked over to a pond, beside this pond was a man's head made out of stone and water was coming out of his mouth. I took a drink. As soon as the water hit my lips I felt a surge go through my body. I could hear someone saying "The park is closing now." I was back on earth. I felt like telling the park officer where to go, that I wanted to get back to Reach One. I looked at my watch. It was ten fifteen. I had been sitting there for five hours. KOZ: YOU WILL SEE ONLY WHAT YOUR MIND IS READY TO SEE. DON'T LET YOUR MIND BE STOLEN FROM YOU BY BUSY MIND LOOPING. I yearn for the day that I may enter the blue doors. Stay with me we will travel to places only few get to see.

* * *

Brain Stirring

I was lost or at least I felt that way, which way was south? I had felt some really good gravitational anomalies but I did not know which way was south. Koz had instructed me to face south when I was focused over the top of a gravitational anomaly. This would assure the correct alignment of the electrons and protons in my brain. That if you did not stand facing south that you would suffer from brain stirring. Brain stirring would be like taking the parabolic dish out from under your satellite receiver or the lens out of a flashlight. The signal or the light would just scatter. We have all heard somebody call somebody else a scatterbrain. We can sense brain stirring in others but not ourselves. We must tune into the mirror image of ourselves that is fed to us by what other people are saying and how they are acting towards us. If you can see that other people think that you are just not with it, you must take action. There could be external reasons why you are not clicking along with everyone else. The first thing to look for is an electrical appliance next to your brain, such as an alarm clock, a night light, an electric blanket. These three things are big ones because of the amount of exposure time. Any type of florescent lighting is bad because of the stray electrons emitted by the ballast. No wonder so many people feel so drained after sitting under florescent lights for eight hours or longer. They head to their favorite regeneration stop and crash. For many this is a bar where they think numbing the brain with alcohol will help, but it just adds to the problem. Get away from the water cooler, and the electric pencil sharpener. Don't hang your head over the copying machine or hang around the microwave oven while you are waiting for your food to be done. Don't eat it for at least one full minute after you have micro-waved it. Find a seat in the break room or lunchroom that is the furthest away from the microwave and line-up of vending machines. Your best move is getting what you need and getting out. Go outside or back to your workstation and eat. Don't use in the ear earphones, such as telephone headsets, Dictaphone, radio, or tape player. Keep the volume to the bare minimum. All these things are bad for children as their brains are growing. If it will affect a compass needle it will effect your brain and the rest of your body. Where have all the great brains gone, gone to stirring everyone. Where are our geniuses, name five off the top of your head. Don't feel bad, I can,t and I bet you if you asked around the same question they also could not.

I was in the hunt for a small inconspicuous compass, something that would fit on my key chain or… there it was just what I was looking for, a compass that had a bobby pin attached. The compass was one of the liquid filled ones that was a ball in a ball. It was designed to wear on the outside of your shirt. If put at a distance of your focal length it becomes a no hands access tool. I put mine in the inside of my coat. Not because I was worried about what other people would think, but I just would not have the time trying to explain why I had a compass pined to my jacket. Gee I am having a hard enough time trying to write about it, with all the time I want to take. Now I could check out my newly relearned gravitational anomaly sensing against a scientifically accepted measuring device. I was headed to a set of dome structures built by the city and the forestry department along the Big Sioux River that runs through Sioux Falls, SD. When I got there it was noon and there was a school field trip going on at this designated outdoor classroom. I stayed clear. I will come back some day when my back and forth walking patterns will not attract attention. All I would need is a school teacher calling the police on her cell phone and report that there is a man around my children acting funny; like he's drunk or something. I could see myself trying to explain to the cops what I was doing. Who knows where that may lead to, even a trip downtown?

I went inside the information center, looked at some of the transfers of fishes the kids had done and went back to my car. I was just sitting there trying to think of another spot that I wanted to test out. I fell into the haze, I looked down, I was wearing a blue shirt and there was a door opening in front of me. I was not alone. There were green shirts and tan shirts. I was at the next level back on REACH ONE. There was a plaque on the wall that everyone read. It said, THOSE THAT SEEK SHALL FIND IT IS JUST A MATTER OF TIME. I knew to head to the blue door, now the color of my shirt. I also didn't waste my time on any doors that were not blue. It was only a short distance when I reached a blue door. I noticed written on it WHAT ARE YOU SEEKING? I thought about that, and I wished that I could have something that I could bring back with me to show my son and others so they might believe. I opened the door. It swung open before my hand touched it. I was in some type of storage facility. But there were no shelves or drawers; each item hung suspended in space. I was able to move among them in any direction. A big sign that was blinking at a disturbing cycle rate read "Choose Only One." There had to be thousands of things to choose from; what kind of time frame did I have? I got busy. I reached out to hold and examine one of them; my hand went right through it. It was a holograph, I should have known that it was not going to let me that easily take something that was physical. All around each article were words in a ball describing what it was. I started to read it was an inner self-seeing scope. The next article was some type of skin meter for testing atom structure. The next item was a mind-focusing device. I knew immediately that this was what I wanted. It was a curved shaped item that looked like a turned inside out bean pod. It had five indentions on each side. I saw a holograph showing a person using one of them. In the writing it explained in great detail that the size and bone density of each person's hands when positioned correctly could compensate for that person's cranial dome defects. I was intensely trying to absorb everything about this item. I wanted to build one when I got back. It had to do with the positioning of the fingers, fingertip to fingertip, and then the correct way for it to be held in relationship to the head. This device was also a spacer, an insulator, that would calibrate the spacing of the fingers from themselves and from your head. After reading all that was there I just stood there soaking in every little nuance, even down to its color. I wanted this even if it did not seem like something that might convince anybody where it came from. I wanted it for myself. This tool could change my whole way of thinking and open areas that I had never thought of before.

As quickly as I had arrived on Reach One, I was back sitting in my car, it was 2:45: I had been sitting there for two and a half hours. Where had the time gone? I should move on. I don't want anybody to think that I am a stalker or something else even worse. I wondered why I was feeling more and more paranoid. KOZ: THOSE ON DIFFERENT PATHS WOULD LIKE TO THINK THAT THEY ARE ON THE RIGHT PATH AND EVERYBODY ELSE IS GOING THE WRONG WAY. BE TUNED INTO YOUR INNER FEELINGS. THEY WILL WITH THE GUIDANCE OF THE GIVING GREATER KNOWN BRING YOU TO KNOW THE PURENESS OF THE UNIVERSAL COSMIC LAWS THAT HAVE NO BEGINNING OR END. Every day now I feel that I am getting a clearer and clearer picture of why I am here and what I should be doing. I hope that you will reach this state of awareness. I know you will if you will tune into what Koz has been saying and what he has not been saying. I have never felt that there is some kind of secret agenda. He has never asked for anything that would embellish himself. He always just acts as a conduit for the Giving Greater Known and the Cosmic Universal Law. Who else have you been listening to that you can say that about? The stench of pork barrel politics is sticking in people's noses; they are looking for some way to blow it out. I know I am, how about you? Are you ready for a kinder way of life where we are working together instead of killing each other? If so you are on the right path. To turn around now is to throw away hope.

***

FEAR OF THE WATCHERS

It starts very early in life. They are there watching. I tried to think about the rest of Mother Nature. Who was called in to baby-sit when a fox or a bobcat had to go hunt while they had a litter? Some dads stuck around but the majority of dads are nowhere to be found. What animal after the age of three has constant hands on carrying? It all starts with the report from the baby-sitter to the parents. There was no chance that they would listen and believe what you had to say over what the baby-sitter said. This feeling of resentment toward the watchers builds early and grows. It seems whatever they do is OK but when you do it, you will have no chance against the system of the watchers. At a very young age we become a split mode of operation. There is how we act when we are not being watched and then in a split second we can switch into the being watched mode. Can you remember when the teacher left the room were we all good little boys and girls? I don't think so; it would be against a basic cosmic common law of freedom. This two-faced acting goes on through our lives. It is done between husband and wife, between employee and employer, the populous and the police, the police and the judges, the judges and the next higher court. Between the private and the sergeant, the sergeant and the captain, the captain and the general, the generals and the commander in chief, the President of the United States. Between the president and his cabinet, the USA and the rest of the world. Then to make the circle complete between the President and the people. We all have this mode of operation shift in all of us, some to a higher degree than others.

    I am trying to reach a place that has only a destination in your brain. I am trying to stir your neural soup to bring back feelings. I am trying to establish a way of thought that is so pure that it is not even thought about. This mode of thinking is so automatic you tend to skip over the thinking of it. Take your time and let my examples work as tools to bring these thoughts to the foreground.

    These thought shifts do not have any borders. I remember one day my son and I were looking out a window watching a group of men go through their martial art forms at the command of their instructor. The instructor was called away for a moment. He had stepped out of sight. The small talk started. Men left the ranks and started visiting. As soon as the instructor returned they were back to their ranks as if nothing had happened. Now as Paul Harvey would say, "the rest of the story". We were in the Crestwood Hotel, about four blocks from Tiananmen Square, Beijing, China. The men we were watching without their seeing us were the national police force. They were playing the two-faced game. These of all men were some of the most up-tight people in the world. This reinforced my thoughts of the being watched mind shift.

    I also remember a time when my son and I were out side the train station in Fussa, Japan. The Kentucky Fried Chicken manager was dressing up Colonel Sanders like Santa Claus. He had just pulled up his red pants with the white fur and gone inside. From around the corner of the building came two young Japanese children, hands over their mouths, laughing; this reminded me of basic training when we were laughing at the drill instructors. The children went over to the Santa Claus Colonel Sanders and pulled his pants down, and took off running and laughing when the manager came out yelling something.

Just the other day I had a cop on my tail. A rush of "Oh no, what did I do now? Hit me. Was I going too fast? His lights aren't on. Better look at my speed, that's OK. I wonder if I have a light out. I sure hope my insurance and registration are in order. Hell! I don't even remember if my driver's license is up to date. I hope that I am not fitting some kind of profile that he is going by. What could it be? Gee it's been four blocks now, I wonder if he is running my plates. My mind is thinking of when was my last moving violation. Hell I haven't even had a parking ticket in ten years in this town. They're just looking for anything to zap you with. All they want is the money. I could not take the anxiety anymore I turned off and watched in my review mirror if he was still following. He went by; what had happened to me? I was a mess. I wondered if the cop really knew how much he took from me. What he had just put me through, it made me feel violated. He had trespassed into my mind and made me fearful. It was not his fault, it was because of the stacking of the watchers over many years that was boiling over into a mind that wanted to shift modes. We must recognize this deep ingrained fixed action pattern and control it and use it as a tool. It is not just us that feel this way it is everybody. We as young children knew it. "I'll tell mom on you" was the cry that filled your brother or sister with fear. Then it was I will tell the teacher you are cheating. Then came I'm going to call the cops on you. Then we shifted into a sue happy society, I'm calling my attorney he will take a chunk out of your ass.

I find myself these days using the "stay away from it" mode. Where do the cops like to hang out in wait for their next score? It's one drink and I'm out of there I can't afford a DUI or any kind of run in with the cops, who knows what it might escalate into. The way they like to push you around and twist arms to hand cuff you. It's their right to be able to assault you in the line of duty and heaven forbid if he is alone not being watched what he might do, it's his word against yours. I don't want to be the newest member of the Special Olympics because they did a Rodeny King on me. Fear, fear, fear, is this any way to have to live. KOZ: THE LOWER MIND IS TAPPED INTO DIRECTLY WITH THE USE OF FEAR. USE THE FEAR FEELING TO TURN ON THE SHEILD OF PROTECTION. I my-self can't wait to get to the next writing session. I want to let you know that the influence of Koz has been increasing. This is way beyond my control. Just a year ago I was computer illiterate and was not planning to write anything surly not a book, about what? Fear struck me, what would happen to me if I stopped writing? What would he do; not wanting to say his name right now? I was thrown a curve ball three days ago. The fan is not coming on in my laptop computer. What do I do? I called a factory repair center and they said that they were just a level one repair station and my problem would be a level two problem. That meant that my laptop would have to be sent to Minneapolis for repairs. He did not know the cost or time frame as far as when I would get it back. Now what? I can't be without my computer, not even for one day. I knew I was not in control of this whole writing thing. I should have seen it when I bought the printer and soon after the scanner. I had better places to put that money like paying my back property taxes or credit card. There the answer was I saw it on TV the new cool one just released by Compaq. I wrote the phone number down. That's what I'll do, I will buy that one and have it in use before I send in my 14- month-old Compaq Presario 1275 for repairs. The next day I got on the phone to call the number on the TV advertisement. I must have written it down wrong. The number was for someone in Boca Raton in Florida. She said that she had been getting other people calling about a computer, too. Maybe it was an 888 number not an 800 number. I tried that, no luck. Maybe something is trying to tell me something: that I should not buy this computer. Was Koz trying to help now? But then I found myself punching in the numbers 1-800-555-1212. This is the information number for company 1-800 numbers. The computer voice asked for the company name. My computer will be here in ten days. What had I done now? By the time the extra battery, carrying case, 3 year extended warranty and shipping were added on it came to just a little over $2000.00. This has gotten way out of hand, who is in control? KOZ: THE FEAR OF THE WATCHERS WILL DRAIN MIND ENERGY NEEDED TO TAP INTO THE GIVING GREATER KNOWN. AN INTERNAL SELF-MADE WATCHER WILL BUILD MIND ENERGY WITHIN YOU. I could sense and feel more than understand about the watching of others and how it added an element of uneasiness. I want you to forget about my examples of being watched. I want you to go back into your past and remember a time when being watched made you feel on edge. How being watched made you think and do things differently. Take this feeling and use it to build an internal watcher. From now on whatever you do there is a watcher watching what you are doing. I pick a person like my father or grandmother as the watcher. These steps that I have taken in my life have made a difference in my performance throughout life. I look over to my mental toolbox and I see myself putting in a large eyeball.

***

THE SHIELD

For humans there is a built-in system of survival. When we got cold we wrapped ourselves in blankets. We found caves that would protect us, and keep us warm. We did things as soon as we could. We were taught to think on our feet. And by all means if you could talk your way out of something, do it. These methods worked just fine when everybody was on a level playing field. The gap or disparity of knowledge was not that great. It was your cunning and wits that made the difference. We loved hearing about someone getting over on someone else. That was neat and cool. The movie Cool Hand Luke was this type of slickness. We had Zorro and Sergeant Friday to help us think about how to use our minds to solve things. People for many years did just fine using their own wits to keep away from or get out of trouble. It was during the Second World War that they started to use a person's words as a tool against them. They made a science of talking to people and getting the information that they wanted. They became very good at it; sometimes so good that it seemed unfair. When the war was over these interrogating methods that the government had developed to use on our enemies were adopted by the private sector. The police, employers, private social clubs, and even churches used these methods. The government, seeing this, thought that it was surely something that they did not want to unleash on their own people. They went about setting up safeguards against such practices of trespassing into people's minds and thoughts. They knew very well that the human mind could not withstand this type of questioning, that it could be led to believe and say anything you wanted it to. All it would take is enough mental and physical pressure. Even our forefathers many years before this had taken steps to protect us from ourselves. The Fifth Amendment to the constitution was one thing that the government inacted. This was a law dreamt up by lawyers and implemented by lawyers. It was presented in the light to protect the people. In fact it was really to protect the pocket books of the attorneys. How could they earn any money on an open and shut case, supplied to the police by there clients. Attorneys need some way to keep their clients mouths shut. Attorneys even went a step further, this was fine for the courtroom but attorneys needed something for the street. Attorneys needed something to protect people from themselves and the police. Attorneys came up with the Miranda rights. This tool should be studied very closly. Your Miranda rights should not be mentioned at the point of confrontation. This will only alert whoever you are talking with that you have these tools and understand your rights. This is where you can have a chance to have things go in your favor, not in the short term but further down the road. If you did not open your mouth and insert your foot or say things that you shouldn't have your attorney will have a better chance of defending you. This is not a contest of what is right or wrong, but who can prove their position.

    I want you to go into your movie picture mind. I want you to see yourself hiding in a closet under a blanket. You are playing hide and seek, or you are hiding from the bad guy. You are very quiet you are even breathing quietly so you can hear everything that is going on outside the closet doors. You hear, "I know that you are in there! Come out!" You don't. He is just trying to trick you. "Where are you? Tell me!" See? He didn't know where you were, he was lying. Now reach into your back pocket and pull out the remote control to your toy car in the next room and make it make some noise. You hear "I hear you" and footsteps leaving the room.

Now you are sitting in a theater watching a cowboy movie. There are two men in the bushes trying to shoot each other. One of them picks up a rock and throws it in the bushes some feet away from where he is. The other man shoots at the sound and doing so gives up his hiding spot. The stone thrower shoots him.

Now reach into your pocket and pull out your protective shield. It has written on it, "protection from mind trespassing and invasion of thoughts." Pull this around you. This will stop you from aiding the enemy. See yourself. You are in a trench passing bullets to your lawyer with your right hand and when you are saying something you are sucking them back away.

Now you are back in the real world. This person has asked you a question like where were you at ten p.m. Tuesday the third? This is not a good time to plead the 5th or ask, "Aren't you going to read me my rights?" This is the time to be the confused child in the closet that has been found. Your answer should be no answer at all and confusing as hell. Like; well was that a holiday? If it was I was not at work because I work half days on Mondays and Wednesdays. This will surely make this person think that you are on drugs or not with it mentally. This should stop them in their tracks. If they still ask you another question like, are you on any type of medication? Answer; the last time I had a full meal was four days ago and that's when people should take medicine that's what my sister told me. You have given nothing and at the same time given him enough to show that he tried to question you without reading you your rights. If this sounds like just plain foolishness that's good. Your mouth had something to do besides saying things you should not and you are not challenging the questioner personally. The more confusing the better. Let him be the one that is running his mouth, he will be hung by the tongue. The wonders your attorney can do with the right information. Couldn't you see that my client was confused and needed medical help? Why did you persist in questioning him? Why did you not assist in getting him the proper help? KOZ: THOSE THAT TASK THEIR MIDDLE MIND WITH OUT THE AID OF THE LOWER MIND TAPPING INTO THE GIVING GREATER KNOWN ARE ON A PATH OF DOOM. Are these things that Koz is telling me so hard to understand? Why was I not told or taught these things in school or by my father? Maybe the teachers or my father were not taught, and had no idea how to pass this information on to their sons or students. Their way out was saying that, that is something that can't be taught, you just have to learn that for yourself. This way of thinking is presuming that somehow that you can teach yourself. If this were true then there would be no need for schools, teachers, or books. I am going to let Koz be my teacher. I have learned more from him than in 17 years in school. Tag along; there might be something that you might learn, too.

***

CIRCLES OF INFLUENCE

I was always the loner, the outsider, the new kid on the block. My father was a military man. We moved a lot. I belonged to no group, I had a built-in self-reliance that was cultivated over the years of being plucked and planted. I had been to ten different schools to just get through high school. I was suffering from post-traumatic stress syndrome by the sixth grade. I could remember trying out for basketball in junior high. I was cut, the tallest kid there. I was by no means a star or even a good player, but I should have beaten out three or four other guys who made the team. As we looked at the cut list taped on the wall we started to console each other on the way back to the locker room. Boy I'm glad that it is over now I can do what I want to do after school. One boy next to me changing his clothes was crying. He said that it was his second year that he was cut. That He and his father had practiced all summer. He was dreading telling his father when he got home. He said it was just like last year; the guys that made the team were the kids that had well connected parents: the mayor's son, a police officer's son, and the rest of the parents who were in business.

I was left out one more time; I blamed it on my father and his damned military career. This went on through my life, this rejection. There was the Junior Chamber of commerce that I was not welcomed into. It was just a way that businessmen could hire each other's kids and give them a nice paying job for the summer with all the write-offs allowed by the IRS. I felt like I was in the wilderness alone with no support group and nobody was handing out maps how to get to town. My dad was no help at all he was more unconnected than I was, being seen as a warmonger in the late 60's.

We are all in the cosmic wilderness at the outer edge of our galaxy. We are being held at a long arm's length while being observed. I want you to go into your movie picture mind. I will only be able to transfer this information as I received it from Koz in picture form. Bear with me as I try to put it in words.

You are walking through a large hallway. You reach into your pocket and put on your eye filters. Coming to a door you put your hand on it and a panel blinks twice and the door opens. You walk in. A great round of clapping is performed in your honor. It looks like they are bowing down to you but in a seated position only using their upper body. You are seated in the middle of the holograph dome. There are 125 regional delegates who are sitting in their holograph domes. Each of them is in contact with 125 district delegates sitting in their holograph domes. They are in contact with 125 local advisors. Do the math 125x125x125= 1,953,125 members at this meeting. You are the chairman. You are the one who has the last say on the vote. This vote only comes around every 20 yaves, which is 253 earth years. There are 10,478 candidates for upgrading in six different levels of advancement, from full membership to first contact level one. This is your 14th session. You are down to the last category level, first contact level one. The planet being considered is called Earth. Being discussed is whether another mentor should be assigned. This planet was not in line for consideration for at least another 12,000 of their earth years. Why are we even looking at this? His name is Koz and he is very admired and will be glad to take the time to mentor this transformation. He has good connections and a big circle of influence with the regional delegates. There is a short timeframe for this planet because of an up coming asteroid collision factor.

  The vote is in. Earth has been recommend by a 14 vote margin. Look to your right. On your armrest there is a button that reads hood. Push it. From an arm sticking out of the back of your chair comes a viewing hood. It comes down over your head. You remove your eye protection, and start to view the history of this small distant planet called Earth.

  Now come back to your middle mind, how did you vote? I voted yes only because of the spot Koz was in. Surely I would have voted no looking back on the history of mankind. Who in their right minds would even consider such a race? Whatever could have been done wrong has been done and many times. What would make anyone think that this would change in the future? I would have voted for total annihilation without blinking an eye if I could have stayed in my movie picture mode. KOZ: MEMBERS OF THE FAMILY OF THE GIVING GREATER KNOWN ARE VERY KIND AND PATIENT. THEY WERE ALL PUT THROUGH THE COSMIC GENIAL TEST. I don't know about you but I'm going for it. I want to see the transformation go forward. This chance that we have been given is a real gift of the cosmos. Without the help of Koz we will be led down a path of sure destruction. I want to try something else, a new direction.

***

OUTSIDE CHANGE

I was living in Biloxi, Mississippi. My dad was stationed at Kessler Air Force Base. We were visiting some friends out in the country. These people were dirt poor but I envied them for their roots. There were the horseback rides down to the swimming hole that cost nothing to take the heat off you. The horses had horse sense. They knew what they had to put up with and from whom. The warning came, watch out for that one, he will try to dump you any way he can. Sure enough, under the clothesline he went, but I crouched low and stayed with him. There was a lot of rib heeling and words said before getting to the swimming hole. The water was going to feel mighty good after riding bare legged and bare footed bare back on a horse that had never seen a brush. The water was cool and clean. The sand was called singing sands because when you walked on them they squeaked. It was time to go to another swimming hole. This was a secret one that only the kids knew about. On the horses we got. The ride was quite brisk; it was all I could do to hold on. There came a fork in the path. We were going to the right. That's where everybody else went. Everybody else except my horse. He went left and there I sat on the ground. They came back for me and I rode double with someone else. They said they should have warned me about how the horse I was riding had to be stopped after the left turn and turned around. Then he would go left to the secret swimming hole. I was told that he was so used to going home at that junction that he would not take the right path any other way. This swimming hole was special. It was a virgin swimming hole. They called it the Garden of Eden and only skinny-dipping was allowed. The day was long but went by far too fast for this was a magical place and time. Not only did our clothes peel away but also any cares of the outside world. Congress and the House of Representatives, along with the UN, should be mandated to do this simple act of saying I'm human just like you.

* * *

They came in every other day: TCTOs, technical changes to orders. After you had gone through security, they were handed to you along with the tech manuals you were going to need to fix the problem. I was headed to P-0, a launch control facility. They were having water problems. I wish I could say more. But I'm not too sure what the boundaries are on talking or writing about a nuclear weapon system. At the time I had a secret security clearance status and was made to feel important. After changing out the pages in the manual the new procedures were in place. The next person who checked out the manual, unless he read every word step by step, would not know of the changes. There were people who had the job of looking over your shoulder and making sure you were reading every word, QC&E Quality Control and Engineering. But they were not there every trip so it was common practice to fix something the way you always did. Those damned books were just too much trouble to haul down a sixty-foot ladder and back out. I could remember carrying what I was going to need in one hand and using the other hand on the ladder. One missed grab of a rung and it would be over.

* * *

There were problems in the heartland. There were going to be big changes. Farmers were going to be removed from their land for lack of payment. First came the auction. This is where it started: the resistance to change. The banks, the government and the laws were the outside threat that built up the inward cohesiveness of the farmers. At the auction they could not get anyone to bid much over a dollar for anything, not even a tractor. The banks weren't going to get their money that easily. At the end of the auction whoever had bought something would sell it back to its owner for the same dollar at a payment date of whenever you get around to it. There was a lot of hand-shaking going on in the days when the handshake was better than the written contract. If your handshake was not any good you might as well give up farming because you weren't going to make it through the tough times without the help of your neighbors.

This is about as good as any time to say that the art of change was developed into a management tool. Somehow I think that our own American Indians and a lot of other people would point out how change for change sake has been used to control people for a long time.

They are called fixed action patterns. These are the feared, deep-seated, very hard to change, automatic actions of people who have not been controlled by change. If change happens enough, the mind will accept change. This allows the rules of the game to be changed in the favor of the government. If the government is not getting the desired results from the established laws, the government will change the rules or laws. And remember, ignorance of the law is no excuse, no matter how often the government changes them. This is brain stirring at its best. If the populous can't be out smarted out of their hard earned money the government will hoodwink them out of it by changing the rules. If the government would like to get rid of someone the government will show how incompetent they are by changing laws or rules without notification. This is setting a trap that will blind side the best of them into making mistakes. KOZ: THE CONSTANT CHANGING OF THE COSMIC SOUP IS WHAT GIVES LIFE A CHANCE. THOSE THAT EMBRACE CHANGE AND SEE THE GOOD, WILL IN A MATTER OF TIME REJOIN THE COLLECTIVE FAMILY OF THE GIVING GREATER KNOWN.

Oh! How my life would have been different if I could have learned this concept early on in life. I have lent you see some of my sign-posts that change was a thing to be dealt with. Go into your movie picture mind and bring back some of the things that changed your life. Sit with your eyes closed and see yourself going through those memories of unwanted or unexpected change. Then rewrite them with you in control. See yourself leap-frogging over those problems and see how your life could have been different. Now return to your Middle Mind(the everyday you) and know that you now have this powerful tool working for you. Survey everything that is the now and know that it is going to change. You start building contingency plans for every aspect of your life. You will never be the victim of change again. In fact you will be seen as a person who can foretell the future. They will talk about you and your far-sightedness long after you pass on.

***

MONEY LOOPING

Why is that baby crying now? I fed him and changed his diaper. Let's see. I will give him his pacifier and rattle his rattle. Well, that seemed to work. He will be quiet long enough to maybe fall asleep. Five minutes later; why is that baby crying now? Let's see. He is dry. Maybe a cookie will work. This is the moment that will affect that baby in a big way the rest of its life. The looping starts at a very young age. This is a human brain that you are dealing with. It will learn quickly how to get the next rush of endorphin to the brain. It's not the item or the action or the thought behind it that counts. The thing that counts is another hit of self-synthesized drug into the brain. There are no laws against body-made drugs. But if there becomes an identifying abnormal trait due to the over-indulgence of self- built drugs you may need to be medicated, to counteract this self-drugging. If it gets too far out of hand you might need to be put under supervision. And if you have done anything that was against the law while getting that rush of endorphin, off to jail you go. This cycle of feeling down and finding the next hit of body-made drug can become just as addictive as any man-made drug. In fact, this self-made drug surpasses anything on the market or illegally marketed as far as a supply route. The brain can give itself a hit of enjoyment any time it wants to. All we would have to do in our minds is think of something in our past that gave us enjoyment and relive it. This works for a while but then the brain wants something new.

There it was. Little pieces of brain stuff splattered against the wall. There is a true way to read someone's mind. It is plastered on the walls of their houses or apartments. You can see it in the curio cabinets and on the knick-knack shelves. I worked cleaning carpets and later fixing air conditioning and heating systems. This gave me access to all the parts of a person's house, thus his mind. Every mind and every house has its junk room. The thing that I noticed most is what I have coined A.C.E., Another Capital Eater, I'm talking about money. This ace will put you in the hole and keep you there. This person has been using buying small little knick-knacks to trigger the self-made drug hit to their brain. I'm not talking about a few little pieces here and there, I am talking about hundreds of junky items in the $5 range or less. I also saw a correlation between that and the person being overweight. They were also using food to trigger their inner drug habit. This type of brain looping can get into vicious circles. The person can feel bored and go shopping, spending money that was meant for something else. Now they worry that there is not going to be enough money so they get depressed. They treat themselves to some ice cream and this adds to their weight problem. They get depressed about their weight and set a goal that if reached will get them that little gift that they have been wanting.

The hardest thing to do is to see that you may be trapped into this type of mind looping. When you can see yourself in this trap you must do a mind pattern shift. You will have to find things to eat or spend money on that work in your favor and still give you that inner drug hit. As a man, tools that I could use in doing my own car repair were a good spending shift. Also just buying something that I would need like toilet paper or garbage bags put something in my hands and made me feel good that I had bought something. I also used a savings account as a place to fork over some cash. This was also spending and got me out of the house. I ate fewer sweets and ate more carrots and celery. Sunflower seeds can put the mind and body to work without packing on the weight like those little cookies can. I was still spending and eating and getting my hits of inner drugs and now knowing that I am doing it in a way that will impact both of my bottom lines. The little thought that I am really changing will grow inside and someday replace the worry and depression that fuel this destructive brain looping. Beta-endorphin, an endorphin of the pituitary gland with much greater analgesic potency than morphine, is now under your control. Your body intelligence is at your command when you have recognized the problem and done the mind-shifting. Sometimes I think that this has to be against the law some how. You are not spending money on junk. You are eating more healthy and saving money. And you're getting your drugs free from your inner factory. This is going against all the rules of the rich getting richer. I feel like I'm cheating the system and way down inside of me I want to keep it a secret and tell it to no one. I have found a tool that I can use at will at no charge. If I let everyone know about it they will surely outlaw it or tax it. I know that I don't have to worry for knowing a secret and using it are two different things. Many people who read this will still be stuck in the state of nothingness and stay doing nothing. For those who act, they will find powers of many kinds that will build off of this mind shifting technique.

 Now go into your movie picture mind and see yourself buying things that are not junk and feeling good about it. There is a man standing at the end of the checkout counter he is handing you a diploma as he is shaking your hand. He says welcome to your new way of thought. Congratulations on your mind shifting abilities. You read the diploma and it says: Let it be known to all that _____ has passed the test of mind shifting. (Put your name in the blank spot.) He/She will no longer be a slave of the system and will not be swayed into brain looping again. Do not even try to lure this person into these types of practices for they will get into your face and put you in your place. This person knows the power of the free mind, stay out of their way. As you leave the store there is a crowed of people there welcoming you to an elite group of free thinkers. One steps forward and hands you a check for the sum of $250,000 and says, this will be yours to cash at the end of your new path. They open the door to the limousine that will take you into your new life of clear thinking. Now I want you to come back to your Middle Mind and find a place to be alone and think. Hold your hands together in front of you. As you go over your mind movie I want you to squeeze your right hand with the left one until it hurts and hold it until your mind movie picture is over. Then do the same to the left hand. Do this three times, then release your hands and lay them on top of your head and go through your movie mind pictures another three times. As you are doing this I want you to push on the top of your head and say to yourself, this is for the Lower Mind. Do it between each viewing of the mind movie. KOZ: THOSE WHO CAN MASTER THE MOVIE PICTURE MIND CAN MASTER ALL. HAND SQUEEZING IS A DIRECT LINK TO IMPRESS THE LOWER MIND AND SHOULD BE DONE WHEN TRYING TO DO A DEEP IMPLANT INTO THE LOWER MIND. I wish somebody else had been chosen to write this book long before I was born. That way I would have had it in my younger life to guide me. How different my life would have been. I find myself rereading my own book as I am writing it. I wonder at times if they might have a clinic somewhere to help writers stop writing. Koz has assured me that I have a lot more to write. This at times bothers me because I at times don't have the foggiest idea what I'm going to write next, like now. Stay with me. At times I feel like I'm the only person in the world going through this transformation. It makes me feel lonely.

* * *

HEAD POUNDING

There's a lot of fighting going on out there. We start our training very young. At first it doesn't look like fighting, it looks like playing, those first pulls and tugs on the rings hanging above our heads. We know instinctively that it is going to take some hands-on manipulation to get things going. If things aren't working like we think they should we throw them or pound on them. If we have a brother or sister, we throw things at them and pound on them. It just feels like it works better that way. When we want to make something perfectly clear we always raise our voices or reach out to touch someone. This combination of words and physical contact is a short cut to the Lower Mind. We learn when we are very young that crying and rattling the bars on our crib together have a better response time than crying alone. Most fighting was meant only so that you could impress the Lower Mind of others. This is also throughout the rest of the animal kingdom. The loser of the fight just walks or runs away.

It took the superior thinking of man to take fighting past its original purpose into an art form. We deduced that more was better even if it meant death. It started with the correct and most efficient way of delivering a hit with the hand, Karate or fighting hands. Then came weapons and the blood started to flow. We have pushed the envelop on self destruction to a point of assured extinction. Now is the time to push it toward the inner direction, toward the Lower Mind.

I want you to find a quiet place to yourself, which will provide uninterrupted space. Sit in front of a table and put your hands on it. The brain has its own laws and rhythms that govern its interplay with the outside world. I want to teach you a rhythm that will greatly reduce the time needed to impress the Lower Mind. With your right index finger, tap on the table to the song "Old Mc Donald had a farm". The rhythm is what you are after, not the words. Do this until you can do it without the words. The next step is to pound on the table as if you were pounding on bread dough. Think only about the amount of force that you are using. This amount of force is very important, too little or too much will send the wrong messages. Then I want you to think of duration, the length of time spent pounding, before a pause and then resuming. The pause is where you insert the message that you want to impress on the Lower Mind. Turn the fight inward. Direct it at yourself. This will put your Lower Mind on notice that something very important is coming its way. After you have taught your right hand the rhythm, the amount of force, and the pause, it won't take you long to teach the left hand. Now scoot up to the table so that you can put your elbows on it. Put your elbows on the table, forearms straight up, your hands balled up in fists, fingers facing toward you. Put your head between your fists and place your fists on a spot above and behind the ear. The placing is important. Think of your head as a box and your fists are on the top back corners. The fleshy part of the hand should be the spot where the hand touches the head. Hold your left hand firmly against your head as you softly pound out the rhythm with your right hand. When you get to EIEIO, stop and insert your message to your Lower Mind. For example, "I need to start saving at least ten percent." Then resume pounding with your left hand, keeping your right hand firmly against your head. Do this three times on each side. You must make sure that you do this three times throughout the day for three days.

    Now go into your movie picture mind. See yourself getting your paycheck and as soon as it touches your hand you turn into a robot. You will not turn into a person again until you have taken the check to the bank and put 10percent of it into a savings account. See yourself walking like a robot to your car. Driving straight to the drive up window at your bank. Hear yourself say I want to put ten percent of that into my savings, twenty dollars cash, and the rest into my checking." As soon as the bank teller says OK you are yourself again. The twenty dollars is your reward for doing this task and can be spent only on yourself or given away. Every night when you go to bed use the inward looking eye that glimpses the future to see if your head pounding sessions are getting through to your Lower Mind. Make sure that you keep this a secret. You do not need to have your Lower Mind getting mixed messages. You may ask someone if they are reading this book. If they are you can ask them if they have gotten to the head pounding yet and share your experiences but never give out your information about any on-going processes that you are working on with the Lower Mind. You do not want any unwelcome visitors at night trying to help you, but not helping you. The secret is not meant to keep things from people, but to keep them from sending you things that will disrupt your hard-fought for deep-implanted instructions to your Lower Mind. You can't let one "I bet you it won't," or "it can't work" into your on-going transformation. The Lower Mind is very vulnerable to outside suggestions. It is a child that is very naïve and will take in all as truth. If the answers are out there why are they still fighting and killing my brothers and sisters? The true power is within you; don't let the fighting children in. KOZ: MASTER YOUR INNER DISIPLINE THIS WILL MASTER ALL OUTER ACTIONS. DO NOT LET THE CHILDISH FIGHTING MIND STIR YOUR LOWER MIND. I find myself taking, what I see other people doing and saying that's just like what I said in my book. I have noticed a shift in my awareness and how it's able to see the brain stirring and looping in others. They are being blown by the winds of other people's Lower Minds. I feel at times that they are a breed apart. I wish I could hand them this book and ask my brothers and sisters to start the inward transformation.

***

FOCUS INWARD

Look around you. What are you seeing? What are your brothers and sisters doing? What are you seeing on TV or reading in the newspaper? Are you seeing people coming together or are they still fighting like children? Do you want to pin medals on them or send them to their rooms until they are good little boys and girls? What can you do to correct the problems, anything at all, or do you feel helpless? When I look outside myself I do not want to have any part of it. The whole world, social, economic, political structure is rotten to the core. To me that means that there is a lot of stinking thinking going on and there must be a major shift in thinking before things will get better. I want you to find a quiet place and go into your movie picture mind. I want you to see yourself as the supreme ruler of the world. You have powers that are unquestionable and can change things at will immediately. You are turning off the fighting, as you would turn off a TV. You are stopping all the hollow words by not buying another newspaper or reading or buying any written news publication. Your vote is too precious to waste, so you do not vote. Your religion is so dear to your heart that you will not speak it aloud outside your house again. Your children are so dear to you that they will be instructed to abstain from any kind of outward fighting, not even throwing stones. You have taken all the war budgets of all the countries and invested in our real assets, our children. I want you to see lines of children being cleaned and given new clothes and shoes. They are handed a new lap top computer and they are shown their new classroom and teacher. They are led down the hall to the lunchroom to be fed. Their next stop is a full medical check-up including state of the art dental and nutrition. A counselor as to their personal lives then talks to them. If their family needs a house they get one. If the father needs a car or transportation, it is provided and whatever else that is needed to heal the physical and mental wounds of this precious child. Now that you have only spent one tenth of your yearly budget there is much more to do. All war materials manufacturers will be bought out and transformed into childcare industries. All military personal will be retrained to support any on-going program to establish a permanent foothold in space. All money will be standardized to one common unit. All countries will become states of the World Group. The new direction that our energy will be spent on will be the up bringing of our children. They are to be readied in all ways to take on our new collective enemy, Space. I want you to see all of this complete and in working order. The only fights that we will have going on will be in the mind, trying to outdo other teams in the space leap to freedom. We as brothers and sisters will start building our string of pearls across the cosmos. We will be perceived as kindly, trustworthy citizens of the cosmic family. And many will come forward to help us.

  I want you to come back to your Middle Mind. I want you to think about what you just built in your mind. Do you think that it would be possible with the way people are using their minds today? Do you think you could sell this package of ideas to the people of the world with their present mindsets? As for me I'm not going to waste my time trying to change the world's thinking processes. I'm going to change my thinking and try to change as many others' way of thinking in my circle of influence. And get us thinking that space is our real challenge and not each other. Now is the time to take the collection of tools that Koz has given to us and focus inward.

So far you have just been introduced to a list of new tools and been given a brief idea how they work. Now you will be given a set action patterns of how to put these wondrous tools into working format. I want you to think of these instructions as a life or death proposition, because that is exactly what it is. If we don't get it right, we as a genial pool will not join the cosmic family. We will just be another strain of bacteria that did not evolve to a point of assured propagation. I don't want to think of this experiment called man being thrown into the incinerator of an on-coming asteroid never to be heard of again. Now listen and heed my words. They come from the Collective Giving Greater Known, through Koz. These instructions will and must be followed to the letter; every word, every number, every pause. When cooking eggs the instructions may go like this. First turn on the stove and find a frying pan. Put it on the stove. Add one egg. Cook until done. Remove from frying pan and turn off burner. Now if you changed it by just one step it would read, turn on the burner, add one egg, put a frying pan on it, cook until done. Remove from burner. You can see that the second set of instructions will produce something quite different than the first. You will be digging a burnt egg out of the burner and saying that person does not know what they are talking about. The instructions now being given to you are of a class of their own like no other set of instructions you have ever followed. We are not talking about scrambling eggs, we are talking about scrambling one's own neural mass. This should not be done in a half-baked fashion or you will feel like you have not been given the whole process and have been disenfranchised. If at any time you don't feel like you are on the right path or not getting the results that you should be, all you have to do is to back track in this book until you bring yourself up to speed. I do not want to leave even one of my brothers or sisters behind. Please remember that as I am writing this I am not alone and that at times Koz will keep me on the true path. These adjustments will have to be made by you and me.

The instructions really do not have a beginning, a middle or end. You have already started just by reading up to this point. When you started only you will know, there is not a set starting point or time. I'm going to start with what has been my starting point only to get this started. It starts for me in the pre-planning, as I am getting ready for bed. I have to set the environment so as not to upset the process. There are night-lights that light the way to the bathroom so as not awake my Middle Mind when going to the bathroom. There is a water bottle and some aspirin within arm's length, a flashlight to help me see anything that I may want to write a note with, and two felt point pens and a pad of paper next to me on the bed to capture any and all messages from the Giving Greater Known. If there are some things that you can think of that will keep your Middle Mind out of the forefront, have them within reach. Put on your stocking cap and find your sleeping position. If you have not established one, try this one. Lie on the right side, this will take pressure off of your heart and give it a break. This may help you sleep and live longer. Put a pillow between your knees; this will take pressure off your back. Put a small pillow between your ankles; this will take pressure or your knees and stop the shifting of the feet. Put a pillow under your left arm and lay it down your right side, fingertips out flat on your upper leg. I always start myself out in this position.. This position will change after you have gone through your transformation steps and drift off to sleep. After getting your position set apply a slight pressure to the right eye, looking at the light spot, looking for any mind pictures that may be coming through. These pictures are a direct link to the Lower Mind and will let you know what it has been impressed with. If you see something that you do not want in your Lower Mind's memory bank go through these steps. First see it very clearly on a piece of paper. Then wad it up and throw it into the bottomless crevasse of no return. With it gone, then look for any other pictures. There will be some pictures that you will want to keep. Look at them and turn them over like flipping a page in a book and look for more. There will be pictures that will need adjusting. See yourself picking up a big gum eraser and removing and then replacing bits and pieces. If your mind wanders off on some worry track, see it on a piece of paper and throw it into the bottomless crevasse, and get back to work looking for pictures. Do this mind control process as many times as it takes to stay on track. This natural bleed-through is normal and will become less and less as time goes by. Some pictures that you see will be messages straight from the Giving Greater Known. Study them well and see yourself walking over to a copying machine and making three copies. Send one copy to your Middle Mind, one to your Lower Mind and one to turn over. Some pictures will be classified under bewilderment and studied for a short time and put in a folder marked Top Secret and sent to a vault room in your Lower Mind. This vault room will be revisited after each session of picture viewing. After all your pictures have been processed, even if there were not any, go to the next step. Think of the day to come and prearrange it in pictures in your movie picture mind. See yourself getting out of bed and getting dressed. See yourself doing the things that need to be done with ease and you see them completed and you are standing there clapping your hands. Go through everything that you need to get done this way. This process will make your brain more organized and give you a feeling of control. Now I want you to paint a picture of your future. Think of what you would like to be different. Think of the person that you would like to meet. Do not try to think of what is possible. Don't prejudge. Think of only what you would like to see. Make sure that you are very specific down to the last detail. You are trying to give your Lower Mind its instructions. Without these instructions it does not know what you want it to do. Don't just ask for a car for you may get a real piece of junk that is more of a headache than an asset. This car will be the car of your dreams. You will get everything that you ask for. Make sure that you can afford it or you may not have it for long. The son of my buddy got his Ford 5.0 only to find out that he had to put out $1700 for a transmission job and that he could not afford the insurance. He finally sold it for a loss. At the age of fifty a person should be thinking of boiling things down, not buying things that are only going to have to be sold at a loss in the near future.

After you finish your future building phase go to your healing stage. Think in pictures of what the problem is, letting your Lower Mind know. Then tell it to go out and find the answers that you will need to solve your problem. Build up your plan of action down to the last detail. See yourself talking to a doctor. He is telling you what medicines to take. See yourself taking them and like some wonder drug you are healed on the spot. Don't let your mind slip into whether this is realistic or not. Keep your Middle Mind out of this process. It does not understand and will never understand the power of the Lower Mind. This process should be linked to something that you do on a routine basis so that you can think of your self-built mind movie many times throughout the day. This is done to impress the Lower Mind and to keep it on track. Go over this mind movie until you fall asleep. Do these steps every night. From now on you will be putting your sleep time to work. The days of play sleeping are over. The full extent of your mind will be summonsed to search the Giving Greater Known for guidance.
KOZ: THE INNER FOCUS HAS THE POWER TO

CHANGE ALL. TO MASTER THE CHANGE OF YOUR LOWER MIND IS TO MASTER ALL.

* * *

Banana Food

The banana was a genetically engineered plant to supply 98% of the nutritional needs of the human race. The potato supplies the rest of your mineral needs. As more and more species were introduced more plants were brought along. Many of these plants could crossover into a variety of different life forms needing nourishment. This place called earth became a runaway pieced together ecosystem that was taking a lot of time and energy.

I want you to go into your movie picture mind. See yourself standing in front of your battle plan file cabinet. Look at the next folder after DRINK: it reads FOOD. Pull this folder out and open it up. You can see that the first thing on the list of foods is the banana and the second is the potato. At the top of this list of only two the headline reads DAILY. See yourself getting up in the morning, pouring an eight-ounce glass of room temperature distilled water, popping a small potato half the size of your fist into a brown paper sandwich bag and microwaving it for 3-5 min., pulling a banana out of the refrigerator and peeling it. See these three things lined up on a table and a standup card next to them that reads, This I offering to my Lower Mind. Look to your right. On the wall is a handwritten, signed contract written by you pledging to do this daily. This is a contract between you and your Lower Mind and only has a three-day fudge factor. By following this routine you will establish a trust with your Lower Mind and give your body the materials to build a stabilized platform for the Lower Mind to work from. This small offering to yourself should not be taken lightly. These are magical foods that work in ways that the Middle Mind does not at this time have the ability to grasp.

Come back to your Middle Mind. Before going on this new path I want you to think about your state of health and well-being. Take a few notes after being on this new path for a week. Take an accounting of how you are feeling, both mentally and your level of energy. In my life, I felt that I was in control. Even though I could see many things that I still needed to change I knew they would come to pass; it was only a matter of time. With my (Change Machine) fully fueled and running at a slow even pace I could see change daily. I felt a power that I had never felt before. This gift of change now properly set into motion was transforming me in ways that were way beyond my own comprehension. I would stand in awe of things that I had done, that were not what I would recognize as something coming from me. I was able to use at will the tools Koz had given me and it brought me to tears many times. I would be overwhelmed by how these tools worked as they said they would. I have read many self-help books in the past but never anything that became a part of me like the word of KOZ.

She was walking her dog. At first glance anyone would have just let them go by with only a good morning dribbling from their lips, just a formal nicety. No, not me. This was not something that I could let just fade into the cosmic void. I was in the Haze. I knew that this person was brought to me through my connection with the Giving Greater Known. I was like a detective at a crime scene. I was asking questions as if I were going to qualify her as a good mate candidate. At one time I reached out and grabbed her by the elbow and she let me know that, she felt uncomfortable with that not knowing me. I backed off but did not let her go without her committing to a lunch date the next day. I knew that this was my next cosmic pearl and I was not going to let it pass by. We were both from out of town. She was visiting her parents and I was visiting my aunt. She was from the San Deigo area and I was from South Dakota. Here we were standing alongside a road in Lucerne, Ca. My mind was racing over the probability of us crossing paths. What was the chance that we would have ever met? At lunch the next day she told me that she almost did not come but that it was her intrigue in my book that brought her. She had eaten a late breakfast and only had some tea and some cheese and garlic toast. I pigged out talking with my mouth full at times. She could sense my drive and passion toward writing my book. I had programmed myself that this was going to only be a meeting so that I could get some feedback on my book. I was not looking for anything else. She saw right through me, saying when she first met me that I seemed to be looking for something more than that. I told her that I was sorry that I had interrupted her life that I felt I had no right to do so. I was using her as a brief contact to the real world and that I would not wish me on anybody. She asked, "What part of me would I not wish on her?" I said that I had fallen into a black hole called writing a book and that I had become very selfish of my space and time. I would wake up between 3 and 5 a.m. and start writing. I would be in bed before 9 p.m. She looked at me with searching, understanding eyes as if she was saying that she saw no problem with it, that she could handle those type of actions with ease, even with a level of enjoyment. I didn't want my heart to wander at that time. I must focus on my book. I mentioned that she said earlier that she had some errands she had to do and maybe we should go. She let me know that they could wait. Would I like to catch a cup of coffee? She would really like to read some of my manuscript that I had brought at her request. We found a coffee shop that was closing but they let us in for coffee. She read about 20 pages and asked me for a piece of paper so she could make a note to herself. She liked proofreading and that was something that she could really get into. Then it happened. She asked me if I would consider having her as my proofreader and said that she would enjoy doing it. She was attracted to what I was writing. It had happened again. Out of the blue, someone was reaching out to help me. I was crying inside. I think that she new it. She told me to quit putting myself down, that I had as much right as anybody to express my feelings and not to worry about disrupting other peoples lives; they may need it. After going through my origami dollar bill folding ritual, them making their choice and me seemingly having guessed what they wanted, we left. I did not want to let her go. The parking lot was getting closer and closer. I dragged my feet. We talked a while and she said, "thank you for coming into my life." I fumbled through my notebook wanting her to write down something so I could keep in touch. When I got to the next clean page I saw that she, when I was in the bathroom, had already written down her E-mail address. I was so happy that she wanted to stay in touch with me. She said how else was she going to be able to proof read my manuscript? We shook hands. Oh how I wanted to kiss her on the cheek but did not. As she drove away I knew that there were still some very special ladies out there and I had just met one. I cried as she disappeared into the cosmic goo of life. I do hope I see her again. I do hope this world treats her well. She is a true cosmic pearl. KOZ: THOSE WHOM YOU MEET ON THE WAY ARE ALWAYS WITH YOU. THEY HAVE CHANGED YOUR LIFE. YOU ONLY GIVE UP THE BODY, NOT YOUR SILVER THREAD THAT CONNECTS YOU FOREVER EVEN AFTER THE BODY VESSEL HAS LONG FADED AWAY. As you take this journey with me I hope that you too are having more connections with a linkage to what Koz has given us. I hope you are starting to swim in the wonderment and are feeling good about where this is taking you. My life has a new spark to it and I wish to pass that on to you. It is a feeling of wanting to turn the next corner without fear, in fact with joy. I want to live this life that I have now for as long as I can. In my past all I could think of was how I wished it would end. I hope that I will meet a lady like Diane who will stir my heart again and make me cry. Some day it will be the cry of joy and not loss. I will have found my cosmic partner and have a built-in giving machine that will make my heart sing. I know she will come my way. I have programmed my Lower Mind to bring her my way. I wait knowing that it will come to pass. There is only the working of the Universal Cosmic Law that I must wait for.

***

Time Line

      Sunday the 26th of . 2000, I found a camping spot where I feel that I can really be productive in my writing. As I was reaching for my wallet and glasses I checked my compass. I was so glad to see that my head was going to be pointing north when I got in bed. I took the camping spot. My head pointing north when I was lying down meant that when I was propped up in bed writing on my laptop that I was facing south. The first night I was on my third trip to Reach One. I looked down at my shirt. It was a gray one. I was at the third level. The trip getting there was skipped. I was at once looking for gray doors. The first one I came to had written on it, Forward And Backward Are The Same. My mind was so intrigued that I had to go inside. There in front of me on the wall was a stretched out timeline looking format. There were no dates but a set of dots, six in all. They looked like the shape of the Big Dipper, the star constellation. The wall turned to a blur as it sped past me to the right for what seemed to be about a minute. It stopped and I was able to see that the dots had shifted a small bit, but the dot and dash inscription underneath it did not change. The wall again took off to the right, somehow knowing that I was finished looking at that section. It seemed more like five minutes before it stopped. I could plainly see that there were only five dots now and they were shaped more like the outline of a straight-backed chair. The dots and dashes were the same. The wall took off moving to the left I did not think it was going to stop. I was about ready to leave. My eyes had wandered from the timeline. I could see a small button on the wall labeled stop. To the right of it was a button marked with an arrow pointing to the right. To the left was a button marked with an arrow pointing to the left. There I stood wondering what I should do. The question was to push or not to push. What would you have done? Was this a test? Was someone watching? Was this my only chance to be in this room? My hand came up by itself without my telling it to do so and pushed the stop button. By this time eight or ten minutes had passed. There were only three dots and one was much larger than the rest. The dot and dashes below were the same. I ran this timeline back and forth looking for some type of pattern or something that resembled anything that I could understand. I wish that I had an astrophysicist and a mathematician with me. They may have seen something that I did not. I was wondering if the dots were stars and their arrangement a constellation? Were they using the change in star patterns as a timeline? When there were large shifts in the star patterns did that mean that the dot dash pattern was in a different location or even on a different planet or different solar system? What were the dots and dashes below? I thought that they could be a coded message of some type. I

wished for a geneticist. Maybe this could be some kind of DNA or genetic code thing. Those were my guesses. I remembered what the door had said: Forward and Backward Are The Same. I left after about three hours of working with this timeline. In my mind it was trying to tell me that there was a constant. The dots and dashes stayed the same. I was taught the paradigm that nothing stayed the same. That's what the best minds of the time were expousing. When I first heard the word paradigm, the saying going around was that it did not equal twenty cents. Now I believe that it could equal anything that you wanted it to be. I remembered what Koz said, that all things would have to be re-evaluated according to cosmic law. If the dots were star patterns this timeline was on a scale of immense proportions. The number crunching would be way beyond my feeble attempt to corral the speed of light. I'm going to say what I think this timeline was trying to convey. Maybe some day if this book ever reaches print there will be greater minds than mine that may ponder and extrapolate. Your DNA code is the focus. It was the same in the forever past and the same in the forever future. Location and planets and stars will change but your first name of your gen- etic type will stay the same. That this cosmic test of our genial code has been run many times before and failed. We are all part of the forever past and forever future. That this test will continue on until it succeeds. That you might very well have been part of this experiment in the forever past and you will be called up in the forever future until we all pass this cosmic test of our genial code. There are many that have taken this journey before us and are waiting on the banks of a celestial sea with milk and honey for the soul and body. They await our arrival with open arms. The gates will open and our wandering of the cosmos will be transformed into a pure direction of joining the Giving Greater Known.
KOZ: WHEN YOU ARE FOLLOWING THE PATH OF

THE GIVING GREATER KNOWN YOUR THOUGHTS WILL SHAPE THE FUTURE AS YOU SEE AND WISH IT. If you feel that you are being left behind please go back and scan over the things Koz has said. Things will really start to pop for you when your Lower Mind has put your new tools to work. Your link with the Giving Greater Known will become stronger and stronger.

***

CHANGE

His name was Joe. Some called him Doctor. There he was, sipping his neurons into oblivion. He and one of the partners of a new steak house in California, and I were talking about his new 2000 Corvette. I found out that he was a psychiatrist for young children. He was saying that teenagers had too many legal problems that he didn't want to deal with. The time that he had to spend in court because of some type of trouble they had gotten into were too draining. He said that is why he only works with young children.

Earlier that day at Quail Run fitness center I met a young man who said that he was going to go to an academy in New Mexico to be a tribal police officer. I mentioned that I one summer worked with Indian kids at a boys ranch and that it was a whole different world working with the clash of cultures. One time I had been missing my gas cap off of my Jeep. I was talking to another counselor about how I must have left my gas cap somewhere and it was going to cost me $18 to replace it. He said that I should talk to, (using a fictitious name,) Running Bear. He likes stealing gas caps to sniff. I called him into the office. He was a small boy not much over 100 pounds. I told him that I did not care about his gas sniffing, all I wanted was my gas cap back. I said that I was not going to write him up or dish out any kind of punishment if when I returned in about ten minutes from my break my gas cap was on this desk. If it's not I'm going to go through your room with a fine tooth comb and you know how messy that can get and I assure you it will be messy. Who knows what else I might find? It could be enough to rotate you back to Juvenile Hall. When I got back, there was my gas cap. I did not write him up or shake down his room, but I went to talk to him. I said that I did not care about him or his gas sniffing but that was not true, I did care. I asked him why he was sniffing gas? He told me that his grandfather died of drinking gas and his father died of drinking gas and did I think it might be an inherited genetic thing. He had blown me away. This beautiful young man was crying out for help and it made shivers run up my spine. I knew that there was no way an Indian boy would ever see the inside of a child psychiatrist's office. Where would the money come from? The system? Ha. His support group had been stripped from him by the government's actions against the Indian community at large. The man at the health club said this young man was the product of his social dilemma coming to light.

I would have hoped that by now, some forty years later, we would have been far enough advanced to stop using our children as just another money machine lining the pockets of the attorneys, health care providers and counselors. I myself was caught up in that system in the middle sixties and now I can see that this stink hole of injustice goes on its merry way pumping out the derelicts and sucking money out of the system. Oh! What a sweet deal these so-called professionals have. They mis-diagnose and treat the young to insure a future people base to play their money games on. They are eating our young so as to be able to drive new Corvettes. It makes me mad to think that we are letting this scam go on. How many great minds are we losing to these hucksters that are themselves walking the thin line of sanity? Who watches the hand that can with a bit of ink, dole out psychotropic drugs that shape our future. How far have they infiltrated into every nook and cranny of the system? What kind of medicines did the person have in them that you got in the fight with? What was the officer on who handled the case? The court appointed attorney was not talking to you but about how to beat the system. What was he on? Who knows what the judge is going to do who just popped his pill again to hold his anxiety at bay? The collective neural soup has been tainted by a bunch of self-medicated bozos who should be burned at the stake for their modern day chemical witchcraft. The only reason why the drug runners are still in the running is that they supply a steady stream of new candidates for the system to chew on and spit out more money to the players of the game. The real drug wars are between the drug suppliers. Who can sell the most drugs? If you can get them off the street how in the hell can the system capture the market and make the big bucks? It's our druggie market. We built it. No one is going to take it from us. And I mean no one. And believe you me they are in it for the money. How can Mexico sell prescription drugs for 75% less than the U.S? And where do you think they are getting their drugs from anyway? Not from the good old USA. No Way.

    Koz has assured me that there will be a big shake down and this goody bag will be exposed and a lot of people will be replaced and many sent to jail. The hand that controlled the ink will be slapped and tied. These chemical mind games have to be stopped or we as a new gene pool will never join the cosmic community of the Giving Greater Known. KOZ: THE TRANSFORMATION OF THE LOWER MIND INTO HIGHER LEVELS OF THOUGHT IS A SET PATTERN OF COSMIC LAW. A PURE BRAIN WILL MAKE THIS

TRANSITION ON ITS OWN. BE PURE OF MIND, BODY, AND SOUL. STOP ALL TAKING FROM THE COLLECTIVE NEURAL SOUP. THIS WILL TAKE A MIND REVOLUTION. If you feel as I do that there is a lot of work to be done and a lot of things to be changed, stay with me. You will get your chance to help. The process is already underway. There are a few who will be joined by the collective thought of the many. Your first assignment will be to get your brain back and put it into natural working order. You will be called on later to put it to work in a collective Lower Mind stacking that will shape the future. Be ready. Time grows short. Be part of this leap to a higher level of thinking. Come help push us into the cosmic family of the Giving Greater Known.

***

Thumb Pinch

The mind is not alone in its work. It coexists with how the rest of the body is feeling and what kind of chemicals it is producing. Koz has taught me how to push my Lower Mind in ways that will direct my body to produce self-synthesized, brain-stimulating chemicals. Hold your hand out in front of you, your left hand palm facing you. Look at the thumb and its structure from the tip to the first joint. Think about it as if this were your head. Squeeze it with your right hand using your index finger and thumb. Put the tip of the thumb in the center of your left thumb and your index finger on the nail fleshy part touching. Pinch with enough force that it starts to feel uncomfortable to the count of five. The release is just as important as the pressure, slowly backing off to a count of three. Do this five times to both thumbs, then put your index finger and thumb together of both hands and place them on your head forward of your temple. You will find a little indention alongside of the eye socket. This is where your thumb and finger go. Go into your movie picture mind and see a stream of blue light flow from your fingers to every cell in your brain. Do this to the count of eight. Then put your fingers above your eyes on the eyebrow, seeing a green light flowing from your fingertips to every cell of your brain to the count of eight. This process will align neurons in your brain so that your Lower Mind is more responsive to your seeded implants. As you are thinking of what you are trying to impress the Lower Mind with, I want you to go back to pinching the left thumb in the same process mentioned earlier. This combination of head-thumb manipulation and suggestion will greatly speed up your Lower Mind's acceptance of your seeded implants. Do not take this process lightly. If used correctly it can become a very powerful tool. Use it sparingly on things of great importance so the Lower Mind will not read it as a false alarm. Don't be crying wolf at every little problem you have. Save this process for the big ones. If you abuse it you may lose it.

* * *

There I was standing in a gas station at three in the morning. I had been hitting the bars and doing some writing about the oilpatch. In came a man and put up a notice of a possible job called (worms corner). What in the hell was worms corner? He told me it was a job on an oilrig that paid $10 an hour. He explained that it was the man that stabs the end of a ninety foot string of drill pipe into the stand of pipe coming up through the drill floor. The driller was coming to pick him up here at five o'clock A.M. but he had quit and if I was there I would get the job because they would have to have a full crew or the tool pusher would run them off. I had my work clothes, hardhat and steel-toed boots in the trunk of my car, I was ready. I stayed and met the driller and was hired on the spot. Throw your shit in the trunk. SHIT, let's go. Wow, that was quite the greeting and introduction. He was mad. This meant that he had a new man to train. I had never worked on an oil rig before. What was I in for? Oh! Boy. We left Sydney, Montana, at a faster than normal pace and it just got faster as we got out of town. The driller was driving, the derrick hand had shotgun, the motorman and chain hand had the door seats in the rear seat and the worm, me, was stuck in the middle of the back seat. The driller said, "the shit that I was talking about last night is in the glove box." The derrick hand pulls out a film canister of marijuana and proceeds to roll a joint. When it got to me I said that I didn't smoke. I was trapped in a marijuana den with no way out. It was winter in Montana and I would have frozen to death before I got back to town if someone did not pick me up. I did not think things could get worse but they did. The next thing that came out of the glove box was a .357 magnum hand gun. Great! There I was in the middle of nowhere going like a bat out of hell to who knows where in the middle of winter with four dope heads wheeling a .357 around. I did not think this was the time or place to try to expound on how drugs were bad for you and your brain and that they are short-circuiting the whole system of tapping into the Giving Greater Known. All types of thoughts went through my head. How if they would have bumped me off no one on this whole earth knew where I was. I think I will just keep my mouth shut. OK! I guess there are times that your only control is knowing that you have no control. The driller puts his foot into the gas pedal and speeds up throwing us into a fish tail on some god forsaken gravel road. Hell, I'm not going to last the trip, hell with them shooting me. The derrick hand rolls down his   window. The wind chill factor at 70 mph plus at a outside temperature of –28 had to be –100 degrees or more. What next? Was this some kind of dream or what? Boom! I got him up the poopchute. Did you see the fur fly? This dope-smoking, gun-toting, hunting icebox car trip was the worst ride in my life. Even with all this going on around me I was able to calm myself and have a level of inner self-control that most people will never reach. I was using the Fist Pinch, a way of being able to detach oneself from reality.

    Hold your left hand up in front of your eyes in a fist, the fingers facing you. Look for a tit of skin pushing out at a point a little lower than the base of the little finger. Pinch across this tit into the sub layers of your flesh. You are looking for a sharp nerve that feels like something between a burning and a needle poke. When you find it do the five count pinch and the three count release. Do this only three times to begin with. As you get the feel for this process you may use it as much as needed. There is no overdose factor. After each release do a sinus-clearing swallow. If need be do both hands. This will give your Lower Mind the feeling of control. KOZ: YOUR LOWER MIND CAN AT WILL CHANGE REALITY TO WHAT YOU WISH IT TO BE. YOUR MIDDLE MIND CAN ONLY MANIPULATE THE REAL. YOUR LOWER MIND CAN JUMP FROM COSMIC PLAIN TO COSMIC PLAIN WITHOUT ANY TIME FACTOR. The next time that you find yourself in a bad, out of control situation, I hope that you will stay calm. Use the Fist Pinch to get you through it until you are in a spot to regain control. Your actions in an out of control plane can make things worse if you do not control the Beast. You and your ideas may have to be put on hold through this cosmic scramble. Stay on this course of transformation and you will become a master of the inner and outer self.

***

Shift to Non-Reality

I awoke but did not stir; I was using the Inward Looking Eye that Glimpses the Future. I was on Reach One (dream state), but this time I was met by what is called a permanent go between. He was the first real flesh and blood person that I had ever met on Reach One. I had so many questions to ask, I did not know where to start. We were sitting at a clear table and he reached over and touched my hand. Then the table turned into a moving picture display. As he was talking, pictures were being shown on the tabletop. He had an electric stick-on patch next to his left temple. A clear wire ran down to the table. He was telling me that he had contracted a rare virus and he could not leave Reach One until it was eradicated. As he was speaking, the table was showing him in an operating room – or maybe an examining room. He was hooked up to all sorts of devices and on the display monitor there was a red light blinking. He said that he was a hydro-engineer and in Chad a lion mauled him, and this is when they believe that he contracted the virus. This virus was not contagious, so I had nothing to worry about. The reason that he was here was to speed up my progress in reaching my levels so that I could go to Reach Two. I asked him his name and he gave me a number, which was one number less than my Social Security number. I asked him where he was born and he said, "Santa Rosa, California" the place I was born. I asked him what date he was born, it was the same day I was born but two hours earlier than me. He directed my attention back to the table with a wave of his hand across my face and then across the surface of the table. As I looked down, he told me that it was not the virus that they were worried about, but what type of viruses the virus might be carrying. Any type of virus hitchhiking was of great concern. There are very few people who do not have some kind of virus in them. He said that I was virus free because of Koz. That he had wiped out all of my viruses for his self-preservation and mine. I was a very rare person and slated for many advancements. I was going to have to undergo a lot of tests even a virus scan, just to make sure. The hardest test to pass was the test that determined how flexible and receptive your brain is to change. The brain that can stretch and be fully open was the highest goal sought after from the beginning of time. There is so much to be assimilated into your present scope of reality. The blocked mind was as good as talking to a rock. My trips to Reach One were higher knowledge transfusions. The antiquated word was too slow and may carry with it ambiguities and double meanings. My trips to Reach One would be more often. So far, what I had learned was just the foundation of the up-and-coming transformation. We got up from the table and I was led hand in hand. My feet were not moving, I was floating along I could not move or speak. I was placed into a machine and Velcro strapped in, I could not move. I was tilted to all sorts of positions as two paddles that looked like Ping-Pong paddles waved over my body as a person looking for something with a metal detector. I felt lightheaded, it was like being on a carnival ride called the Zipper.

I must have fallen asleep in the real world or on Reach One or I was drugged on Reach One and am just awaking. I looked at the time it was 9:36 a.m. I had lost some time, or I had fallen to sleep and that had chewed up the time. My use of The Inward Looking Eye That Glimpses The Future and the trips to Reach One have blended with my dream state and my sleeping state. This blending has never happened before where I did not know which one ended and the next one started. As they became one I had a feeling that the reality scale had taken a dip to the non-tangible side. My true life was on the other side of tangible reality. I had gone through a major transformation in thinking. This level of thinking was going to change how I conducted my life. My awake life was just a mode to secure a stage for my non-tangible life. Anything that was in the way of my transformation would be dealt with posthaste. That anything that would ensure an environment that catered to my non-tangible self was materialized. I was pulling away from the so-called real world and slipping into my own self-built reality. I was more comfortable reaching for the stars than dragging my feet on this rock. I was starting to sense this higher level of thinking in ways that I was unable to in the past. It flowed over me like a new idea. It captured my whole body and made me feel very small and very powerful at the same time. The body from now on will only be a vessel and the thoughts the real world. There was so much to do. I had to start getting rid of a lot of baggage that owned me. The '70 Chevelle went, the '65 El Camino went, my '92 Harley went, I sold my house and moved into a camper. What the hell was I doing, was I nuts or something? Had I lost my mind? I had spent a great deal of my life putting those things together. I was way out of control and liking every bit of it. The weight that was lifted off of me was freeing me to be more with less, much more. There are a lot of people who will expound on a new way and how things should be done out there. But when you look at what they are doing, they are a bunch of hypocrites. They are asking you to give and give until it hurts as they are driving around in their new cars and living in their new houses and preaching from their multi-million dollar pulpits. KOZ: DON'T BE LED ASTRAY IN THE JUDGMENT OF OTHERS. STAY ON THE PATH OF THE GIVING GREATER KNOWN. THESE FALSE WITNESSES WILL FADE ON THEIR OWN. WALK TOWARD THE LIGHT OF SELF-AWARENESS AND INNER STRENGTH. BUILD ON YOUR LADDER INTO THE HIGHER LEVEL OF THINKING OF

THE GIVING GREATER KNOWN. You will not be able to make transitions as easily as it sounds in this book. These transitions have taken me many years with a lot of non-transformation dead time in between. There would be a lot of blank pages in this book if it were on a true time line of this transformation. Take your time, be kind to yourself and loved ones. Incorporate what you can when you can in an order that will fit you. True law will be true in any order of exposure. I would like to bring you up to light speed as far as your transition, but I don't want to blow you away. Think of me as a tool that is outdated trying to pass on the newest ideas of the time. Without Koz, I would have nothing to say.

* * *

M.O.R.T.

There I was sitting alongside the road, my little truck had broken down again. I was waiting for it to cool down. I was in the Haze. I was the chief engineer of a magnet lift induction coil orbit insertion accelerator. It was called M.O.R.T. What the hell was I doing here? I had not the foggiest idea what needed to be done. Koz told me not to worry, that with the tools that he has given to me and his guidance, I would do great wonders. I was sitting at a desk where I could see out of a big glass window. I could see hundreds of men and woman working on M.O.R.T. Lying on my desk was a folder marked TOP SECRET. PROJECT DIRECTIVES. It had a red seal on the three open sides of the folder. It was one of those military folders that had the clip on the top of the pages. I opened the drawer looking for a letter opener, I then opened the TOP SECRET folder. I was half expecting the red lights to come on and a squad of guards to come rushing in to arrest me. On the first page, the cover page, it said, "Directed by" and I could not believe my eyes, there was my name with a GS 23 rating. There was a knock on the door and in came three white-coated engineers. Doctor of physics James Wilt, Doctor Of mathematics Mike Ingals and Doctor of chemistry pyrotechnics Jerry Thomas. Using the first letter of their last names I coined them the W.I.T. team, they were going to be asking for my help a lot in the future.

They were having a problem on the testing of the first stage of acceleration. The problem was that we were tearing barrels apart. The first stage in M.O.R.T.'s acceleration was a fuel combustion stage. They had reached an upper level as to how much combustion material that they could use without tearing things apart. I opened my mouth and the words came out like I knew everything there was to know about their problem. "Gentlemen, I have a team coming in from Germany, from the Bosh Company. They will explain to you how to boost your muzzle speed by using high-pressure computer controlled fuel injection nozzles. They will be landing on helo pad 2 this afternoon, I expect you to meet them and show them to their quarters. Tomorrow, you will set out in a new direction. I will expect to see you in my office at 5:00 A.M. sharp, see you then". They marched off talking amongst themselves. I was able to hear every word. "Where did they find this guy? I looked into his past and there were no records on him. It is as if he appeared out of thin air. Who cares! If he can keep this project moving? I'm going to get a paycheck. This guy is always coming up with off the wall bullshit that no one else has heard of before, and it works."

The next morning the W.I.T. team showed up with the three-man team from Bosh. They explained that there were places where more combustion fuel could be added after the first explosion that could boost the acceleration of the projectile. They could even use different types of fuels. One was a hydrogen peroxide that had an extra electron added, that made it act like a mini-nuclear explosion. Off they marched going about their business. Where was all this information coming from? I was scared and confident at the same time. I knew that I had some out of this world answers to give to these people that would keep them astounded for many years to come. It was the next day when a different set of engineers came knocking at my door.

    They were having a heating problem on the magnetic induction coils. These coils had the job of further accelerating the projectile after it got through the combustion acceleration stage. I explained to them that the banks of coils were too far apart and that a coil should only fire every tenth time. That would give it a cool down time that would be compatible with the liquid hydrogen cooling system. They marched back to their test labs, talking to themselves. I wished just once that he could not come up with an answer. When he speaks the words seem to flow into my brain as if it were a pure knowledge that was unquestionable. He gets on people's nerves, he acts as if he knows their problems and the answers even before they have said anything.

    The next team of engineers was having a weight load to projectile ratio problem. The main thing that was going to have to be put into orbit was water. The weight of the water and its freeze factor were making the slosh factor unmanageable by the time the projectile reached the acceleration induction coils. I told them that they were going to have to think about prefreezing the water to a super cold. They should build a tank within a tank. The center tank would contain water and the outer tank liquid oxygen. They said that they would run into cost over runs that would put them over budget. And that there was not enough return shuttle bay space for their reuse, that they would have to have with such an expensive tank. I told them that they needed to report to the training room on the sixth level at three p.m. That I was putting a special cognitive fluxing pool together to handle this problem. They went on their way talking amongst themselves. I get spooked when he knows our problems before we do. How long was he going to let us stew over this? And what the hell is a cognitive fluxing pool anyway?

At three p.m. three teams showed up: the space station structural engineers, the water people, and the liquid oxygen team. They all were involved in using M.O.R.T. to get things in orbit. I entered the room and snapped a ruler on the podium. This was a tool of mine to get their undivided attention. I got the beast out and ran him around the room. "I'm only going to tell you this once". Somehow that little statement was a shortcut to their Lower Minds. "You will work together as a super team. I want a one-way projectile system. The projectile will be designed so that its parts will be incorporated as part of the space station structure and along with it the shipping of water and liquid oxygen. And I want an integration of all things being M.O.R.T. shipped". I snapped the ruler and left the room. I could hear them in my mind, they were at work without delay. They were talking about how they could design the projectile in many different configurations. Each configuration could supply a range of parts from decking to shelving and a lot of other things. KOZ: FUTURE BUILDING IS DONE BETWEEN THE LOWER MIND AND THE GIVING GREATER KNOWN. BY WHOM, WHERE AND TIME DOES NOT MATTER. IT BECOMES PART OF THE COLLECTIVE KNOWLEDGE. YOUR TIME WILL NOT BE WASTED. YOUR MIND IS A FUTURE BUILDER SUPREME. IT CAN PULL THE FUTURE INTO REALITY FROM THE NOTHING. "I want you to start thinking of what you would like to see in the future. Write it down and share it with others that are on the path of the Giving Greater Known. This power of bring the future into reality is a natural process of your mind. Don't let your Middle Mind steal this gift from you. Work with it, make it a tool of the mind that you use daily. Come, help me build the future that we together can build at a grander scale than one person alone. I will give to you so you can give to me, and together we will be synthesizing a future with no boundaries."

* * *

Gap of Change

I was sitting in a bar called the Leaky Teaky in Nice, California, when I fell into the haze. The bar was packed but I was alone. I felt that I had stepped into a different parallel world. The pool table was going game after game but I did not put my quarters up. I was not talking to anyone. I was not even in the room, my mind was someplace else. I was thinking of places and people who I clicked with. I was there but I was not with-it there. I felt that I had to make an adjustment. I felt I was not shooting at the gap of change. There was one man in his middle sixties who was known as Smurf. I asked him if he minded if I called him Smurf; because I did not want to take from him possibly the only thing of value he had, his dignity. He said, "Why not? Everybody else does." He was staying in the same trailer park campground that I was. I asked him how long he had lived there and he said, "Four years." I asked him if he had a car and he said, "No." He told me that he could not get a driver's license because of his past DUIs. In a sad voice he said "I will never leave BJ WALLS", (the name of the trailer park.) I gave up my seat so that a man and his wife could sit together at the bar. This put me closer to the door, the thing that I really wanted to hit.

I headed for my camper and went right into using the Inward Looking Eye That Glimpses The Future. It was not long before I started to see circles hooked into circles. It looked like the paper chains that we used to make to decorate the Christmas tree. But these were made out of a thin metal, like the stuff the toy Slinky was made of. Each circle had a small gap in it and next to the gap was a key held by a hand. Next to the hand was a drawing of an eye with an arrow pointing at the hand. Then I saw a stick figure of a man. The man started walking past the eye and the arrow and started talking to the hand. He asked where the gap was. The hand turned the key and the circle turned until the gap aligned with the key. The man walked through the gap and started talking to the next hand. He asked where the gap was and the hand turned the key and the second circle turned until the gap aligned with the key. The man walked in and found a chest. He opened the chest and started jumping up and down with joy. I then saw myself looking into a book and writing something down. I was on the phone talking to someone I seemed to be very happy as I was saying, "Great great!"

The next thing I knew there I was on Reach One. I was alone, standing in the middle of a large circle of doors. I looked to see what color shirt I had on, it was white. There were many doors of the same color, but there was only one door that was white. I started walking toward it. When I was close, I could read the words printed on it, "SEEK OUT THOSE WHO KNOW." I opened the door and there, three steps away, was a carburetor type of thing. I picked it up and read the tag. It read, "Get help to fix or replace." I looked to my right and there was a line of people standing there. I looked at the first person, his back was turned. I went to tap him on the shoulder but he was only a hologram. I walked around to the other side of him and I saw that he was scooping ice cream onto an ice cream cone. This was not anyone that I thought could help me with my problem. I went on to the next person. She was ironing clothes, the next person was cooking, the next person was decorating a cake, and then I saw a man with greasy hands and a pair of pliers in a holster attached to his belt. I showed him what I had and he said, "Oh, a three gpm oscillator. I have rebuilt ones, new ones or the do it yourself overhaul kits. I suggest that you go with the rebuilt one if you have never worked on one of these before." He took me over to a door and we went inside. On the door was written, "The Right Person For The Job."

I had fallen asleep and the next morning, I awoke at one A.M. the small electric heater had gone on the blink. I grabbed my laptop and starting writing at five a.m. I was sitting at the Marina Café grumbling about how I was still having problems with my S10 CHEV pickup. They convinced me that it was my catalytic converter that was plugged and that I should get rid of it. I went home and pulled out my saw and cut it out but the truck still ran like shit. I went back to the Café and had a piece of pie and coffee. Sitting next to me was a mechanic. He said that he would look at it for me. We went out to the parking lot. He looked at the catalytic converter and said that I did not have to take it off, it was OK. He thought that my problem was that I was getting too much fuel and it was flooding. I remembered what I had seen on Reach One and when I was using the Inward Looking Eye That Glimpses The Future. KOZ: BE NOT LED ASTRAY BY THOSE WHO KNOW NOT THAT THEY KNOW NOT. LOOK FOR THE GAP, THIS IS WHERE LOWER MIND TO LOWER MIND SYNTHESIZES THOUGHTS. REMOVE YOURSELF FROM PLACES WHERE LOWER MINDS HAVE FALLEN INTO BRAIN STIRRING AND MIND LOOPING. I hope that you, too, are using the Inward Looking Eye That Glimpses The Future. This process has taken me many trial and error sessions and many years to develop into a usable tool. When you get a handle on it, you will not be alone in any decisions that you must make.

* * *

Inner Stray Voltage

I have talked to you about outer stray voltage disruption. About staying away from electrical things like a microwave ovens, ect. Now I want to talk about inner stray voltage that will disrupt your Mind Energy. I can remember in school that I saw a science film. The subject was the nervous system. They had cut a leg off of a frog and had it taped to a board. Then, they took a battery and shocked the severed leg and it jumped. This movement proved that the nervous system was using electricity to send messages. Then it showed a person all wired up and they were reading his brain waves electronically. Later on they were using voltage to jump start someone's heart. They showed a mental patient getting shock treatments. Not in this film, but I know that they also use high voltage to take someone's life in an electric chair. These things I bring up only to refresh your memory about electricity and your body. Now I want you to think about a process in your mind that is running on Millivolts. This system runs on the difference of the atomic electrical structure in chemicals. To plug this system into any outside source of man-made electricity would disrupt this delicate system. You would not touch an electrical fence or stick your finger in a light socket.

I want you to go into your movie picture mind and take a little trip with me. You are an electrical inspector for the

Agency of Internal Affairs. See yourself lying on a bed , your Lower Mind is rising up out of your body. You are going to take this trip in an out of body state. See yourself walking through a door and entering a room. Written on this door are the words, Shrink Room. You walk through a bank of infrared lights and are handed a sterile white jumpsuit to put on. You then step into a plastic tube were you become smaller and smaller. You will become so small that you will be in the realm of the atomic electrons. A clipboard with your instructions on it is handed to you. Look at the clipboard. It reads, "find all micro-electrical disturbances and report them to the Lower and Middle Minds. Lower down on the page it reads, "Briefing." (This electrical system is so sensitive that human thought often disrupts normal operations. You, as a visiting inspector, will not think of what is right or wrong because your thoughts will disrupt things. Do not touch anything because the pressure of your touch and your chemical body oils will disrupt the natural process. You are only here as an observer and a recorder, welcome to your body's sub-atomic electronic system.) This system deals with the strongest electrical transmitted messages first and then the next strongest on down the line.

You are so small that you have been absorbed into your body still lying on the bed. You enter through the top of the head. You are inside your own brain. Look at the clipboard, there are a few things to be checked off. You must think about the person whose brain you are in. This should be easy as it is you. You won't be able to lie to yourself, so your answers will be truthful. The first question is, are you a drinker of alcohol once a day or more? There are little boxes to check next to each question. The next Question is, are you a smoker or a person who visits places where smokers are present? Question three, are you on any type of drug that will disrupt things? In front of you are two doors, number one and number two. If you did not check any boxes go into door number one. Inside, you see things are running smoothly and the electrons are giving off their charges at even intervals. Now, if you have checked any of the boxes, go through door number two. Inside you see a cross between a New York traffic jam and a Fourth of July fireworks show. You can hear the complaining electrons saying, "He has gone and done it again. How in the hell does he think we are going to get our jobs done with all these chemical disrupters in here? I can't remember when the Lower Mind has been able to tap into the Higher Mind. How does this person ever expect to be able to tap into the guidance of the Giving Greater Known?" Write on your clipboard a note to yourself of things that are going just fine, and things that need to be changed. Now, I want you to drop down to your earlobes or any other place that you have poked holes into and put in some kind of metal. I want you to see the electrons being introduced into your body. Not large enough to be perceptible to the Middle Mind, but the Lower Mind sees it. The Lower Mind is trying to figure out what you are trying to impress upon it by this type of action. You are doing a mind stirring and you don't even know it. These seemingly small actions on your part have big repercussions when you are talking about the impact they have on an atomic level. Look at your clipboard and write down your plan of action. See yourself now entering your mouth. Are there any metal filings? If there are, are there some that are gold, silver, and who knows what? The reaction between these dissimilar metals using your saliva as an electrolyte can give off interfering electrical pulses. Take up your clipboard and make note of this. Now I want you to go anywhere that you have jewelry on and see what type of interference this may be producing. If you don't think that this has any bearing on your system, I want you to try and talk a person out of their copper bracelet that they wear for aches and pains. Now, see yourself leaving your body and getting larger and larger. When you have reached life-size, re-enter your body. Grab the pad and paper next to you in bed and write down your report on your atomic electrical system. For those who need to do some changing I suggest trying this experiment.

For three days don't drink any alcohol. Do not wear any jewelry or do any mind-altering drugs. Go to a sporting goods store and buy a heat-to-fit mouth guard. Wear this guard when you sleep at night. On the fourth night, I want you to be aware of your sleeping environment. I want you to go right into the Inward Looking Eye That Glimpses The Future. Stopping and writing down anything that you see. Do this until you fall asleep. When you wake in the morning, I want you to go into your daily future building programming. And, as any bits and pieces of dreams come to you, write them down. I want you to write an account of your dream activities, whether they have increased or not. Do this experiment three times in the next month. The body intelligence will now have a choice of paths to follow and change will happen whether the Middle Mind wants it or not. KOZ: THE LOWER MIND IS EASILY LED ASTRAY. STAY TUNED TO NATURAL SYSTEMS. THE SMALL IS THE LARGE IN THE REALM OF INNER THOUGHT. I wear a mouth guard at night, to prevent me from grinding my teeth down to nothing. There are some nights I forget and don't wear it and this may lead into many more nights. When I remember to start wearing it again, I have vivid dreams. Hold your Middle Mind at bay and move into another light of understanding. Work with yourself as if this is the only chance that you will have to get it right.

Gathering of Tools

Fist Push

There are things that I know about that I have no idea where they came from. The only answer that rings true in my brain is that I was fed this information from a natural outside source. This source could have more than one pipeline of information flowing into it. The three that I have identified that are pulling in new information for me are: KOZ, the GIVING GREATER KNOWN, AND BODY INTELLIGENCE.

I was walking by the washroom in BJ Walls Campgrounds. I could see a man whom I had met before. I just wanted to make small talk, so I asked him how well the washers and dryers worked. He said that they were the best that he had ever used. Then he asked me how my book was coming and what it was about. I told him that it was coming along just fine, that I had written 1300 words that morning. The book was about metaphysical cosmic law and how we should be using more of our brain. We should stop brain playing and start making the brain work for us. He asked me what my claim to fame was. Why did I think that I knew so much is what he was really asking. I told him I was just another person getting through life just like the next. I was on my way to the bathroom, I could sense that I was not going to be able to spell out my whole story so I said, "Catch you later." I felt that I was very much alone, that I was different. I did not need a list of degrees or in-depth field study to be able to have a vast knowledge source. I could see that this person was tuned into the outer and not the inner. I wished that I could have talked to him with his Middle Mind set to the side. I would have told him this story that I am going to tell you.

    I was sitting in a 20ft by 20ft shack that was under construction. This is what I called home. One end wall was not complete, it was the fall of the year and it was cold. I was three miles north of Watford City, North Dakota. I had set up a wood-burning stove that had a six-foot stovepipe. The smoke would hit the peak of the inside of the roof and billow out the end of my shack. I did not have the money to buy the triple insulated vent pipe that was needed to go out the roof. I did not have any running water. I would sit on a folding chair in front of my wood-burning stove and scoop water out of a pan on the stove over me to clean myself. I had no electricity. The next morning a mouse awakened me. He was pulling at my hair, taking the oil out of it. I did not move. I let him and me just exist. I went into my future building mode. The first thing that I was thinking and seeing was a better lifestyle. Oh how nice it would be to have a shower and a toilet.

    I had fallen into the Haze and was hearing voices. I heard Dream Your Dream and Your Dream will carry you away. My head was cold, my feet were cold, I was dirty and hungry, I did not have time for this cosmic media-physical bullshit. Then I heard, "Push your body out of the reality and let your inner knowledge step forward." This sounded great but just some more bullshit that I had no time for. Then I felt my body falling and I was standing in front of a pure white wall. This wall transformed into a movie screen and started showing me people in great pain. A man would walk over to a person and take his hand and the person would stop screaming or moaning in pain. He was doing this to one person after the next. I watched very closely to what he was doing. He was pushing with the tip of his thumb on the fist between the second and third knuckle. The person would stop and look at what he was doing and start doing it themselves after he left. A voice said, "this is a tool to use when you need to get your body out of the way of your dream-building." I awoke and tried this process, it worked for me in ways that are hard to explain. The first thing it did was to fill my mind with ideas of a higher knowledge that I did not question. That if I really wanted change, there was no stopping me. I dreamt my dream and I was out of there in less than thirty days. I had my shower and toilet.

In the future, I would use this body removal technique many times. I have found that it works in many magical ways. It can wipe out pain in other parts of the body. It can be a mind-altering wake-up call. And what I have used it most for is to impress the Lower Mind after a session of Dream Future Building. The amount of pressure that is applied is different for different uses. For pain, use the hold to the count of five and the release to the count of three, as many times as necessary to override the pain. When you feel that you are between a rock and the hard spot, use it in sharp, hard jabs three times. When you are trying to impress the Lower Mind, use a gentle constant push while planting your suggestion seeds. KOZ: BODY / MIND LINKS ARE A SOURCE OF POWER THAT IS AT A HIGHER LEVEL OF UNDERSTANDING. THE MIDDLE MIND WILL NEVER UNDERSTAND THIS HIGHER LEVEL OF UNDERSTANDING. DON'T WASTE YOUR TIME TRYING TO TEACH A TURTLE HOW TO FLY. Don't let minds that are not on the path of the Giving Greater Known steal from you your gifts of cosmic law. Keep working on your inner understanding of yourself. Arrange these tools in an order that best fits and works for you. See how I use them and then shape them into your life that only you know of. Go back and refresh your mind about the tools that Koz has given to us.

***

Suspend Fear

There have been quite a lot of times that I was afraid and had to back down. As a boy and a young man I was very thin and weak. As I hit nineteen I was able to bring the beast out at will. This was an internal switch that I could flip and mister bad guy would come out to play. I want you to listen to a story , that will make tools out of thin air, that will make fear disappear. I had just gotten a job with Black Hills Trucking as a swamper behind a gin truck. These trucks were what they used for moving oil rigs. It is hard, dangerous work. Your job was to hook-up and unhook whatever the trucker was moving. There had to be a lot of trust between the swamper and the truck driver. You looked out for each other and the truck and equipment. The swampers were the low dogs on the totem pole. Every once in a while you would get a truck driver who was new or didn't care. They will get you killed. The best thing to do is just to walk away let him hitch his own loads. This happened to me only once and it turned some of the other truck drivers against me. But some of the truck drivers said not to worry about it. I told them that he was very close to getting punched. They said, "Yeah, by who, you ha!" It was a few days later and things had blown over, I never had to work behind that truck driver's truck again. I was headed to the Sage Brush bar in Watford City, North Dakota. When I walked in, there was a table full of truck drivers who I had been working with and was on good terms with. I said that the thing that I did not like was a bunch of brake stomping, blinker switching, horn honking, truck drivers. I was saying this in fun and they knew it. But what I did not know was that there were a few truck drivers I didn't know sitting at the bar. One grabbed me by the arm and asked, "What if some of those #$%^%$ truck drivers were to take you outside and beat you up?" I fell into the Haze, my mind was thinking about the odds that it may not be a fair fight. And I also thought if it got too out of hand that I would get some help from my friends. And besides that these were the truck drivers who had in the past, questioned my skills in the fine art of self-defense. I moved like a cat with cunning and speed. There were only two of them who wanted a piece of me. They only wanted to teach me a lesson about talking about truck drivers in a negative way. I was showing off and these guys didn't stand a chance: I had something to prove. It was a full out effort on my part where they did not want to get hurt. The outcome of this fight was going to be talked about amongst all the drivers. This might be the fight that would make people think twice about picking a fight with me again. Here, I might get thrown out of the bar, at work I could lose my job. The fight only lasted about three or four minutes but when you are fighting, it always seems longer. I was kicking one man all the way to the door and then threw him out. The other one left by the back door they had had enough. I turned to the table where my co-workers were sitting and asked them why they did not step in and help. They said, " It look like I had things under control and that we would have been in the way."

  I am not a believer in fighting, but sometimes the beast comes out to play. This story I have told you is not about fighting or how I felt about truck drivers, this story is about how my mind was able to shift and suspend fear. I was not in a normal rational thinking mode. I was able to transform reality in my mind and, therefore, transform reality in the real world. This tool was a gift to me from Koz. I have questioned other people about this brain reality shifting. They told me that possibly they had felt something like that in their past. I asked them to take a little mind trip with me. They did not understand, so I had to phrase it differently. What would you do, if you were confronted by three people larger than yourself? I want you, the reader, to go into your movie picture mind and see yourself in this story. What would you do? Most said run. Now I want to just shift the story in your mind a bit. Let's say that you have just left the back door of the restaurant with your grandmother or some other loved one and these three larger people wanted to hurt them. What would be your frame of mind? Well that's different, you say they would have to kill me to get to them. What happened? Why and how were you able to overcome that fear? This is what they said, that's just the way it is. They were not able to see that this is a tool that could be used at will. The things that we fear can be controlled from within. KOZ: THE MIND IS THE CONTROLLER OF REALITY. THE TRAINED MIND CAN SHIFT AT WILL FROM PERCEIVED REALITY TO A COSMIC FLUX OF INNER REALITY. I hope that as you are reading my story, that you will pause and let your mind wander. Let it wander over things that you have experienced. Your story has the inner links that will impress upon your Lower Mind the message, the tool, to be put into your mind's toolbox. With this tool you will be able to reality shift at will. You have already done this in the past, whether you whistled in the dark or looked for animals in the clouds.

* * *

Repetitive Exposure

I can remember when Koz told me that it was repetitive exposure on a non-scheduled interval that put things into the Lower Mind. I became an A and B student using this method. Before that I was lucky to get a C, what a waste! If only I could have know of this in grammar school instead of having to wait until my last semester of my junior year of college. Going to college is a time management problem, not a smarts problem. Some of the best sociologists and physiologists working for the big corporations knew about it; they used this Secret to instill all sorts of self-promoting ideas in the brains of the masses. "I'd walk a mile for a Camel" "Fly the friendly skies of United" "Let Hertz put you in the driver's seat." The reason that I did not learn of repetitive exposure on a non-scheduled interval was that the teachers were not taught. I remember they told me how to study. Lets see; ah find yourself a quiet spot. Sit at a desk with good posture and make sure that the lighting is coming over your left shoulder. Make sure that you will not be disturbed and study for two hours for every hour of class time. All this sounds good, but I found it to be unrealistic. What worked for me and will work for you was just almost the opposite of these instructions. Forget about the desk and light. Put your optical extension of your brain called your eye on whatever you have to store on a short-term basis as many times as you can before the test. Read out loud standing, lying, sitting, walking or jogging in good light or bad. Read out of the book only once, and then transfer what you have underlined to three by five index cards. Put on them anything that has to do with places, names, numbers or ideas and anything that you can remember that flowed over the teacher's lips. Take all your class notes on three by five cards. Keep these cards with you wherever you go. The trick is to capture small segments of time and put them into the brain exposure mode. Don't worry if you are getting it; if you expose your eyes and ears to it enough times, it will get into storage if you want it to or not. This system of studying will make you feel like you are cheating, that's how good it is. I see this tool as a printing press running at high speed. I'm putting this into my Mental Toolbox. Now anybody can put this billion-dollar SECRET to work in his or her own lives. That's presuming that you still have a human brain that you did not fry it on drugs, alcohol, or all the additives in highly processed foods. These foods include HOT DOGS, PIZZA, CHOCOLATE, and MEAT IN THE CAN. OR ANY FOODS PACKAGED IN PLASTICS. A must see is the documentary that was on the Public Broadcasting System, called "Assault On the Male." It will explain to you why the sperm count is down 50%. That the phenols in plastic are mimicking estrogen creating males with very small penis's or none at all. Wow! Where is the World Health Origination, are they wearing the blinders of fear of the big chemical companies? There is a small piece of tissue that links the left and right sides of the brain, the corpus callosum. This pathway is about the size of a pencil lead. The messages are of an electro-chemical construction; they are highly susceptible to drugs and drug like substances. A lot of people have turned themselves into a non-human, human – node, this benches them in the game of life. The perception powers of the non-drugged automatically discriminate against these people. This is done on a subconscious level. Watch very closely what you eat or ingest, it could change you forever.

* * *

A Place To Regenerate

As I walk this world I am able to feel without feeling anything. My Middle Mind doesn't have a clue as how large masses of homogeneous matter affect my Lower Mind. I find myself being regenerated after a trip to the ocean, mountains, or lake. In my past as a child these were weekly events that were done with the whole family. Now I find myself having to push myself to do these nature-regenerating visits. When I find myself in such places, I know that I have found a special balance between my mass and outer mass. My sense of wonder goes on high alert. As I sit and ponder over how a rock was made, I can feel the drifting of my mind into a direction that has no direction. This side looking drifting feeling is a warp in time space reality. I call it Drift Looking. As I drift my vision is tunneled and my body finds a flow down spot to relax in. Time is altered and an afternoon leaps past, as my mind restructures my world. This is the warp in reality that will let vast amounts of Cosmic Law flow into your Lower Mind. As the world around you swallows you up, you become smaller and smaller. Your Middle Mind is overwhelmed and it fades into the shadows as your Lower Mind takes center stage. You have brought your whole body to this place but your Lower Mind sees this as its workshop. It will go into hyper speed functions as you lazy the day away. It will take over, throwing your body into a stupor. The Lower Mind is straining and compiling the whole of your brain neural soup. It is using so much Mind Energy that there is none left over for any other type of brain or body function. Someone may come up to you and shake you and say something like, "Are you all right, you seemed so far away, are you feeling OK?" As you get up, you wonder how your body ever thought that the position that it was in was comfortable as you stretch out and rub out soreness. You feel light headed and it takes a few minutes to get your earth legs. You hear people talking to you but it is not registering. Your Lower Mind wants to hold onto this niche, this warp in reality that it has claimed as its workshop. It wants to stay in this other side of reality and do its work. This state of being removes all Middle Mind reality and clears the way for a true cosmic fluxing of one's mind and Cosmic Law. Seek these places out not for your walk around Middle Mind but for your Future Building Lower

Mind. Don't go for what your eye can see of the outer but what your inner eye can see of the inner Lower Mind at work in its workshop. It doesn't have to be a mountain, a lake or an ocean; it could be next to a wheatfield or cornfield. You could find yourself sitting in a hay mound in a big old barn. Look for other people in these places staring off into space. You may find another person on the path of the Giving Greater Known.

Come along with me as I take you into a dream that has become reality and pushed my Lower Mind. I have had this dream for many years and it still haunts me to this day. I am driving a car in my dream and I see a very thick shelter-belt of trees. These trees are planted on the north and west of a farm site of the northern Great Plains to protect it from the cold winter winds and snow drifts. They also act as a privacy fence and in my mind a fence of secrecy. I drive down a long driveway and the farmer is there to meet me. He seems starved for someone to talk to. All I wanted to do is to ask for directions, but things got carried away. I notice an old Ford truck and make mention of it. I told him that I at one time had an old Ford truck, a 1950 flat head V-8. He led me over to a barn and there was an old Ford truck just like mine, even the same color. As I was looking at it other cars came to mind that I had owned. I walked over to a door opened it and they were there too. The farmer was gone and whatever I was thinking about appeared behind door after door. The one that I remember vividly is the room that had a group of small airplanes hanging from the ceiling. I had this recurring dream from the late 1960's to 1999.

I was in an antique shop in the Empire Mall in Sioux Falls SD. I had mentioned how nice a piece one of their bronze statues was. And how I liked to pour bronzes. She said that I should meet a lady she called Em. She poured bronze and that her and I would have a lot in common. I kept it in the back of my mind and some time later I went back to the antique store and got Em's phone number. I called her up and she was happy to talk to me and could not wait until I would come and visit. One hot summer day I called her and went to visit her out in the country north of Crooks, SD. As I was driving down the road to her place, I saw the thick shelterbelt of trees and fell into a sense that I had been there before. I remembered my dream and it spooked me. She lived on a dead end road and as I got around the corner of the trees I could see three large barns, two houses and three other out buildings. She showed me the blast furnace that she wanted to sell. We struck a trade for labor deal. One hundred hours for the blast furnace. As we needed a board or a light fixture or whatever, we would go hunting through the barns. There she had just about everything. She was an auction junky. She never missed the auction that South Dakota State University at Brookings SD had yearly. On top of her buying the barns had a lot of stuff in them when she bought the place and her husband use to own a machine shop that overhauled engines. My dream had come true and who knows what would have had happened if she had of been a single lady. One day after putting in my time for the day we went just looking. I could feel that side ways drifting into a warp that led into non-reality. Here it was a place to keep everything there did not have to be any rhyme or reason and there was none. As a boy and a young man, I had always shed things that were not necessary, we were on a perpetual move. My father, a Military man, moved often. My Lower Mind wanted to take over and flow the body down and take all the time and energy it needed to absorb this feeling of forever space to linger in body, mind and stuff. KOZ: THE MIND HAS NO BOUNDRIES AND WILL BRING TO YOU THINGS THAT YOU HAVE LONG PAST FORGOTTEN YOUR DREAMS AND HEART FELT DESIRES ARE THE

LOWER MINDS FUEL. I hope that you can find a nearby spot to do your Drift Looking, and do it often at least weekly. Drift Looking is a very important tool for the Lower Mind. If you can find someone that you can walk with down the path of the Giving Greater Known and share your Drift Looking with, you will surely have found a place that will bring to reality all your dreams.

***

Lower Mind Butterfly Catching

I have reached another level of thinking, which I would like to share with you. This type of thinking pulls in different parts, pieces and elements of the teachings of Koz. The Middle Minds actions impress the Lower Mind, which through the Higher Mind taps into the Giving Greater Know. The Lower Mind takes this information and sends out a calling for a link up with other Lower Minds. In this "Link UP Call" there is a cosmic coded message that only brings in Lower Minds that have what your Lower Mind is looking for. The body comes along for the ride and you have to let it float. When somebody comes your way you must shift your mind into a butterfly net, designed to capture messages from their Lower Mind. You must get by their Middle Mind!! To do this, I use these words as I am talking to someone. "May be you won't understand this, but I would like to talk to you about things that I don't talk about with just anybody. I have a place that I go to that helps me get my thoughts together. This place makes me feel good and regenerates me." These few words are not words for the Middle Mind. These few words are for the Lower Mind letting it know that you want to talk about things that the Middle Mind doesn't and will never understand. Listen to me well, this is a junction that you must master. You must hold back your Lower Mind if you don't, the other person's Lower Mind will sit still and be happy to draw in Mind Energy from you. Your Lower Mind has a built in self-protection that wants to transform other Lower Minds to what it has gathered from the Giving Greater Known. It wants to be heard and it wants to share and it likes the feeling of using and giving Mind Energy to other Lower Minds. This is where the problem is; it is hard to get it to shut up.

I want you to go into your Movie Picture Mind and see along with me a story of catching Lower Mind butterflies. Leave your body behind and come and take a walk down a new path. Look to your left and then to your right, there are no butterflies to be seen. Look in your right hand you have a butterfly net at the ready. Now look straight ahead down the path, you can see a large building coming closer and closer. You are now standing in front of this building and you can see that it is full of butterflies. You reach out to open the door and it is locked. In fact they're many locks on this door. A sign on this door reads; ONLY TRAINED LOWER MIND KEYS WILL WORK. And below this sign is a picture of the human brain. As you look at this picture it transforms before your eyes. The brain starts to grow skull and skin and hair. It turns towards you and the face develops into the face of the person that you are talking to. Their mouth opens and out comes some of the most beautiful butterflies you have ever seen, they are like from another world or dimension. (THEY ARE).

Now come back to the words, (and it regenerates me); and stop. Remember this sentence? (This place makes me feel good and it regenerates me.) Get your mental Lower Mind Butterfly Net at the ready you will surely have some to catch. If this mind is still locked say just a few more words. The ones I use are; have you ever experienced anything like that before?

STOP! SHUT UP!! Get your net ready. There may be many locks on this brain and there may not be any butterflies in there that will fill in the empty spaces in your Lower Mind Butterfly collection.

Come along with me on a little side story of Lower Mind Butterfly catching. My Aunt had tripped over a blanket on the floor and fell knee first into a large coffee table. She was glad to see me and asked me what I was doing that afternoon. I said that I had to pick up a part for my truck and that I was going to work on it. She said "Oh". This was a different kind of "Oh". I could hear a let down in her voice. I said that the truck could wait and what did you have in mind. She let me know that she did not feel comfortable driving with her hurt knee. That she would like to go to the Moose Lodge and have a few drinks and stop and get a Philly steak sandwich. I was in the haze; lets do it. I could see a twitch of joy in her movement and her voice. When she got into the car she asked how the gas was and maybe we should gas it up. We went to the gas station, I filled her tank and handed her the credit card back. She then handed me forty dollars and said to get her some cigarettes. Oh did you pick up my mail at the house; yes I did. Good, we will stop of at the post office on the way and pick up my mail. I let her buy me a drink and left her alone at the bar to talk to friends.

I went over and talked to some men decorating a Christmas tree. I was still in the haze and was wondering why my life had taken this turn. Out of my mouth in an automactic mode these words flowed. Do you know of anybody that could loan me some tools I'm looking for a breaker bar and a torque wrench. One man pointed towards another man and said "Leroy over there is a retired mechanic". I asked him about bowering some tools. He said "come over to my house 10 a.m. tomorrow.

I invited my aunt out to eat and she accepted. She had shrimp and I had steak. She was enjoying herself and I got my Lower Mind butterfly net ready. I said that I had broken the 60,000-word count in writing my book. And I said that I was writing about thinking places. She looked at me with her Middle Mind tuned in and said, "I don't understand what you mean." Oh, just places where the body shuts off and the mind can regenerate itself. STOP! This is where you say not a word more.

Now I want to share with you this story this beautiful Lower Mind butterfly. She said that there was a time of great loss and she was depressed over loosing her mother, my grandmother. She would go to the beach and relax. Now listen to these words closely. I would see myself flying around with my mother and looking at things. This really helped me get over my depression. There it was the Lower Mind, I had used the right words and reaped a cosmic butterfly for my collection. I knew that my Lower Mind was out there working for me and it had brought to me this next pearl on my string of cosmic pearls. KOZ: LOWER MIND HUNTING IS A GIFT THAT WILL BRING ABOUT A NEW REALITY THINKING BASE. LOWER MIND TO LOWER MIND FLUXING WILL COVER YOU WITH A DOME OF ENERGY. LOWER MIND FLUXING ENERGY IS THE FUEL OF THE COSMIC LAW OF THE GIVING GREATER KNOWN. Come with me into this higher level of thinking so that I may show you things that only your Lower Mind can grasp. Stay with me, you as the student is soon to pass. You will be at a knowing level that will put you in a higher plain of understanding. That these words that I use will melt away and be nothing but sign posts along a grand journey that is just getting started.

***

Mirror

I, at anytime, can now shift my reality and find myself Drift Looking. I have had to leave a parking lot not knowing what I came there for. I would have fallen into a total relaxed slump and passed hours away. It happened more often when I would look into my rear view mirror. At first it was to see if my hair was combed or if I had sleep in my eyes. Then one day I found myself looking at something in the rear view mirror and trying to refigure it in my brain as if I was looking at it straight on. This trying to pull something in your mind from the backwards to the forwards is a key thought process. You see what your eye sees but you know that this is seeing it backwards and your mind without hesitation tries to bring it to the straight on looking reality. This shifting in the mind is the same shifting that the mind does when shifting from reality to an altered non-reality. The paths of thought are so close together that there is a good chance that there will be bleed over akin to what was learnt about the Yes-NO rebound. The mirror can play tricks on the reality-based mind and bewilder it to a point of frustration. Try this simple test with a mirror to see what I mean. Put a small desk in front of a wall mirror. Sit in a chair at this desk. Supply yourself with a piece of paper and a pencil. Put a stack of books between you and the paper on the desk. Do this so that you can only see the paper through the mirror not directly. Reach around the books pick up the pencil and draw a square on the paper only looking through the mirror. When doing this I don't want you to worry about getting the square drawed, I want you to feel the feeling that your brain is feeling. This feeling is the Key to The Other World. Put this feeling in your toolbox of tools that Koz has given us. This tool is a tool that will build a bridge into non- reality. It will let you slip in the back door of non-reality piggy-backing your way in on a feeling that will bleed over into the mind-set that is needed to do reality shifting.

I had been setting for hours and did not come back to reality until I saw the store manager locking up. I jumped out of my car and ran over to him and said I need to get some; my mind turned blank I just walked back to my car shaking my head. I had done it again, I had been Mirror Gazing. I looked into the mirror and it all came back to me. I had been on Reach One (day dream). I had gone into a circular room. The walls were mirrors and I could see hundreds of me, my reflection. Around me was a circular table and I was sitting on a swivel chair. On this table were hundreds of little cell phones. I picked one up and the label on it read (For Calling Other Lower Minds Only). Underneath that it read these are think activated communication lines. There were not any numbers on the phone. I held it to my ear and a voice said that if I wanted to call in a Lower Mind all I had to do is to think of the person releasing his Lower Mind and it flowing into me. I thought of my Uncle Frank. I felt a rush go through my body I had the Goose Bumps. When I looked into the mirrors I could see my Uncle coming out of me first one direction and then another. I picked up another phone and thought of my son and as I looked in the mirror I saw him flowing in and out of my body's reflection along with my Uncles. I picked up another phone and thought of Eienstein and he was also there in the mirror. I looked at the phone and there was a disconnect button, I pushed it. A voice said to send a Lower Mind away you must think of them and thank them and say good-by. I did and Eienstein and then my son and my Uncle were gone. A bright band of light sucked the table and phones into it. The mirrors faded away and all I could see were stars. I was sitting without a chair floating and looking into outer space or maybe inner space. I closed my eyes and when I opened them I was standing in front of a door that was gray. The plaque on the door read Lower Mind Link Registration. I walked in and saw a line of people that had no end. And as soon as I stood in line I looked back and I could not see the end of the line behind me or the door that I had just come in. Above was a tele-prompter screen. It said if you know about the Inward Looking Eye that Glimpses The Future please proceed down the white line to your right. I stepped over to a line on the floor to my right. As soon as my left foot hit the line after my right foot I could see that I was passing people in the line where I was standing. This passing became faster and faster until it was a blur. Then I came to a stop in another line and I couldn't see either end of. I looked at the monitor above my head it was asking me if I knew about the Yes-No Rebound. I stepped to the line to my right and again I was off passing up more people. This kept on going on and on until I came to a window. On a small plaque on the ledge read take a piece of paper and write your name on it and put it into the box on the wall to your right. I did so and when I dropped it into the box it fell out the bottom. It turned into sparkles like you would see at a fireworks show, and then before it hit the floor it formed into a ball of light and took off back through the line of people. I could see it flowing through there heads one after another. I stood there watching it until it had gotten so far away that I could not see it any more. The next thing I saw was the store manager locking the front door looking over at me and shaking his head. I just sat there trying to think of what I was there for. I think in the future I would have to comb my hair without looking in the mirror. KOZ: MIND BRIDGES, BLEED OVERS, AND BACKDOOR HITCHHIKING ARE ALL IMPORTANT TOOLS TO TAP INTO THE GIVING GREATER KNOWN THROUGH YOUR DRIFT LOOKING. I would like to think that you were in line with me and got to put your name in the Lower Mind registration box. I think that this trip to Reach One brought up many more questions than last trips. I think it was trying to tell me that I could call in Lower Minds to help me like I helped my friend James with the volunteer fireman's feed. There is a higher level of knowing than people don't even know that they have. They know when a person is in touch with his Lower Mind even if they are not or had never heard of it or thought of it. That is why I saw a light in the people's eyes as I served them their prime-rib.

***

Mall Window Looking

I walk in shopping malls looking to see myself. There are times when the windows and mirrors are arranged so that you see a side of yourself that you never get to see. This person in the reflection you know as you only because as you move it moves. Your mind goes though a fill in the blanks process and moves on, not really looking at this person in the mirror. I have in the past used my camera on a timer to take my picture when there was no one around to do it. I can remember one such time when my son and myself were in a ruin, a temple, north of Bangkok, Thailand. I set up the camera and I and my son stood there pointing as if we were seeing something of great importance. When I see that picture I see my son standing next to a person that I had never seen before. I know it's me but I never get to see me at a straight on from the side and a little from the back angle. I look different but no one else thinks so because they get to see me at all types of angles all the time.

This feeling of looking at yourself that is not quite you as you think of yourself, is a powerful window of control. If you own this different person what would you change to assure that this vessel would not let your being slip away. In walking in the mall I can see this other person many times at many angles in the now, in real time. This is an interactive viewing that surpasses looking at a still camera picture that is of a time frame in the past. I want to know this person in the reflection and place him in my mind as a separate identity from myself. I will at times go back to the same store window to look at that person again sometimes three or more times. I have had store sales people thinking that I had seen something that I had liked. They would come out and ask me if they could answer any questions that I may have about something. I wanted to ask them to move something in their window so that I could get a better view of myself. I wanted to ask him why my brain was attracted to this new view of myself and was this a tool that I could use to control myself by seeing myself as a different person. There were really three views that my brain was jumping back and forth between. The reflection off of the glass window, the reflection of a reflection in a mirror and my minds-eye reflection all came into play. Would this multiple reflection input to my mind give my mind a shift in reality so that it could hold me myself at arms length for inspection? Was this a short cut into inner reality shifting? My reply to the shopkeeper was "no I'm just looking."

    After a session of self-looking I would find a place that I could sit down and see my reflection. I was looking for a spot where there were people passing in front of my reflection and me. The reflection would be off of a window of a store that I could see things inside of and people moving around inside the store. I wanted it so people would be walking behind me and I could see them in the reflection of the window. There would be times when someone else would be sitting in my spot and I would have to wait and I would. I made it look like I was waiting for someone looking at my watch and looking around as if I was looking for some one. I was looking for someone and it was me, my other self my reflection in the window. As I am waiting I have at times funny feelings that I might miss seeing my reflection in the window because it got tired of waiting for me. I might sit down and my reflection would not be there. What would really bother me is who could I report it to and how would they be able to get my reflection back. The seat was mine, they finally left. I sit down and I make it look as if I am reading a newspaper. I'm looking over the top of the newspaper into the window. The Mind Reality Bending starts. The input to the brain is in so many layers that it must shift to a float mode of gathering information. This float mode dose a lot of skipping over of input trying to focus on one thing, but it can't. It jumps from one set of inputs to the next trying to put it in an order that it can feel that it understands and can control, but it can't. This feeling that the mind is experiencing is of the same type when we feel we have no control. The mind will look at all these inputs and start weeding out the ones that it has no control over. The first thing that it lets go of is what it sees in the window the things on display. It knows it can't control the people in the store so it lets go of that. There is no way to stop the people from walking between my reflection and me so that is let go. I have no control of the people walking behind me I must let that go too. I can't stop the noise that is all around me so I don't try to control that. The lights are a bit bright but I can do nothing about that. As someone passes by, they brush my newspaper, I see it move in the reflection. My mind has locked on to when I pulled the paper back toward myself, it also moved in the reflection. The mind goes through a state of happiness in finding something that it can control. It starts playing a little game of see I made you do that. Why can my mind see that it can make my reflection do something, but not my real body? KOZ: THE LOWER MIND IS THE MASTER OF THE INNER AND MUST BE TAUGHT THAT IT CAN ALSO CONTROL THE OUTER. GLASS GAZING WILL IMPRESS THE LOWER MIND THAT IT ALSO CONTROLS THE OUTER. Try some multi-layer glass gazing to impress your Lower Mind that it can also control you're outer self. Do this more than once so that your Lower Mind gets the feel of it. Don't let your Middle Mind out of the strongbox and chase your powerful Lower Mind back into its inner control.

***

Mind Take Over

I was drinking a glass of water; the glass was so cold that it was sweating. As I looked at it I could see the little drops of water on the outside and reflections off of the glass. I could also see the ice in the water and through the water the table that it was sitting on. The thing that held my mind in a state of non-reality was the bend in the straw. I could see that it was bent but my mind knew that this was just a trick of light refraction. I was not able to keep my mind still so that I could just see what my eye was telling me what I was seeing. I wish my mind would leave me alone and leave its tainted view of things to it's self. I would like a switch that I could throw that would shut the brain down so that it would not keep interrupting my eye observations. If I perceived that the sun came up in the east that's all I want it to be. I don't want my mind to step in with it's gathered knowledge and whisper in my inner ear that it's the earth that is turning not the sun moving. This movement makes the sun look like it's moving. I want these interruptions to go away. They are disrupting my concentration so that I can't see anything anew for myself. If I wanted to see things through the muddy water of my mind I just would not clean my glasses. I would try looking at things through a Coke bottle. This Coke bottle image would be so distorted that it would be very hard to see things the way they really were. But then again my mind would step in and straighten things out.

I was at a dear friend's house one day and she was showing me a picture of one of the white deer that lived on the church property. I pulled out my glasses and put them on. I looked at the picture and was astounded as to how much depth it had. It looked like the deer could walk out of the picture at any time. I wondered if it was a special process, some type of holograph or something. I looked at it with only my right eye and it appeared to be now just a normal picture. I closed my right eye and looked at it with my left eye. I had a startle, my left eye had gone bad when had that happened. I don't need this now I am writing a book. I took my glasses off to rub my eye as if this would help somehow. I opened my left eye and it was still seeing things blurred. Then I noticed that one of the lenses in my glasses had fallen out. My eye was OK as far as OK was for my eyes. My mind had gotten carried away with the idea that there was something wrong with my eye. It also had stepped in and compensated for the blurred image that I was getting from my left eye and let me see the picture as being in focus.

It made me wonder how many times in the past had my mind got carried away and deceived me. Why was it always interrupting? And what could I do about this self-mind stirring. I was still looking at the glass of cold water thinking of how far off my mind had taken me. I wish it would be still, all I want is to be left alone so that I can look and see this glass of water.

I was on Reach One, I was in a room that had people sitting in chairs and they were facing a blank white wall and their eyes were taped closed. I could see them moving their hands around feeling something and then writing on the wall what it was. I stood there watching them. They would get something handed to them by the person to their left. They would feel it and pass it to the person to their right and then write what it was on the wall. Then they would reach out to their left moving their hand around until they linked up with the next item. They did this ten times and then stopped. The white wall was shifted one spot to the right. So that unbeknownst to the blind taped eyed person he was not looking at his own writing on the wall when they took off the tape. Not one of them ever said that this is not my handwriting. I have been tricked and my handwriting on the wall was the next one over to the right. They were asked to now rewrite the list of ten items on the wall on the wall next to what they had written on the wall. When they had finished they were asked to step one space to their right and check their neighbors list against what you had written on the wall now to your left. Not one of these persons recognized that the new pattern of words on the wall in front of them were their hand writing that this is what I wrote on the wall.

I was interrupted, a voice was asking me was there anything else that I wanted. I knew that she was only doing her job that's what waitresses are supposed to ask. I wanted to say to her that I did not need her mind interrupting me; my own mind was doing a good enough job of that. Just leave me alone so I can get back to Reach One. I did say "no, no thanks." Which really meant leave me alone can't you see that I am thinking. What does that mouth full of words really mean anyway. Other people can't see that you are thinking that's why they interrupt and disturb your train of thought. Can you feel the feeling of being disturbed? Can you remember how it made you feel? I feel like I wished I had a switch so I could turn them off. Them and their inconsiderate brain how dare they bring that mud puddle of neural soup my way. I feel like telling them to take their brain away and go tell someone that gives a damn. I want you to feel the feeling of your brain being disrupted by someone else. And then think about how it would be if that were a constant thing that went on with everything that you thought. How would a person ever get a pure thought out of their head?

We must recognize that we have this internal disruption going on all the time within us. That many people can't think for themselves and will never be anything but a follower. They will bend with the storm of brain neural goo as it blows through their neural soup.

Koz has taught me a little trick that is a trick within a trick. That when I am disrupted in thought that I see it as something that is a message from the Giving Greater Known that is very important. I should practice disconnecting from my thought and give this interruption my full attention. I should see a hold key like on a telephone that will put my thoughts on hold until I get back to them. By doing this I am not depleting my Mind Energy being mad about being disrupted. This also makes the person disrupting you feel that you value their opinion and they will sometime in the future maybe bring you a real gem of an idea. See them as trying to trick you into being disturbed. But you are going to trick them into thinking that you are glad that they are feeding you all this free information. And that it is too bad that they can't see it for themselves and how far they could get on their own advice if they would only take it. KOZ: INTERNAL BRAIN STIRRING WILL STOP THE BEST BRAINS IN THEIR TRACKS. BUILD AN INTERNAL HOLD SWITCH THAT WILL LET YOUR LOWER MIND TAKE ADVANTAGE OF NEW INPUTS FROM THE GIVING GREATER KNOWN. DON'T LET YOUR OWN LOWER MINDS PROTECTION SYSTEM SHUT YOU IN THE INNER VOID OF YOUR OWN MIND.

When I was on Reach One this time I was impressed by how my mind could possibly be leading me astray not meaning to. That it is not as right as I think it is and that I should be more aware of it's input. That I have to start thinking with a higher mind about what my mind is bringing to the round table of thought. Come and build this type of higher thinking mind with me so that we will be on the same wavelength.

***

Brain Wave Control

Last night I was invited to play bingo at the clubhouse in a trailer court owned by the Church of The Golden Rule. This is where my friends Don and Beth live it is located just south of Wilits, Ca. When I drive to their place I feel as if I am descending into another world. After going up a steep grade on the highway you take a left turn and start descending into a valley of bliss. To greet you there are white deer that if I were a drinking man would get me off the sauce. I came to do an over night visit and head out to the coast. That was Sunday it is now Wednesday morning and do not want to leave. I think the main reason is a young man in his upper 70s that is on the path of the Giving Greater Known. He talks of the looking inward that is where we can change everything outward. This man is living proof that there is a higher level of thinking. If you are ever by this way and you would like to meet a man from out of this world, stop in and ask for Hue. They have a campground there and if you feel that you could keep up with him as he dose his daily rounds of giving see if he will let you ride along with and work with him. Last year when I was there I was able to do just that, I felt blessed. He is a Church member and his work is done from his heart. There is not a set time that he has to start or finish. He will do for anybody anything that he can and make sure the stuff that he can't do gets done by someone else. He does this because he believes in giving,   giving, giving… He is not paid by the hour nor is he even paid, all his needs are met by the church. When my days of wandering are over I have a feeling that I will be there. I would not mind spending my last days with Hue and fall into this world of giving. Although he is a small stature man and his shoe size is not over ten, I feel even with my size fifteen's his shoes would be hard to fill. When this man passes on I will cry and the world would of passed up a chance to bump into a true cosmic pearl.

    I was standing counting out my pocket money I had forgotten my wallet. The cost of a bingo card was fifty cents. I had enough for six and that's all I think I could keep up with. My three dollars was in the pot. It was time to pick out my bingo cards. There were two ladies in front of me looking for the good numbers. I felt that this had nothing to do with playing bingo or its outcome. I was just there to be with my friends. I thought how far removed that this was from being at Harold's Bar in Cave Creek AZ. or the Gas Panic in Tokyo Japan. What was I doing here? I could be anywhere in the world that I wanted to be, anywhere. I looked in the box of cards and took the first six off the top. We were to play six games the last one to be a blackout that paid eight dollars and the rest to pay five. I counted eleven people playing and they all had eight cards and one lady had ten. I figured I didn't have much of a chance of winning anything. What the hell was I even doing here anyway? I got my cards ready and was going through the movements but not thinking of bingo. I was looking at one card and noticed that it looked like one of the translucent slide windows that slides to mark a called out number looked different from the rest. It looked like it had been sun degraded or someone had put a cigarette out on it. I picked the card up for a better look.

It was just how the light was hitting it. I flipped the card back and forth a couple of times and fell into the Haze. I started to think about what Koz had told me about Mind Energy. And how that the Lower Mind used this energy to tap into and talk to the Higher Mind and how it used it to tap into the Giving Greater Known. I started concentrating on the numbers that I needed. I won the next game. And I won the last game the blackout. It was passed over by the rest of the people as just luck and I said nothing as I walked out the door ten dollars richer. I knew that they were not anywhere near the level of thinking that would be needed to even entertain a discussion on this matter of mind over matter link with the Giving Greater Known. Most people would call it luck and not even give it another thought. I want you to put your Middle Mind into the strong box and take a walk down a different path of thought.

Close your eyes and see that the other side of no sight is darkness. Open your eyes and see the other side of darkness is light. Think of space and think of the matter. Look closely at the matter and see the space in it. See a board that is dry and weighs 2 pounds become three pounds when soaked in water. See a piece of steel hard and shinny and see mercury slip down into the pores and spaces. Now see something so small that it goes straight through the steel with ease. Something like an x-ray or gamma ray or your own brain wave. That if this type of energy can traverse the distances of space that the short trip to the bingo balls would be easy.

I want to tell you a story about a story that will always be just a story. There will be no way to back up this story, this story is one that they do not like talking about. They are the best of the best. They have the right stuff what ever that may be. They some day might make it all the way to Top Gun. There are a few that won't make it past the first week of hands on training. I was sitting in the best USO in the world it is in the Lampert airport in Mo. An old retired officer told me this story of fear and jets. That it took a lot of brain crunching to get through college and through Officers Training School and have the mind set that you need to be selected for Flight Training School Jets. There are a few that have very highly trained brains that will not make it. They will be washed out because of a list of different things but not the real reason. They will be branded as jinx, a person that has the bad touch. Oh! The record will say slow to grasp the required skills. Or a person with out people skills needed for this task. Or a person that is not team orientated. And if you try to fight the system then you develop a Passive Aggressive Personality Disorder and discharged with a General Discharge. These few or maybe not so few highly developed minds are really being let go because of their brain waves effect on the electronics of the jet that they are assigned to at that moment. There seems to be no boundaries to the possibilities of what could go wrong. From one system to another things seem to not be operating correctly when this person gets around a jet. Time and time again no matter what jet or how many jets these types of people are introduced to things go wrong. They are hushed up and washed out to a desk job or out the door. There is something going on with them and their brain waves that will not be addressed. End of story.

    Story two is the same story but just replace the jet with the new bread of electronic computerized car. Oh! Hush this one up we don't need any more problems of the type where the driver says that he tried to stop but the car took over. That his fear transmitted directly to the cars control circuit and made the car run in fear. That the person had no control and even after turning the key off and stomping on the breaks many times could not get the car under control. The police officer even testified that he saw the brake lights come on and it seemed that the person was trying to pull over but couldn't. KOZ: THE POWER OF THE HIGHER MIND LINKED INTO THE GIVING GREATER KNOWN IS WITH OUT BOUNDRIES OR REALITY BASED LAWS. ALL CAN BE DONE WITH THE TRAINED HIGHER LEVEL OF THINKING THROUGH THE USE OF COSMIC LAW. A HIGHER MIND LOW ON MIND ENERGY WILL DRAW IT FROM ANY NEAR BY SOURCE IN THE AMOUNTS NEEDED TO RESTORE ANY FEAR OR NEGITIVE ENERGY DRAINS. Step into this higher realm of thinking by practicing it on a daily basis. Don't let somebody with a few words out of their mud puddle of neural soup steal this power from you. Keep it a secret from the non-followers of the path of the Giving Greater Known. Build on it when you find someone that is on the same Lower Mind path.

***

Change Inside

This is where you must start using this book as a road map to a grand inner voyage. On any voyage or trip the first thing you do when you look at a map is you say. Lets see now we are right here and we want to get here. The first part is "we are right here". Where are you in your minds eye of yourself? What would you change if you knew that you could? I want you to make a list of changes that you would like to see in your life. I want you to list the large and small changes. I want you to think smaller and smaller. I want you to think of something that you know you could change. I want you to think in your mind that it matters not what you change what matters is change itself. I want you to think about change as the most important thing that you can learn to do. That change should always hit your brain in big letters (CHANGE). I want you to think of yourself as a CHANGE Champion. That if you did not CHANGE something today that it meant that you lost that day and it will be added onto the same old you.

The thing that I want you to feel is the power that you feel inside when you have learned the secrets of Change and your eyes open to a new world of possibilities. I want you to think of the last time things changed in your life and think of who made the change and if it was not you what did you think. Were you thinking as I do that it was unfair that they had a power over you that you could not do anything about? Was your rent just raised enough that you will have to swallow it because you can't afford to move or don't want to. Was your electric rate increased? Did the price of gas go up again? I want you to talk about how you feel about those things that are changing. And then hear yourself say, but what can I do about it things change and life goes on. If they raised the price of gas to ten dollars a gallon people would still be buying it, they would have to." Feel the helplessness that is pouring out over your lips as you shrug your shoulders and twitch your head to the side in a jester of oh well thats just the way it is. There's no sense of me wasting my time worrying about that, just pay them the money. I want you to think about change as a spreading and growing thing. That once you get it started that it will grow on its own.

I want you to sit in a comfortable spot and close your eyes and go into your movie picture mind. See yourself standing in front of a large field of rocks and weeds. There is a fence all around and a nice double swinging gate large enough to drive your truck through. You look across the street and there you are standing again, there are two of you. You pay this no mind for two of you is perfectly OK in this world because you locked that book called the Middle Mind up in that strong box and it is not going to disrupt things. Just to the right of the gate is a number counting machine. It reads in large letters at the top CHANGE. And below that it reads DAY and below that it reads the number one. You look across the street and your other self's counting machine is also on the number one. You open the gate and drive in and start clearing a spot to plant strawberries. You look across the street and see your other self scratch his head and drive away. You on the other hand are standing and looking at the thirty plants that you got planted that day and look over to the counting machine and the word CHANGE is flashing. And across the road it is not. You pack up your tools and go home. The next day you come you see that the counting machine is not flashing but the number two is displayed. You see that your other self has arrived but his counting machine is still on one. You weed your plot and get ten more plants in the ground that day, CHANGE is flashing. You look across the street to see your other self playing Frisbee with his dog. Three months have past and your counting machine reads 80 and when you look across the street your other self's reads one. You have put up a sign strawberries for sale and people are buying. They are buying a lot of strawberries from your now 800 plants. Your children are helping and the neighbor kids too. There will be enough money to send the kids to college.

    Which side of the street is your true self on? Are you the on-looker of change or the mover and shaker? Do people see you as going places or is your number staying the same. Are they coming to join you in your adventure or are they staying away because they don't want you asking them to lend you some money?

    Take this challenge and see if you can get in your own pattern of inner self-change. I want you to find a rock to put in your pocket. I want you to carry it with you for a week and look at it and feel it for a week. Then I want you to take that rock out of your pocket and start a pile of little rocks next to the front door of your house or in a pie tin in side your house or apartment where you will see it every day many times. Don't ask why, just do it. There are many powerful forces at work that your walk around Middle Mind will not grasp. As you take a week old rock out of your pocket look at it and feel the feelings of ownership and that how that you will miss it's look and feel. Then look at the new rock and feel it all over and put it in your pocket. I want you to do this until you have transformed your Lower Mind into a CHANGE orientated force that looks for change and changes itself on an automatic basis. KOZ: TEACHING THE LOWER MIND THE POWER OF CHANGE WILL CHANGE EVERYTHING AS YOU KNOW IT, EVEN REALITY. A SHIFT IN REALITY IS A CHANGE THAT CAN CHANGE WORLDS. CHANGE AS A TOOL IN THE RIGHT HANDS CAN TURN WORLDS INSIDE OUT AND START THEM OVER AGAIN GOING DOWN THE PATH OF THE GIVING GREATER KNOWN. Take these small steps in CHANGE and before long you will feel the power of inner change and Change will be the norm. I want you to say to yourself that some day I will drive by here and say I used to live there. And I can remember when I used to work there. And know in your heart that things will change as you see fit.

***

Self-Made Rules

I was standing in front of an ATM and its message to me is that in so many words was; your account has been shut down and to contact your bank. I stood there looking at the screen moving my head side-to-side trying to get a better angle so that the sun wouldn't glare off the glass. What was I going to do now. I was in the land of the rising sun where an apple cost $5. I had brought my son with me to Japan to expand his mind and now find myself short on cash. I had maxed out my credit cards on rental cars and motel rooms. I could cash a check for $150 a day at the Base Exchange. I looked I had only four checks left. I was able to stretch those four checks out by making twelve copies of the last check and using them. This was working out just fine until the teller pulled out of thin air a Self Made Rule. She let me know that it was against the law to make copies of checks and I could be in big trouble. I told her that the name of my bank was on there my name and signature and it was dated that constituted a legal contract and that she would cash it. Now she was not so sure and made a telephone call. She turned to me and said that I was going to have to go to base finance and talk to them. I was glad that I had rented bicycles from the base recreation center. The finance office was on the other side of the base. When I got there the person that I had to talk to said, "I'm telling you right now I'm not cashing that check". I said, "That I understood that and the reason that I was there was that I wanted the regulation number that he was going by so when I went to the legal office that they could look it up before they called you". He said, "He had to make a phone call". He came back into the room and asked me how much I wanted to cash the check for, that he would only cash that one check how much was I going to need. I was going to be happy with $200 and that's what I got. At that stage of my vacation I was just waiting for the next flight out and that should be enough money. I felt like going back to that teller at the Base Exchange and put her in her place showing her that I did get the check cashed. The next day there were seats open on a KC-135 going to Travis and then onto Grissom AFB and we got on.

I want you to think of some Self Made Rules that you knew were bullshit. How did they make you feel? They made me feel like I wished I had a lot of money to throw around so I could prove them wrong. I did not tell this story to prove right or wrong I told it so that it may bring up a simular story in your past that would bring back these types of feelings. These feelings of yours are self realized and the only way that I can transfer the feelings is to have you tap into your past and pull up your feelings. I want you to go into you movie picture mind and think of some of the Self Made Rules that pissed you off. Think of three or four of them and each time recapture the feelings that you felt at the time. I want you to do this until you can pull up these types of feelings at any time. These types of feelings are very important tools to push your Lower Mind into a sped up reaction. If you will pull up these types of feelings and wave them in front of your Lower Mind it will be like giving it a shock of a cattle prod. I want you to give this feeling a one-word name that will make it easy to shoot it into your Lower Mind. I have chosen the word (Jail) and it's all right if you use the same word or one of your choosing. I want you to see in your mind's eye a big cage dropping down over you as you are fed one of these Self Made Rules. Self Made Rule = Cage = feeling = Jail; Jail = feeling. When you think of the word (Jail) I want it to bring up the feelings that very moment. The key is to bring these feelings to the forefront. Now I want you to use this powerful tool of the mind to do, as you will the mind to do. I want you to look and make sure that your Middle Mind is still locked up in the strong box and is buried. We don't need that type of childish thought disrupting us now. This word (JAIL) when spoken in the right frame of mind is a very, very powerful tool and should be used sparingly. When you find yourself pushed up against a task that has to be done but your lazy Lower Mind does not want to get moving, this is what I want you to say. I want you to find a quite place and start talking to yourself out loud. I want the Middle Mind to only say the words I don't expect it to understand them or their higher level of power. Talk to yourself directing your message to the Lower Mind. Say these words. If you don't stop playing around you will feel (JAIL). The time has come to put your butt in gear and get the job done. If you don't it's (JAIL) for you. (JAIL), (JAIL), (JAIL). Every time that you say the word jail think of it as your Lower Mind being whipped with a bull whip. And it does not like it one bit. See your Lower Mind down on its knees begging you not to say that word again. It is saying to you that it will do anything that you say just don't say that (J) word again. And I want you to see it get up with a show of I'm getting to it right now. And see it going to work on this task that it has been putting off. This when done in a head pounding session will speed up and deepen the brain implant to the Lower Mind. KOZ: THIS SHIFT INTO A HIGHER LEVEL OF THINK COMMUNACATION WILL GIVE YOU A DIRECT LINK TO YOUR LOWER MIND. THIS WILL PUT YOU AT THE DOOR STEP OF PURE COSMIC LAW AND BRING YOU INTO THE FAMILY AS A FULL MEMBER OF THE GIVING GREATER KNOWN. If you have been a practicing student of these tools given to us by KOZ you have made some large steps down a different cosmic path. If you feel that all of this is too hard to get into, you are not alone. I myself had those same feelings for many years. You have just peeled off the paper-thin first layer of this new cosmic onion. As you work with these new tools they will fall into their natural working places and become an automatic inner process. This will take time much more time than just one reading of this book.

McCROSS BOYS RANCH

He was a big boy for his age, over 200 pounds. He was still taking things from people or destroying them. He had played this game all his life and now it had to come to a stop. I was working as a counselor at a boys ranch for juvenile delinquents. One of the other counselors came running down the hall, he yelled, "The new kid was tarring things apart we are going to need some help on this one." We ran to his room he was throwing things and breaking anything that he was able to break. He was here because he would not stay in school and he had many minor infractions on his record. We got him held down and were trying to talk to him when the director came in and put a smother hold on him. He would put both his hands on the boys' face covering his nose and mouth so that he couldn't breath. This was held until the boy would be close to passing out and then released. If the boy still wanted to fight after catching his breath it was done again. After about three or four times the young man stopped fighting. Although I thought that this was a little harsh, it worked and there was no hitting or twisting of arms that could of injured the young man. I was left to make sure that there were not any more outbursts. I was able to talk to him and hear his side of the story of how his mother was running around. She was into drugs and was doing a lot of drinking and even some prostituting. That she was never at home and he had to get a job because there was not any food in the house. And that's why he had not been in school. I fell into the haze his story was so close to my own. I went out of the envelope and said things that were not within the guidelines of the ranch. I jumped into my beast brain for two sentences. I know how you feel, those bastards didn't even give you a chance to tell your side of the story before they smothered you down. That shit happened to me all the time when I was a kid, the bastards don't give a shit. (THE SHIFT) I found out that all I could do is play their silly game until I got to a place where I was in control again. That all I had to do is to play their little minds along until I got there. You don't want them in here again snuffing you out who knows what kind of permanent brain damage they could do if you piss them off enough. I don't imagine that it feels the best to be smothered out that way. I saw the young man was shaking his head no. I had made a connection a link up to his Lower Mind. Then we started making out a plan of action. I told him that if he did well in the boys ranch school and behaved himself that he could be out of here and back in control and back home in about two weeks. But you have to play their game. What you have to watch out for is they will try to trip you up. So that you will do something stupid like hit someone. Then they can keep you around for a long time pulling in federal money for your stay. Get the picture you are just another dollar sign no more no less. (THE SECRET TOOL) If you tell anybody that I told you these things I will stop being on your side and make life miserable for you and you will never get out of here until your 18 yrs. Of age. Is that a deal as I held out my hand and we shook hands as I said "do you think you can do that?" (Challenge). The boy did fine and was rotated back home in about three weeks.

    This using of feelings the combination of his and my feelings was able to build a link between our two Lower Minds. It built a kinship and trust on the fact that our Lower Minds were on the same path because they had the same feelings that they shared in common. I have used the phrase, (how did it make you feel), to build direct linking paths to others peoples

Lower Minds. I use lying on of the hands with the use of the common already established acceptable touching called handshaking. This seals the deal or builds a stronger Lower Mind link-up. The handshake also forms a sort of a secret alliance that transcends the mere word. There is also the chemical touch, pheromone link that is in the realm of the body intelligence. This body chemical link is at a very high level of communication that should not be over looked when linking-up with another Lower Mind. All the words will not be remembered but the feel of the handshake will be. The chemical message will carry a higher-level transmission of knowledge of the other person than words could ever do. During his stay I would only have to say to this young man, do you remember our handshake? This would bring up all that was said and I was giving him support with the tool of (Repetitive Exposure On A Non-Scheduled Interval). At times I would only use body language that he and I would only understand (Secret Tool) from across the room I could hold out my hand as if offering it in a handshake, and he would nod to let me know that we still had our secret pact in force and I would give a thumbs up back. And lip the words GOOD MAN.

    I want you to go into your movie picture mind. I want you to think of someone in the past that you wanted to help but it did not work out like you would have liked it to. I want you to find a place in your mind that is a quite place. I want you to see yourself talking to this person and hearing what you had to say and listen to what they had to say. I want you to think about the tools that you had to work with. Can you see the elements of a good structured plan or were you just shooting from the hip. Now use the tools given to us by KOZ and see a different out come. I want you to feel how you feel about this new outcome. I want you to feel inside you this powerful tool that can reach out and change other peoples lives. And I want you to feel the feelings of pride and accomplishment when you see this person reach out to someone else and extend a helping hand using the same tools that you used. I want you to see a large bucket and written on the side of the bucket is the words HIGHER LEVEL OF THINKING. And you are pouring this bucket of neural soup on the north pole of the world and it is flowing and covering it in a higher knowledge. See yourself receiving the highest award given the feeling of self worth and that I can make a difference, just little old me. KOZ: LINKING INTO THE LOWER MINDS OF OTHER PEOPLE AND GIVING OF YOUR MIND ENERGY WILL BRING MORE ENERGY TO YOU. THIS RETURN OF ENERGY WILL COME BACK IN A MULTIPLE AND IN MANY FORMS. YOUR COSMIC PEARLS WILL COME YOUR WAY MORE OFTEN AND THEY WILL BE PURER AND BIGGER. I do hope that some of these new tools will be integrated into your own life to an extent that you will feel them working for you and you will want to share them with someone else. To change you is to change the world. Go forth and multiply, could also mean of the mind, at a higher level of thinking.

***

Hurt Time Factor

There is a place where your mind can take you and hold you there as a prisoner. It will hold you so tight that you will become depressed and thoughts of suicide will rush through your mind. This place your mind will take you will consume your body. You will not only lose weight you will go through a mind stirring that will put your mind and thoughts on hold. You will think that you have lost it. You will think that there is no returning to what you thought was the normal you. People around you will see you being sucked into this mind place and try as they may to help they only make things worse. The pill pushers with their all-knowing minds will try to give you a chemical tune-up. All this does for you is to give your brain just one more thing that it has to deal with. When we are young we rebound out of these mind sink holes easily and go on with life. But when we get older there is so much more neural soup that can be stirred. Our minds will go from neural soup pot to the next neural soup pot straining it for the answers of why and how can I change it, where is the answer. In not finding it, your mind just knots up tighter and tighter. There are neural strainers all over the floor and they have flowed together along with the neural slosh from your frantic straining of the pots. Your mind inside looks like a kitchen that just got done cooking a thanksgiving dinner for thirty.

    Come along with me and see a mind bender that I was swept up into. I was not looking but was not turning anything away. I had not shaved for three weeks and had no plans to until the late spring of the Dakotas would bless us with some temperature above the freezing zone. I was shooting darts and having a good time. Her name was Gail and her mother's name was Carol. She was eyeing me and I her. Then the bumps and brushes and the stand so close that you could feel each others body warmth and smell each others breath and hair. She was going to have to leave she had to feed her horses, but she would be coming back. I asked if she could use a hand and she whisked me into the other world the world that people in love see, a lover's world. She was the type of gal that every man is looking for. She was there with you through thick and thin. It lasted two years and then my mind took me to a place that I was sure that I would never get out of. This place was the next street down from lonely street. There was a knot, lump, rock type feeling in my chest. This story goes on and on it never stops it will always will be present in somebody's life. I want you to leave my story and bleed over into your own neural soup. I want you to think of your own story of feeling rocks in your chest. Bring it to the forefront and its feelings with it. When you are totally wrapped up in those feelings. I want you to let the story fade away along with any names or faces. Take the feelings and hold on to them until they boil up inside of you and bring back the feeling of pain in your chest. Think about how powerful this feeling was that it could take over your whole life. It took your physical and mental selves on a ride to the nowhere zone.

    I want you to go into your movie picture mind. See yourself standing in a workshop. In front of you is a sturdy bench. On this bench are a big anvil and a large hammer. Take your right hand and reach down through the top of your head until you reach that spot where the feeling of rocks and lumps are. Grab on to this feeling and pull it out the top of your head. Set it on the anvil and pick up the hammer and start pounding on it. It dose not matter how hard or for how long your inner feelings will have control over that. When you have stopped pounding I want you to step back and see what you have made. I what you to see a tool that you have never seen before. This tool is both right and left handed. One size fits all. See yourself picking up this tool and putting it in your mental toolbox. As you open the toolbox you can see an outline of its shape. This tool was known by the toolbox even before it was made. It was always yours it was always there. Now I want you to come along with me and let me show you how to use it.

    My little truck that I tow behind my camper is headed to the dismantlers. I have the feeling that I am giving up on it. It needs a new set of timing gears and chain. The 1.9-liter engine is an odd ball one hard to get parts for. The head gasket cost me $32 and had to be shipped out of Phoenix. It took four days and $3.72 shipping cost. I was going to have to change and did not like it. I liked that little truck. I have had nothing but problems with it. I could not focus on liking it. I was going to miss it. I had to make a change.

I reached into my mental toolbox and found the tool that I was going to need to make this change. I call it my Reality Fabric Cutter. This tool is the same one that I had you build in the workshop. I knew I was going to need it. I could see how that little $200 truck had got my brain and rock in the chest feeling all stirred up. I had stop writing, today is the 19th and I can see in my writing log the last day that I wrote was the 16th.

I needed my Reality Fabric Cutter and I should not delay for if I do it will only get worse. This tool opens a time warp in the mind and brings you into the future. Slip sideways with me as we see this tool in action in your movie picture mind. I see myself standing in front of my little truck. I reach into my mental toolbox and I pull out the Reality Fabric Cutter. I raise it like a two handed sword and I cut through the fabric of reality. I see the air, the blue sky, the truck, and the ground in front of me split open as if it were on a movie screen. The cut peels to the side and I see my new truck. I see myself getting into my new truck and driving away. I feel myself in this new truck and it feels good. I'm hear myself saying why was I pounding my head on a brick wall over that other truck I'm sure glad that I made the change. I look out the window of my new truck and I see a sign that is twenty feet tall and the word (Change) is flashing on and off. And I see myself getting out of the truck and standing by it and smiling. I am thinking of how powerful of a tool the Reality Fabric Cutter is. And how when used to make a change that it can make change feel good. And it can let you feel the power of Change. It will let you pre-live change and let change, change your life. This pre-living of change will let change flow into your life easier with less impact on your Lower Mind that does not want to change. KOZ: THE POWER TO SHIFT TIME TO SEE CHANGE IN THE NOW IS A POWER THAT WILL MOVE YOU THROUGH A THOUGHT REALITY WARP. THIS REALITY FABRIC CUTTING TOOL USED WITH CHANGE WILL MAKE OUT OF YOU A WORLD SHAPER. This Reality Fabric Cutting tool works for me every time. I can make changes quickly and without the long drawn out heart ache of the past. Try this tool given to us by KOZ and see your life become a field of changing colorful flowers that will transcend you over this playing field they call reality.

* * *

Seeing The Not And Nothing

There are times that I wonder what types of wonders my mind is passing by. I know that it steps in and does it's own will without being asked. Like the time it compensated for my left eye that was out of focus. I was looking at myself in a mirror when I noticed that the reflection off of my glasses of my hair was magnified. How could a mere reflection be magnified? I could understand if I was looking through the lens and the hair was on the other side that it would be magnified, but a mere reflection being magnified. Then my mind wandered off thinking about those magnifying mirrors. The small round ones that has one side a normal view and the other side a magnified view. My mind wanted to move on; it did not what to think about something that it could not understand. How many other things has my mind skipped over because it did not want to be bothered? I stood there trying to get my mind to focus and give me an answer. I was going to have to give up on a well-known statement. The seeing is believing statement and the statement,

I won't believe it until I see it.

There I had done it again; mirror gazing I was on Reach One. Their skin was as white as the lab coats that they were wearing. They were looking at a screen that was showing pictures of a set of eyeballs. Then they would look down into a viewer. They turned and looked at me as if saying I was supposed to be looking too. I looked in front of me and there was a viewer. I stepped forwards and looked into the viewer I was seeing what and how the eyes were seeing that were on the screen. I stood there for a long time looking at the screen and then looking at the viewer. Each time a set of eyes came up on the screen we would look in the viewer and then we would mark on a pad of paper a check next to corresponding number given for this set of eyes. I think that this was some kind of choosing session of which type of eyes should be used. The vote was in and a set of eyes was blinking on the screen. We walked into an adjoining room and I could see a team of men and I'm using the word men only because I did not know what else to call them. When we were coming to this new room I was able to see one of their eyes and they didn't look human. We got to see the finished product. It was a human man and he had human eyes. We again looked down into a viewer and were able to see what this man was seeing. It was to me a normal view how humans view things. I was saying that I though that there were a few other selections that would have been better. Like the set of eyes that could see energy coming from or going to a person. They looked at me and shook their heads as if I had come from a different planet and did not understand and couldn't I see that these eyes could see energy flow. I wondered what they had seen through their non-looking human eyes that I did not. I was looking at my hair again, I was back on earth. I sat down and wondered about what I had seen on Reach One and Koz came booming into my brain. THE EYE MUST BE DIRECT-

ED AS TO WHAT YOU WANT IT TO SEE AND WHAT YOU DO NOT WHAT IT TO SEE. THE SEEING OF THE NOT SEEN IS THE VIEW THAT MUST BE SEEN TO SEE MIND ENERGY FLOWING IN AND OUT. THE SEEING OF THE NOTHING AND THE NOT IS SEEING. BRING THE NON- SEEING EYE INTO FOCUS AND SEE WITH A NON-SEEING EYE. FOCUS ON WHAT YOU ARE NOT SEEING TO SEE THE FLOW OF ENERGY. I had to read this many times before I could see what the hell it was trying to tell me.

Right across from where I am staying in my camper is the Leaky Teky Bar home of the low life club. My next door neighbor about three spots down stopped me one day and asked to borrow three dollars until he got some money that he had coming in. He said that he had some walnuts sold that he had cracked and that as soon as he got paid that he would pay me back. I was there in the bar when I saw a lady slip him a twenty-dollar bill. He walked right passed me and did not say a word or pay me. I saw what I did not see. I did not see this man giving to himself I saw him taking from himself. He had bellied up to the bar and had a tap beer and was putting a cigarette in his mouth at the same time shaking some salt into his beer. He just sat there thinking of how he had it made with his newfound wealth. I was seeing his Mind Energy flow from his body by not seeing the things that brings Mind Energy in. Just earlier that day we were talking about Richard a man that lived between us. And how that he should stay in the Hospital and give his lungs a rest. This is what he said; his smoking was going to kill him and he won't quit. I sat there looking at him and could understand that he could see Mind Energy flowing from Richard but he could not see it flowing from himself. I wondered if when I passed this way again would he still be with us. The hell with the three dollars. KOZ: TAKE YOUR NON-

SEEING EYE TO A MIRROW AND SEE WHAT YOU ARE NOT SEEING IN THE REFLECTION. DOES THE INNER EYE SEE A SMILE OR A HEAD SHAKE IN DISCUSS? I hope that you will practice seeing the not and the nothing. That you will not throw your Mind Energy at someone that is throwing it away. Train your eye to see the non- seen and you will see things clearer than you have ever seen before. Choose to see what your brain has chosen not to see and start seeing it all.

* * *

FUTURE BUILDING

BRAIN FUTURE BUILDING TOOL

The mind first of all is a future building tool. It has powers of reality shifting and future building from the on set. I want you to think of yourself at play when you were a child. Remember all the self-made games from playing house to fighting off the bad guys. Come along with me on a story of mine as you link into your childhood past and pull it into your present. Re-feel your past in your present to re-establish these thoughts of future building. I as a young man always dreamt of going to the Far East and seeing all the sights, and how with my height that they would think of me as a special person. I would become a very important person and that they would hold me in high esteem. I saw myself drawing crowds were ever I went. I was a leader of a large group of people and I had a lot of power.

I did travel to the Far East with my son in the 90's. I did draw a crowed one-day in downtown Tokyo. I was standing on a busy street corner folding origami figures out of dollar bills and giving them away. I had enough of a crowd that the police had to come over to see what I was doing. When they saw what I was folding they wanted one too. I along with my son was invited along with the group to have coffee at a Donut shop. I remember a young girl folding two napkins into a man and a woman figure; I still have them in my photo album. The reality was far from the dream but close enough that my mind was impressed with future building forever more. Think of some of your childhood dream playing and future building. Focus on one that did come about and fold this over and over in your mind. Think the way you were thinking as a child with no limiting bounds. Feel how natural this type of thinking came to you as a child, how easy it was to side shift into a dream reality. Think about this for a lengthy time span. I want your Lower Mind to re-connect with the sensations and feelings that went along with this type of future thinking process. Think about how natural it was for your young mind to think in the future building mode. You came equipped with this thought process, you did not have to go to school to learn it. In-fact you had to go to school to un-learn it. I hear myself and others expounding on how they can foretell the future. I hear them saying things like well I could of told you that was going to happen a long time ago. And how if I did not change my ways that I was going straight to hell on a run away freight train. I remembered one time when a lady and I left a bar at the same time. The few people that were sitting there had built up in their minds all types of future happenings. I could hear her in the back ground with a few words shutting down their future event thinking process. I heard her saying "I'm leaving he's going to the bathroom we are not leaving together". When I got to the parking lot she was in her car looking at me and lingering long enough that it would of given me a chance to talk to her. I pulled out my notebook and made note of the goings on and she drove away, I never saw her again. I sat in my car and was trapped in a mirror gazing session. I found myself on Reach One. I was in a pure white room it was very large. I could see many groups of seven people sitting in a circle with their backs towards each other. They all had a hair dryer looking hood over their heads. Out of the top of the hoods were a bundle of fiber optic strands. These strands merged into a central box above there heads in the center of this circle of seven. Written on the side of the box were the words Dream Fluxing Chamber. Coming out of this box was a single blue fiber optic tube about four inches across. This tube manifolded into seven separate smaller tubes that led to a screen in front of each of the seven people in this circle. The screens were hooded and as I tried to get close enough to see one I was stopped. I was held, one on each arm I could not feel any tugging or pushing. My feet were not moving but I was. I was floating towards a Dream Fluxing Group. I could see that there was an empty chair. On my own I walked towards the chair. Before I could set down the other six people were rotated in front of me so I could see who they were. I recognized all of them, they were friends. When the open chair came back around I sat down. The hood slipped over my head and the screen lit up in front of me. I saw written on top of the screen Dream Fluxing Recapturing Session. I saw myself talking to each one of these people and I found out what their dreams were. I had my Lower Mind Butterfly Net at the ready and was scooping in their dreams and putting them in the top of my head. Then I saw a finished view of this dream fluxing session. At the end of the session were the words Trial Run flashing across the screen. The out side lights of the bar had shut off and I drove away.

  KOZ: DREAM FLUXING IS A NATURAL FUNCTION OF BRAIN COSMIC LAW. DEVELOP YOUR DREAM ENOUGH THAT YOU COULD EXPLAIN IT TO ANOTHER. SHOW IT AROUND TO AT LEAST SIX

OTHER LOWER MINDS AND HAVE THEM SUPPLY THEIR LOWER MIND PRESSURE TO YOUR DREAM.

I thought a long time before I was able to get a handle on this trip to Reach One. As I was trying to figure out how to apply this to a workable format in my own life KOZ came booming in. DREAMS OF DREAMS BUILD YOUR FUTURE. DREAMS OF OTHER LOWER MINDS DREAMS SUPPLY MIND ENERGY TO OTHER LOWER MINDS. BRING YOUR DREAMS TO BE ENERGIZED WITH MIND ENERGY. I understood, it was as if I was given a shot of cosmic law directly into my brain. I will put this process into action and let the Cosmic Winds blow me away.

* * *

NEW CAR PROJECT

I was up early and so was the hangover crowd. There was so much smoke in the bar that I left with my Sprite and stood out back next to the lake. I could see the garbage the cans and an assortment of other things that people had thrown away. It was on the bank and in the water and as the sun was shining on the ripples I fell in to the Haze.

I was walking up to a door as I got there I could read on the door Project Director and underneath that the letters T N C and then my name. I was wondering what the Sam hell I had gotten myself into. I saw my name on the desktop name plaque and a stack of papers. Written on the top page were the words, "The New Car Project." In came a man that seemed a bit bent out of shape. He was telling me that he could not get the other project engineers to come to an agreement on the TRI- Piece link-up. I told him that there was a meeting with a team of NASA docking engineers and that I wanted him and his group to be there. Nine o'clock the next morning I had assembled the Cognitive Fluxing Pool. We were looking at options of how to mate-up the parts of the TRI-PART NEW CAR. We were all given a project brief and as I looked at mine I could clearly see the date it was the year 2124. After looking at a few different options we selected a cone hydraulic locking system. All a person would have to do was to drive up to the selected front or back sections and the self-guiding self-locking cone system would lock onto it. If you wanted a luxury car front section and a pick-up box back section that could be an option. Or if you were going to the dump or hauling landscaping and building materials you could select a pick-up box front and rear. If you needed to take the ball team to the game you could rent a couple of Van sections for the trip. The new car was a three-piece configuration. There was the middle section that was the main drive and engine. The front section and rear sections were inter-changeable. The individual owned these inter-changeable parts but the mid-section was leased from the car company. The car company did all the up keep and repair of the mid-section. They had built it with repair or replacement in mind at its concept development stages. Since it was their nickel being spent they engineered it for quick turn around. There was no more waiting for your car to be repaired you just dropped of the mid- section and a different one was issued to you. The problems with the one that was turned in would be dealt with at a later time best suited for the car company. The engine was the property of the car company and its workings were held at a high level of secrecy. The engine that I got a look at was a tri-fuel hybrid that had a real punch to it for being a four cylinder. It was a diesel, hydrogen, and LP electric highbred. It would shift back and forth between these fuels as it was running and you did not feel a thing or even know it. The hydrogen was produced on board a by-product of the battery section. These batteries were designed to store and break down large amounts of water into hydrogen and oxygen. During the summer the condensate water from the air conditioning coil was used to keep the batteries topped off. During the winter the condensate from the exhaust was used and a back up of an on-board water tank. The batteries were mounted on a suspended rack over top of the engine. The engine was tuned to a vibration frequency that was a frequency that aided the batteries to produce more hydrogen. The internal combustion engine crankshaft and the electric motor shaft were one in the same. They were both inside the same motor housing and sharing the same oil lubrication system. The electrical motor shifted over to a generator when the diesel kicked in. The diesel motor would turn into an air compressor until a high pressure air injection tank was filled and then a compression release kicked in letting the pistons to travel freely. The heat from the exhaust was run through a heat reclaimer-cooker that producer a methane gas that was burnt as a fuel. The cooker would turn plastic pop bottles and a list of other things into a useable fuel. The oil was never totally changed out as today. The oil filter had a pop out button on it that would close an electric circuit that would light a light on the dashboard telling you to change the filter. When the filter needed changing it would do it by it's self by shifting over to a fresh filter bypassing the partly clogged one. The oil sensing transducer would kick in an oil pump that would pump in more oil from an oil reserve tank to replace that, which was trapped in the old oil filter. This oil addition method was even better than the old oil change method. New oil did not have the engine processed microscopic molecules that the old oil did and would allow wear until it was broken down. There was also an oil pump to pressurize the oil gallery inside the engine. And would have to reach a psi of 60 before the control circuit would be completed and the electric motor-engine would start. The car tires had magnets imbedded in the rubber and as they passed coils in the fender wells they generated voltage for the electrical system. These engines would routinely get a million miles or more on them before a sleeve, ring and bearing overhaul.

We were led to another room where there was a running prototype of the future engine. It was made entirely of ceramics and was just starting to warm up at 1500 degrees F. I saw the total workings but was told not to write about them yet. KOZ: WHATEVER THE MIND CAN THINK CAN COME ABOUT. THE FIRST GATHERING OF COSMIC BUILDING MATERIALS IS IN THE MIND AND THEN AND ONLY THEN BROUGHT TO REALITY. TRAIN THE MIND TO GATHER COSMIC THINKING GOO AND YOU WILL BECOME A MASTER BUILDER IN THE MATERIAL REALITY WORLD Bring in as many of the other tools that were given to us by KOZ to help you on your quest. Keep a written record for I will ask for it in the future. Now get to work building your new future.

I had gotten to a place that would let me warp time. I could see a section of my future. This was a sub-system in a system. As the masses drove by they only saw the happy campers. They didn't see the little men in their little boxes their self-made prison cells. Hell most of them would be better off in prison. In prison they would get the basics food, clothing, health care, and a non-leaking roof over their heads. These little camper trailers and motor homes were in such bad shape that they were put in the back of the park. These poor souls were pushed to the back so no one had to see them. The management did not want to scare off the over-niters with this group of junky campers so they were shoved away from view of the road. The over-niters at $17 a night would bring in four times the money that the monthly renters would. Along with this sub-class was the middle class that had their full size mobile homes. This middle class was not much better off than the camper. This was a whole sub culture that not one politician would like to address. Many of these men had work hard some of them for more than forty years. The system didn't want any thing to do with them. At any given time these end of the liners could be picked up for public intoxication. There was no money to be had. The jails would be filled to the brim and you would have to set up tent camps like sheriff Joe did in AZ. This slice of humanity is well hid from the rest of the world. This land of milk and honey has swept its dirt under the carpet where the drive-by eyes will not see it.

 I wanted my Lower Mind to see and to be impressed. I wanted my Lower Mind to get a full dose of this slice of reality. I decided to stay over the Christmas and New Years holidays, I would pay and stay for the month of January. I wanted to see and smell and taste this life of boozes and crackers.

 The scuttlebutt around the park and at the local bar was where the free food was going to be and what they were serving and at what time. I tuned in and had it all mapped out. I had fallen into this sub class of diggers of the goodies. I was on foot with two other men headed to a bar called the Boathouse. It was only three hundred steps away. When I got inside all the seats were taken at the bar. When a lady saw us looking at a few open stools she said that they were taken. There was something in the way that she said it that turned me off. All I could see after that was a group of people out to get something free. This was not a get together of old friends to share food and tell stories. This was a grab what you can get and don't get in my way gathering. It reminded me of the time at the creamery when the boys grabbed at the box of pop-cycles. I left and started counting my footsteps, I was wondering was it really three hundred steps between bars or was this just a saying. My count came out to 280. It made me think that at one time that there was probably a person that did count out the steps, as he was drunk walking. That their world was so tight that they measured it in steps, the count needed to get to the next watering hole.

I could feel this pull of easy street. A dimension that was as simple as walking itself. How nice it would be not to have a car, with all of its costs and problems. Walking distance to two bars and a fishing hole, what else could a man ask for? Maybe someday, but I am not ready to start counting steps between bars yet. I want to shift my mind over to a different reality and run away from this land of less than nothing. I want to do this in a flash of cosmic time not a lifetime. I am going to step back and look at myself and see what the eyes are seeing. These portholes are the drawing in points that can lead you anywhere. Eyes are the windows to the Lower Mind. Lower Minds are where you can reality shift at will at a speed that is truly mind stirring. I must go into this behind the Seeing Eye realm and take a real good look at myself. As I am seeing me I also will be tapped into the Lower Minds fitting department. Lower Minds are always on the look out for there next pearl for the string of cosmic pearls. As I am looking out of their eyes I am also looking at their pearl collection and reading it as a road map for me to tune my visual perception by. I will also be tuning into the non- seeing eye and feeding the Lower Mind.

Come along with me as I shake up my mental toolbox and do some cosmic reality shifting. I am making sure that my Middle Mind is in the strong box and will not come out to play its, that can't happen game.

I'm going into my movie picture mind. I can see myself in a floating bubble. Inside of this cramped bubble is a 360-degree view of my life as it is now. I don't like what I'm seeing and I am reaching for a tool in my mental toolbox. As I am thinking of this tool goose bumps flow over my body and a feeling of dread. I touch it and I am already at a state of fear. Out it comes the Whip. The helpless I can't do anything about it feeling whip. The one that I gave the one word name to that starts with the letter J. I don't want to even think about it let alone write the word (JAIL). I remove myself from myself and see myself cowering. Snap goes the whip and I can see my Lower Mind fast stepping in place with it hands held out begging me to stop. I snap the whip again and it tries to run away. It can't run away I have a whip that knows no distance. I snap the whip again and the Lower Mind is now crying and begging me to stop. I snap the whip again and I see it peeing its pants and squirming on the floor and a picture of my father beating me comes flooding into my mind. Then I go into the whip shaking and yelling stage. I'm telling it, (my Lower Mind) that if you don't get your act together that you will be one of those little men stuck in their little dirty boxes. That if you don't start now to see yourself as the eyes see you, you will not know were you are or where you want to go. You with your non-plan are planning a box of your own. You need to find and tap into a Lower Mind that will shift your reality away from those boxes. I place the Jail tool back into the toolbox and I reach for the next one. Out it comes the Reality Fabric Cutter.

I see myself holding this tool at the ready. I am watching for the right bubble one that will have the right float to it to take me off this path that I am on. There are many bubbles going past but there are few that are going in the right direction. When I see one, I want to pop the bubble that I'm in and join with the new one. I see in my mind's eye the bubble that I am looking for coming my way and I slice up the inside of my bubble and it disappears and I am looking at the inside lining of my new bubble. (I have found her or she has found me and we are very happy that we found each other. She thinks that I'm the cat's meow and I think she the best thing since apple pie. We click and work together as a team. We share a nice home and we do a lot of nice things together. We both like to travel and see new places or just stay at home and enjoy each other's company.)

I'm going to reach into my mental toolbox and pull out three more tools. Yes there they are the Secret, the Challenge and Future Building. I'm going to keep this process to myself so that it will be well guarded against the Middle Minds of others and make it stronger. I am going to challenge myself to do a Future Building session every morning before I get out of bed. Now I want you to hear my secret story of a man that challenged himself to change and used Future Building to do it. Did you hear the story? Why of course not, it is a secret, but if you keep reading you will find out along with me how the story unfolds. I 'm writing this on Christmas Day 2000 I don't even know how the story is going to play out. This will be a test to see if these tools really work or are just so much bullshit. I want to see what kind of time factor this will take. I want to see if there will be much more added by the Giving Greater Known to my Future Building then I even thought possible. KOZ; HAVE NO QUESTION OF THESE TOOLS THAT I GIVE YOU THEY ARE COSMIC LAW AND ALWAYS WORK. TIME IS NOT TIME AND SPACE IS NOT SPACE, THERE IS ONLY MIND CONTROL OF SPACE TIME. DO NOT THINK OVER THIS WITH THE MIDDLE MIND IT HAS ONLY MAN MADE TIME AND SPACE CONCEPTS. Now I must keep working and writing with this because my mind wants to see the on going process unfold. I can't put this book down now I have to finishing reading how it turned out for me. I would think I would have to already know I'm the one that has to write it. This is even getting a little crazy for me and at times scary. I think I have bitten off more than I had bargained for. Where in the hell is this book taking me now.

***

Mind Number Blowing

I want to talk about number blowing. And how the large is the small and how the small is the large. The wind in the northern plains of the Dakotas will stir you inside and out. The wind can turn the small into the large. The snowflake is small enough that we only measure them as a group. The weatherman will tell you how many inches of white stuff accumulated overnight in inches or feet. I felt that they had lied to me somehow. As I was getting ready for work I was listening to the school and road closings. There had been three inches of snow and drifting in the country. I was able to get the truck started so there was not going to be any problem getting to work. This was a snow country pick-up truck. It was jacked up in the air so the body parts were up and out of the snow. The tires were 275R16s this was a high sidewall tire that gave you more clearance under the differentials, those round things that the drivelines went into. It had a 454 cubic inch big block engine in it. It was four-wheel drive and had many ditch scares on it. This poor truck had been flipped over on its side and top more than once. It was equipped with all the right stuff. Lets see tow cable (check), jumper cables (check), highjack (check), coveralls (check), snow shovel (check), and survival kit (check). I felt that I was going on a cross-country survival run. And many times that's what my eighteen-mile trip into Sioux Falls SD became. Every thing was ready truck warmed up and down the driveway I was headed. Thirty feet later I was stuck. The truck had jumped up on a snowdrift and broke through the crust. This left it high and dry with no traction, it with all the right stuff was going no where fast. What had happened is that the wind had blown the numbers around and made three inches into three feet.

I felt that I had been lied to that I was not given the true numbers. I felt that the numbers had been twisted and made into a false representation of reality. In fact I felt this way about a lot of things. When they sold me my battery it had a 60-month warranty on it. In my mind that meant that they would replace it without cost for 60 months. Lets see Mr. Cole you bought that battery 14 months ago so that is lets see on our chart will be a charge of twenty seven fifty to replace your battery with a new one. I felt that the numbers had been blown around and twisted one more time. As I looked around I felt that I was in a storm of blowing numbers and none of them were blowing my way. The election was decided by the popular vote. What the hell did that mean when only 20% of the people voted and only half of them voted for the winner? A 10% factor was blowing the greatest super power in the world around like a leaf in the wind. I was not going anywhere so I made a few telephone calls one to work and one to my girlfriend in town. There was nothing to do until the snowplow went through. I was down stairs feeding the fire when I fell into the Haze staring into the flames watching them licking on a piece of wood.

I was on Reach One the door I was standing in front of was blue and all it said on the door was the number one. I opened it and walked in. To my right was a box with numbers in it. A person came over and took one out and carried it away. I followed him he went behind a white draw curtain and I went in too. There was a man lying on his side on a table. There was a crank handle sticking out of the top of his head. The number was rolled into a thin tube and inserted into the ear of the man lying on the table. A large hammer was pulled out from under the table and was used to pound this number into the mans' head. Another person came up and started to turn the crank. There was a hole in the table so that the mans' ear that was down was over a catch pan. I could see all types of different sized colored and denominations of numbers coming out. This catch pan was then brought over to a balance scale and weighed. I could plainly see on the other end of the scale was a human brain. They did not balance out not even close. The pounding went on but the man on the table showed no signs of pain or even discomfort. More numbers came out and were added to the scale. It still did not balance out. The person on the table was led away and a person said this one passed. Another person was brought in. I went to see where these people were brought in. A person was sitting on a chair and was being hit with a stick on top of his head. This was more like if you were tapping out a tune on a drum. The person sitting in the chair was looking at a pile of numbers on a table. When he was hit with the stick he would with his hand sweep them off onto the floor. A person standing next to the table would pour some more numbers out of a bucket onto the table. The stick fell and the numbers were pushed to the floor.

    I was sitting there the fire had almost gone out, it was cold. I heard the telephone ringing up stairs. I got there in time to hear someone say I think I could save you a lot of money on your next vacuum cleaner can I come out and give you a demonstration? I did not have even one carpet in the whole house and how in the hell was he going to get here anyway. For a moment I was going to lead him on then I saw myself sweeping the numbers off the table and saying no thanks. I saw this as a new tool and gave it the name of Mind Number Blowing. KOZ: PERCEIVED NUMBERS ARE ONLY A MAN-MADE SHAPENING TOOL TO DEFINE REALITY AS BY THAT ONE MIND. STAY AWAY FROM NUMBER STIRRERS AND STREACHERS. NUMBERS ARE A

PLAY THING OF THE MIND AND ARE EASILY CHANGED AND ARE DESIGNED TO BE CHANGED. You can change your reality in an instant by Mind Number Blowing. Become a person that can see the numbers behind the numbers. Numbers are for you to chew on and spit out in any form that you would like to see them in. If you are not a good number chewer find a champion.

* * *

Hose Draining

I am a misfit, I go to bars to meet people and I drink coffee. Some people feel sorry for me as they ask if I had in my past had a problem with liquor. Sometimes I say yeah and I say that I can't afford a DUI. Other times I say that I was not feeling well and I'm staying of the booze for a while. I find myself siting alone just starring out a window or starring at the mirror on the back bar. The Boathouse bar in nice California is a nice place to window and mirror gaze. I was sitting there with some other people but I was truly alone, here it was the 27 of Dec. just two days later and things have already started to fall into place. My personal future building session using the Reality Cutting Tool was already kicking in. I stopped in and talked to a lady that owns Talley's, a camping and cottage resort on Clearlake in Nice Ca. She has been a widow ten years and said that she was praying for an angel to help her. We struck a deal lot rent for labor trade and I told her that her angel had arrived. I moved in on the 28th of Dec. and she went on a two-week vacation. Her daughter is living there and looking after things. I will keep you informed.

As I was window gazing I fell into the haze and I was on Reach One. I was looking at some type of assembly line. At the first station there were little men drilling holes in the side of an elephant. The elephant moved forward to the next station and a group of small men were putting hose bibs or faucets in the drilled holes. The elephant went to the next station where hoses were installed onto the faucets. In the next station I could see the hoses being put into the mouths of large piggy banks. I could see the piggy banks getting larger and larger and the elephant was getting smaller. At the next station the hoses were being replaced with chains. A lifting crane picked up the elephant and transported it to a storage rack above my head. As I looked up I could see elephants forever, there were millions of them. All of a sudden a horn went off and people were running and I followed. When I got there I saw an elephant pulling a hose out of his side with his trunk. It seemed that the little men were helpless they could not stop the elephant breaking one chain after another. I saw the elephant running at full charge speed towards the jungle. I could see at the edge of the jungle a group of elephants waiting for this new arrival. They were jumping and playing around in happiness to see him coming. I heard the horn go off again and off I was to see what was going on. It was another elephant breaking away and running for the jungle. Then the horns started to sound one after another. I then saw a herd of elephants rush the assembly line and the little men ran in all directions. I looked up and I saw that there were men and not elephants chained. And as I looked over to the jungle they also had changed to men.

 Barbara was calling me back to the real world now on her third hot rum. She said that I seemed so far away and asked me if I was mad at her or something? I wanted to tell her about Reach One and what I saw and what I thought it meant. I knew that this was not the right time or place she was not ready for such a high level of thinking. I could see and hear her rattling along about something but I turned away and started looking at the window again. There it was all the elements that the brain would need to bleed over into the non-reality zone. In one view I could see about eight layers that my brain was shifting back and forth to and from. There were the things hanging in the window and their reflections off the glass. That's two. I could see myself and people walking behind me. That makes four. I could see the dock and the lake. That makes six. I could see the reflection off the water and the lights from Lakeport on the other side of the lake. That makes eight. I could see mountain Konacti and the stars behind it in the sky. That made ten. I wanted to tell her about neural path bleed over and about window gazing but she was on her own shifted reality trip as I saw her dancing with another lady in front of the juke box.

  I had slipped back to Reach One. I was on a speed-walk people mover I was looking at a map. It showed an exit coming up I wanted to get off. When I got to the exit there was a twelve-foot high fence and I couldn't get off. I could see people leaving through the exit. So the sign on the fence saying this exit closed made no sense to me. I go onto the next people mover and started looking at my map again. Again it showed an exit coming up and when I got there, there the fence was and the same sign. I mean the same sign. The exact same sign and I could see people leaving through the exit. I could not do anything but get on the next people mover. I looked at the map and there was another exit coming up. As I was heading for it I looked down at the sign on the moving handrail and it said no sitting or jumping over the handrail. The no bled over into the yes and I jumped over the handrail just before the fence and headed for the exit door. When I jumped over the rail I could hear people still on the people mover saying you can get in trouble doing that. Don't you know that that's against the law? As I neared the exit door I looked back and could see three other people jumping the rail.

I was not drinking and was asked to drive as I was getting into Barbara's car, Cherry and her boyfriend Ron were on their way in. Cherry's mouth was running and taking. Oh you're not going there are you Oh! No yuck. I wished that there were some button that I could of pushed that would have instantly made Cherry feel the hurt that Barbara was feeling but many fold. KOZ: REALITY, REALITY, REALITY, DON'T LET OTHER PEOPLE'S MIDDLE MIND SHAPE YOUR REALITY. FOCUS ON WHAT YOU WANT, LISTEN NOT TO THE CHILDNESS OF THE MIDDLE MINDS OF THE TAKERS. WHEN YOU THINK ABOUT PUSHING THE RETURN BUTTON IT WILL RETURN NEGITIVE MIND ENERGY YOUR DIRECTION. After each time I return from Reach One I feel empowered. I can readily see other peoples hose draining but hard to see my own. The view that I bring back from Reach One has a gripping profoundness to it that seems to reach deep inside and link up with my Lower Mind in a way that it comes through without question as a pure natural Cosmic Law. This outside source builds a tirade with Koz and the Giving Greater Known.

* * *

REALITY WITHIN A REALITY

There are no men that own there own mind. The bad is the good and the good is the bad. It feels good to have something that is in order in your mind. Other Lower Minds will stop and be in awe of such order. These well established neural pathways are there to stay, there is no getting rid of them. Your mind does not want to let them go. They produce and inject a body built self-sensitized endorphin into the brain. This endorphin keys up to receptor sites in your brain the same as an opiate. As this good hits your brain it could be bad, for it has taken thought time from you. Remember the song that you hummed for a full day and could not get out of your head. When you first started it was hitting all the right buttons and it was feeling good. As time went by this song or jingle became annoying as it interrupted all phases of your thinking. This type of brain looping can get to a point of a brain illness that can stop a person in their tracks. They seem to have an answer for everything in their own little world. These answers may have a lot of truth in them but they are out of align with the norm. The established thought paths of other Lower Minds will not tolerate the out of alignment thoughts. Other Lower Minds that feel threatened will classify this out of alignment thought process as an illness. If they can detect anything that seems a little out of order they will try to label it in a way that it will be locked up in a brain dysfunction category. These steps are not taken to help the person that seems to be having the problems; they are taken to protect the established neural soup of the masses. This established neural soup of the masses has taken a lot of time and money to bring it to its present form. How dare anyone try to change the rules of the game now. Oh what would we do if someone came up with the idea that income taxes were unjust and were illegal, and should be abolished? That government should get their resources from the land and not from whipping the backs of the people. Oh! Watch out there I can see them coming with their white coats and bottles of pills. We must shut this one up before it spreads. We can't have anybody talking that way it will up set the whole system. We can't have him putting ideas like these into others people's minds they may have enough truth in them that it might start a thought shift. By the way what is the government doing with 330 million sq. miles of land anyway? And what right dose it have to be holding onto 300 million sq. miles of mineral rights. Don't these assets belong to the people that fought for them? Where dose this money go? Who is managing the managers of such a vast amount of assets? Give these assets to me and I would get rid of income taxes and health-care costs.

These are the type of ideas that can kick in a thought pattern that is linked to the beast. When the beast comes out then all established systems are washed aside and chaos holds the land. Koz told me of a way that I could use these established neural soup patterns to my advantage. I could turn them around and use them for my benefit. I could reap a windfall of past-spent money. All the money that governments and corporations had spent to shape the neural soup of the masses could be mine in an instant. All I would have to do is piggyback other ideas like a virus onto their implanted ideas. I could take the word the thought the song or the jingle and make it a slave. I could transform it into a totally different set of meanings in my mind at will. I would not waste my time in trying to get rid of it on the contrary, I would embrace it as a gift and thank them for showing me a way to control my own mind.

I want you to come along with me and bring your movie picture mind. I want to tell you a story of word reality shifting in my life that will clearly show the how and when and the not. Find yourself side slipping into this non-reality reality and follow this path with me.

It started with a bus ride from Santa Rosa Ca. to Oakland Ca. to the induction center. The time had past my delayed enlistment program was over and I was going into the Air Force. The list was checked twice and heads were counted all present and accounted for. In came the reality shifter. His voice was at a level that would be outlawed in a decibel test for a work place. Listen up children, my name is Sgt. Mad when I speak all I want to hear from you is Sir Yes Sir, do you understand me? Lets hear it. The bus roared with SIR YES SIR. My brain was not going to let this man or anyone else tell it what to say so I did a reality word brain shift to get my brain to flow with this new system. All I had to do is to change the word meanings in my mind a bit and it left my brain unchallenged. They would hear from SIR YES SIR but I twisted my mind reality and it meant NO NO SIR. There they stood with a sneer on their face thinking that they had done some kind of brain transformation on me. It was I that had done the transformation I had used his own training against himself. In his pee-brain a word is a word and it could mean only one thing, I could only think of what a weak mind. Being BI-lingual I could shift easily into different meanings. I thought of the word gift and how it meant poisonous in German. They must have know what a mess they (the government) and the (corporations) had made of our minds that they would have to go to such extremes to get it straightened out. Or at least transformed into their new order of thought process. I did not want to suck much of this bullshit in for I would have to leave it behind when I got back to the real world. When I did get out I was glad I didn't, there were many that did and they could not adjust back into a different reality called civilian life. They were labeled PTSD (post traumatic stress syndrome) and drugged into submission. The government knew what they had done to our minds and set up a whole program of identifying and treatment. They gave it a word or words that made it sound like it had something to do with the malfunction of the person's brain. They could not say that all the stuff that we were feeding your brain was a bunch of bullshit and that you would have to forget it so they made it out that you were the one with the problem. On the civilian reality side they knew what a mess the government had made of your brain and opened a classification of mental illness called Post Traumatic Stress Syndrome. What a mouth full of mean nothing words that was. What the hell did it mean anyway. What it meant to me is that there was a reality collision between the military and the medical civilian sector and they used these letters PTSD as the cushion between them. But is there another reality that is the real push behind this clash of titans of reality shifting. As thousands of our World War Two veterans die every month, how will the Veterans Administration fare. Without the numbers of serviced veterans, how will they be able to keep their funding at its present level? Did they throw us a curve ball called PTSD to keep their numbers inline with the funding or what? What is the true reality but the one that you hold in your mind to be true. Use my story to see that there could be realities inside of realties and your reality is just as valid and is a very powerful tool to be used when needed. KOZ: REALITY IS A MIND FUNCTION OF THE MOMENT THAT TRANSFROMS THE PRESENT TO BUILD THE FUTURE. INTERNAL REALITY SHIFTING IS A TOOL OF THE MIND GIVEN TO YOU BY COSMIC LAW. MASTERING REALITY SHIFTING OF INNER MIND CAN BLOW UNIVERSES AROUND. The brain has been called the three-pound universe. It can transform reality from what it is to what is the meaning of is. Are we all living in a yellow submarine why no and why yes? I will not ever again let someone tell me that there is only one true reality. I am reclaiming my reality-shifting tool and so should you.

***

COSMIC SEEDING

I saw him again that person that is me that I don't get to see often from somebody else's viewpoint. It is as if I am looking at myself through someone else's' eyes. I was in the bathroom at a restaurant named Stars in Ukiah Ca. the mirrors were so arranged that I could see a straight on side view of myself.

    I fell in to the haze and was on Reach One. I was walking down a roped in path. The ropes were like the ones at a theater. I came to a big door and the sign on it said The Cosmic Seeding Of Planets. The door opened on its own and I was sucked in, again my feet were not moving. I was in a theater, not a movie theater but one that was over looking a laboratory or operating room. I took a seat and put on a set of headphones. To my right was a computer monitor screen. On it was the words Glycogen Production Factor Genial Transformation. I could see a person on a table they were as white as ice. A voice came into my ear saying that the thawing process is now in progress. I could see the tubes running to the body that were carrying a warm blood supply. This was done only to speed up the thawing of the body but was not necessary. The group of people around the table stepped back and clapped as in a job well done, they had done it. What they had done was to take the genial code from a frog and tie it to a receptive site in the human DNA strand. This enabled the body to produce its own glycogen. This meant that a person could be frozen and brought back to life all on its own. The people in the seats next to me were also clapping and getting up from their chairs and leaving the room, I followed. We went down a long hallway I could see that they were walking; yeah you got it, I was floating. We came to a room that looked like we had come to a merry-go- round. As the people in front of me came to it they got on. When it was my turn to get on I was swept to the side and the line kept moving. I could see what was going on inside this operating wheel. First they were taking a skin scraping from the inside of the mouth and putting it in a test tube. To the test tube was added a small amount of frog DNA and it was put in a vibrating machine. At the next station as this wheel shifted the continence of the test tube was drawn into a syringe and then added to a blood bag that was clear and rocking back and forth on a cradle device. The transfusion bag was then attached to the person with a patch that was stuck to their stomachs. They were rotated on this wheel until all of the fluid had left the sack. They then got off the wheel and left through a side door. Above the door it said come back in six weeks. I could see to the left of me a line of people coming in a door. They were heading to a glass wall that had a sliding glass door in it. As each person got to the door it would open and as they went in a puff of vapor cloud would billow out. I walked to the other side of this circular glass room and saw them coming out either walking or as white as ice lying on a stretcher. Those that were walking were crying the DNA implant did not take and they were not selected for cosmic seeding.

  I was told by KOZ that the cosmic seeding was on a cosmic time frame. These people would be frozen and shot into space. They would be injected into a liquid hydrogen comet. And that they would stay there until this comet came close to a planet and then they would break loose and seed this planet with all sorts of life forms. This form of cosmic hitchhiking had been done from the beginning of time. This type of travel could in time take you anywhere in the galaxy. The thing that had to be done was the figuring out of the comet shuttle bus schedule. Then all it would take is the energy to jump from comet to comet until you reached your destination proximity. He suggested that I do some correlation between UFO sightings and visiting comets to our solar system.

  I left the bathroom and my friend Bob was waiting for me he didn't say or let on like what took you so long. So this made me feel like that I had come out of some kind of time compression. I didn't say much on the way back home to Nice

CA. I was lucky that Bob wanted to explain to me about the no minds of Lake Co. that could not see how culture could spur the economy of this area. I had just got done eating and that was my key to help Tina with removing a wart from the side of her head. I was sitting there saying a few words every once and a while making Bob think that I was listening all the while I was calling up the rabbits for Tina. KOZ: THEM THAT DO NOT TAKE ADVANTAGE OF COSMIC SHORT CUTS ARE DESTINED TO GO IN A SMALL COSMIC CIRCLE. My writing has slowed down I feel that I should look for a place with less distractions. I will take out of my mental toolbox my reality cutter and invoke the power of change. I hope some day that you will be as comfortable with change as I am.

***

S.O.L.E.

I want you to join with me and many other people. Lets run a test of Cosmic Law and the Giving Greater Known. Let us do some Lower Mind Stacking, some future building, and using of a dream within a dream. I want to share with you a dream of inner space. I want to test the collective thought process that can pull reality out of nothingness. As you read my dream you will become a Lower Mind that will be putting collective pressure to bring it into reality. As you are reading my dream I want you to think of things that you would like to see come into reality. As you read I want you to use your movie picture mind and see in your mind's eye this dream of the collective Lower Mind Stacking. Now join with the many and bring the pressure of your Lower Mind.

It starts as everything starts with a thought, with a dream. I dreamt of a non-country country. There were no boarders, there was no land. There were no standing armies. It started as a submarine luxury ocean liner. The idea was to be able to take advantage of the many splendors of the under sea world and have a means of escaping terrible weather. The business was so good that it was booked years in advance and there was a four week limit on your stay. This limit was thought to be unfair and was voiced by the customers. The company went to a customer owner status and started to sell shares. As a person collected enough shares he could use them to buy a permanent cabin that would stay in his family until sold back to the company. These cabins and their total contents passed onto the next generation without tax or transfer fees. This included all credits that were held on account in stock in the company or company vouchers that could be used to transact business or buy your next hamburger or pair of shoes. This environment became quite popular; it supplied many things that a species would be looking for to carry its genial code forward to join the collective of the Giving Greater Known. The idea that even a nuclear war or an asteroid hit that would wipe out all surface life would not have any effect more than a bad storm on the Submarine Luxury Ocean Liner, from now on known as SOLE. The people that wanted cabins that could not get them because of supply and demand pushed the company into building more and bigger SOLE. As time went on the SOLE fleet became a bigger economic unit than some countries. This growth and independence did not rest well with a lot of countries that were losing their best people to the SOLE. The company's board of non-leaders voted that to insure their security that they must develop a defense system. There were many ideas from mines to attack mini-subs. The idea of deception, movement and using time warps won out. They developed a under water holograph system that could project thousands of SOLE images. These images would so confuse that any real attack was useless. The SOLE had its own university system and attracted the best teachers and students from all over the world. The proceeds from magnesium nodule mining and undersea oil production supplied an unlimited supply of revenue. If the SOLE wanted you they usually got you. They could offer a cabin or cabins that would be free and clear. People would get education, medical, employment, and retirement (not as we know it) in an offer that would be hard to refuse. As money became available there would be a lottery set up that any one could enter without cost. This lottery was not for money but for paid cabins. This year alone there were six thousand selected people. They selected a signal person and then their family unit. There were quite a few people at first that did not leave their land lives. After 75 years of development the S.O.L.E. have become the tenth most populated collective or country on earth and by far the richest. In another 25 years they will also be the most populous best-educated and healthiest people on earth. About 40 years into development they started a space program. This program was not based on exploration or who got there first or who went the furthest; it was dedicated to the principles of assuring the continuation of many genial pools. They have 256,543 people that have already bought and paid for a cabin in space. There are millions more that are on a share buy in program and the S.O.L.E. trade in program. The building of Reach One will start its third phase the acceptance of people in six more years. Reach Two and Reach Three have also been started. The SOLE collective developed a vertical mag-lift projectile accelerator to put things into orbit. It was built at a 19.5-degree north latitude location. At the depth of 2500 feet on the ocean floor they started the building of the barrel. When it reached the surface it was another 125 feet higher. At the bottom there was an air dome were all the projectiles were loaded. It runs 24 hours a day seven days a week every 15 seconds on average a 2500 lb. payload is put into orbit. The barrel is loaded with fifty projectiles at one time and they are shot one at a time within three second interval. There are six more accelerators being built and plans on the drawing board for one on the moon. The scientists have done some experimenting with eggs and embryos and have been able to freeze them and send them into orbit. At the lab in Reach One they were able to thaw and propagate the eggs and the embryos. This has opened a whole new field in space travel. KOZ: COLLECTIVE DREAM POOLS CAN DEVELOP THE FUTURE. ALL THOUGHT ENERGY IS MIND ENERGY. THE STACKING OF MIND ENERGY CAN BE DONE BY ANYONE FROM ANY PLACE NO MATTER THE DISTANCE. I am like you part of this test and will some day hope to see the outcome. Those that dreamed of space travel in the late 1700's did not live long enough to see men on the moon. But at the speed of advancement that we enjoy today this could all come into reality in a lifetime. I hope that you added to this dream your dreams will build on each other.

***

Cosmic Oceans

I was working in my workshop, this was the day that I was going to put my blast furnace together. It had been setting idle for a long time and now I finally had a place to set it up. Now I was going to be able to pour bronzes. My mind was on a path of creativity thinking of all the things that I wanted to pour. Things that I had seen on Reach One. I threw the main breaker on for the shop; it was up and behind the air compressor. As I threw the switch the air compressor came on and startled me. I looked at it and read the tag on the compression side tube it read CAUTION HOT. I was now looking down into my blast furnace, checking on its progress. KOZ boomed into my head: WHERE THE HOT IS THE COLD AND THE COLD IS THE HOT. I fell into the haze I was on Reach One I opened a light blue door. I was in a briefing room for astronauts. I looked down at my clipboard. I could see that the last space shot had visited two comets. I could see that my team was going to two too. We were going to shoot a probe through the side of a comet. We wanted to see what was inside and then shoot it out the other side and retrieve it. This all sounded like an easy task when it was nothing but words on paper. The comet was going at a speed of 26,000+ miles per hour and had a fallout diameter radius of 1400 miles and a vapor tail that was 267 earths long. Once the probe was inside there would be no way to communicate with it. Its exploration phase and exit maneuvering stage had to be an internal function. The probes time frame was linked to the repositioning of our spacecraft to the other side of the comet after shooting the probe. If we were not in position to intercept the probe when it came out the other side there would be slim chance of catching it. As soon as the probe would clear the exfoliation plume of the comet we could again communicate with it. At this stage of the operation we would do a set of directional and speed burns of the directional vortex rockets. This is done to position it for a docking link-up.

  We were back on earth. We had gone through all the back slapping and fan fare of a job well done. We had gone through all the debriefing and de-contamination isolation. We had been home for about three months and been reassigned to another comet probe mission. We were in the space math stage figuring slingshots around the moon and earth. All of a sudden we were jerked and down briefed and taken out of the rotation and transferred to area 52. This was all done in a fashion that was out of the norm. We were taken from our study lab and taken to the flight line. There we were handed an in-flight lunch and put aboard a C-21 or a small Lear type jet. All we were told was that we had gone into a TOP SECRET protocol and that nothing more was to be said not even talking to another team member until fully briefed. We sat there in a vacuum to ourselves wondering what was going on and what was going to happen next. Three hours later we landed and our jet taxied into a hanger and the doors were closed. I knew that there was something big going down. This was out of the norm as far as putting a plane in a hanger. The usual procedure is to let an aircraft cool down and then pull it into a hanger with a tow vehicle. As we disembarked I could see that this operation had been planned for some time. They had built a cool down station for the jet. It consisted of two large high-speed fans and ducting to the outside.

  The team was pulled apart even though I had the rank of a Colonel my objections were pushed aside by a little man in a white coat. I was led to a small room and asked to wait there. When the door was shut behind me the back wall was raised and sitting there were three men and one women. I was greeted and then the questions started to fly. They all had to do with our last comet probe mission. They seemed to be concerned about breaches in security. They asked me if I had anything to do with the tampering of the probe prior to mission launch. I assured them that I didn't know what they were talking about. They said to bear with them that they were just doing their jobs. After about thirty questions they said thank you and left the room by a side door. In came the small man in the white coat that met us in the hanger. He sat next to me in a chair in a way that made me feel uncomfortable at first and then very comfortable. He talked to me and asked me about things such as what was my point of view of how the earth was formed. And how did I think life evolved or was created. He wanted to know how strong of drive I had to push the envelope of known knowledge to a different level of understanding. What kind of commitment would I be willing to endure to push this envelope of knowledge? I assured him that I was a pure scientist and I would do anything that it would take to open new doors in the field of science.

I brought you here to get your input and your commitment. We what to send a mission to rejoin with the last comet you probed and send in a manned probe. The stakes are high but I want you to see something before you say anything. He raised his hand and the lights dimmed and I watched a movie as he narrated it. This is the probe's read out of the last comet mission. The speed relativity and skin temperature of the probe are on the bottom of the screen. The temperature was reading –240 degrees F. and was rising rapidly. When it got to a –40 degrees the cameras were activated. It looked like we were going through a snowstorm as specks bounced of the lens. The skin temperature was now at 70 degrees and the snowstorm effect had increased. The things that were hitting the lens were getting larger and larger until the probe was dodging them then they became smaller and smaller. The skin temperature was getting colder and colder. After a burst of speed the probe had exited the comet and I could see our space ship. The little man sitting next to me said his first words about the film. We did some computer assisted photo imaging processing and now I want you to look at the film again. I sat there in awe as I saw life forms of all sizes and shapes drifting across the screen. They got larger to the point of having to dodge them. They were of a class that I had never seen before not even in fossil record. The film was shut off and I was again looking into my blast furnace. KOZ: YOUR MIDDLE MIND WILL BLIND YOU TO THE TRUTH. BEHOLD WHAT THE MIND CAN DREAM FOR IT IS THE SEEDS OF THE FUTURE. YOUR LOWER MIND MELDING WITH THE GIVING GREATER KNOWN WILL SHAPE THE FUTURE AS THE COLLECTIVE FAMILY OF THE GIVING GREATER KNOWN SEES IT. Stay with me and KOZ and the Collective Family Of The Giving Grater Known. We as a team of dreamers and future builders will make worlds and universes out of the nothing using our combined Mind Energy, Neural Soup and Neural Leakage Soup. See this bonding flow over you and this world and bring it to a much higher level of thinking.

* * *

Best Outcome

Future building is when you start with the best possible outcome then work you're way backwards to the first step of action. Look at this outcome in your mind's eye, see it, smell it, mind touch it, fell around in it; how do you feel in that position? Those feelings are the key to tapping into the energy force that brings everything into the tangible. That feeling is the magical driving beast within you that will transport you there or to anywhere. KOZ: THE UNKNOWING LOWER MINDS OF OTHERS ARE LIKE ENVIOUS LITTLE CHILDREN IF THEY CAN'T HAVE IT THEY WILL TRY TO DESTROY IT.

The future is the moment after the now. In the morning after the awaking and before the stirring is the moment of future building. At this time you go through your whole day, in word and in mind pictures. This is the final touch on the instructions you have given to your Lower Mind, making sure that nothing from the 360 degree input radius has infiltrated and altered your instructions. Shooting from the hip or making decisions on the fly or doing in the field engineering all sound macho and a good trait but they will get you into trouble more often than not. People who seem to be able to make those on the spot decisions are really not they are pulling from their well programed Lower Mind. From now on you will not be alone. The masters of ones own Lower Mind has the Giving Greater Known in his corner.

Never Ending Journey

THE NOTHING AS SOMETHING

I was sitting in my friends' house in Regensborg Germany. Tommy was one of the German friends that I had met in the 7-11 gas station in Escondido Ca. He handed me a piece of paper. On it was something that looked like an inkblot. Underneath the image was written these words. Concentrate on the four dots in the middle of the picture for about 30 seconds. Then close your eyes and tilt your head back. Keep them closed. You will see a circle of light. Continue looking at the circle. What do you see? I tried it I saw something that was unexpected and bewildered my mind. When I looked back at the image I could see that the thing that I saw was a reverse image a negative of what my opened eyes had seen. But what entranced my mind is that my mind had done some adding and filling to this minds eye view of the reverse of what it had seen. Where had it gotten the instructions to do so? How many other things that were presented to me in the opposite or negative were coming thru as something else than what my eye was seeing. My inner eye was doing a lot of transforming, twisting and adding on its own. I was tilting my head back as instructed I told Tommy what I had seen. He reacted in a way that was more than a yes you are right. His face glowed and there was an eye-to-eye contact that was of a different nature. This eye contact was a link up of inner Lower Minds. In me seeing the same thing that he had seen let him know that I had a brain that was working on a similar format as his. But there was more; this little game of the mind had turned into a test of sorts. This was a test that could let you know if you were talking to an intact fully functional human brain. This little test was also telling you if the person was thinking and using both sides of his brain. This little mind game test reminded me of some of the block and picture tests given by the government when selecting and weeding out new recruits into the armed services. They used these simple little match the picture with the blocks and what was it drawings to see if you were in possession of a fully operational human brain.

This was all to familiar to me it smacked of the yes-no rebound of the mind. I what you to think about these three areas of thought process. I want you to think about them in a way that your brain has not thought or worked in before. I want you to think of your brain as a evolving growing stretching goop. That there are some things that are so far above it's understanding that it must go through a transformation to get to a higher level of thinking. Think of yourself being a bee in a beehive. You know what you know and that is all you need to know to gather honey and protect your family genial code. You are unable to think outside of the bee box. Your bee brain has no idea of the beekeeper and his manipulations. And there would be no way that you could conceive of what that thing that he arrived in called a pick-up truck; what was that all about. Shift this line of thought to yourself and now be aware that there are things going on about you that are above your ability to grasp. You must start a new line of thinking. This new thinking is where the yes is the no and the no is the yes. Where the truth is the lie and the lie is the truth. Where the wrong is the right and the right is the wrong. And you are you and are not you. Gather your wits and your gathered knowledge and through them all into a cosmic blender and put it on liquefy. I want you to go into your movie picture mind. I want you to dream a little dream with me. See yourself as a super being with powers that are so great that you can transform worlds and universes. Look over to your right there is a small box about the size of a cigar box. Open this box and see inside it a group of small boxes. Reach in and pull out the one-marked worlds in the making. Open it and see that there are a group of slides inside of it, the type that are used under a microscope. On one of them is the writing Project Earth. Put this one under your microscope. There is a notebook to your left open it up. You can see that there are many entries. Go to page 64 and read what it says… this experiment has gone in a direction that will not be tolerated much longer these humans have been transformed into killer humans and if they can't be put back on the path of the Giving Greater Known you will have to put this slide in the autoclave for sterilization. Oh! What powers you have to wipe out a whole solar system with a flick of a switch.

      The human keepers would like us to get away from our childish antics of making war and get on with going down the path of the Giving Greater Known. We must start using the power of Oneness. We must start seeing what our minds eye is seeing as we are looking at something or hearing or smelling something. The words that we trusted only to mean what they say have to be looked at in a different light. They could be saying one thing and really be sending a total different message to our inner seeing eye. I saw a commercial on TV it was saying good for you, you are drinking milk good for you. My mind was getting a double message. They were not saying that milk was good for me but it was coming across that way. I saw another disturbing advertisement. This is an info ad that is a non-ad that becomes an ad in the inner eye as it twists and transforms it. This ad is telling you that they are supporting a program to keep cigarettes out of the hands of children. They use the {we card system} and how well it works. As they are saying one thing, the minds are picking up a whole different message. It is showing young kids wanting to smoke and making the teller out to be the bad guy. Now kids you know you want cigarettes but you can't get them ha ha. This is setting up young minds in a challenge mode written about before. This must be stopped who are they try to kid the only way that big tobacco can stay alive is by tricking the minds of our kids into smoking. They are cleverly under the disguise of being the ones not wanting the kids to smoke actually egging them on to find a way to get them cigarettes. Another avenue of mind implanting of corporations is the music video. This slips under any kind of controls using the disguise of art and free expression. The ratings are a joke and are nothing but a smokescreen to keep this maverick brain seeder on the loose. Oh! I think the courts will have a field day with this one someday. KOZ: COSMIC LAW KNOWS THE NOTHING AS THE SOMETHING AND THE SOMETHING AS THE NOTHING. SEEK OUT THE TRUE PUSHED MEANING, AS IT WILL TRANSFORM ON ITS OWN WITH THE AID OF THE INNER MINDS EYE TWISTING. BE MINDFUL OF THE WORD TWISTERS. The transformation of the mind to a higher level of thought processes will take a lot of energy and time. Go and give as much as you can and in doing so gather large amounts of Mind Energy. You will need lots of Mind Energy to leap into higher levels of thinking.

* * *

NEURAL COBWEBS

I was just leaving a stressful situation of having to inform my Aunt that a close friend had died. She took to drinking and had fallen to sleep several times as I was using her ground line to check my E-Mail. It took me about an hour to re-program through Compaq and setting up my computer to recognize and sign on with AOL and answer my AOL e-mail and also answer my Hotmail.com email, which I use for my international connections. When my Aunt woke up from a short nap she commented on how long I had been on the phone and how that it was going to run up quite a bill. Even though I could see that she was of a different generation as far as all this computer stuff I tried to explain to her about the time that I was hooked up to her phone line. That the connection that I had to make with Compaq was a toll free 1-800 number and the registration with AOL was the same. That I had touched bases with a couple friends in Europe and my uncle in Wyo. her brother. I said " I don't think that you understand it all and as I left assured her that I would pay for the long distance charges that I had rung up on her phone from Nice Ca. to Santa Rosa Ca.

    I stopped off at the Harbor bar and restaurant and had my favorite an Oriental chicken salad, it is to die for. I saw a friend of mine come in and sit at the bar. He didn't see me sitting at the freestanding bar behind him. I was in my entertaining mode. A man that was known by the nickname Rooster had introduced his daughter and her boyfriend to me. They bought me a drink and I folded her a whale out of a dollar bill and a rose out of a paper bar napkin. My friend noticed my handy work and joined me. We had talked a while and then a local man was talking about how that he visited the writer of the song that was playing on the jukebox. Before he could say the writers name my friend blurted it out. They then went down the sycophant trail in a deep Lower Mind to Lower Mind communiqué. I was out of the loop and had fell into the Haze. I was in a high state of awareness as to why the meeting of my friend was so timed and that he could be the next pearl on my cosmic string.

    I was on Reach-One I was wearing a gold shirt. I was

being led at a hurried up pace down a long hallway. We passed door after door I was getting tired. I stopped in my floating tracks and protested to the pace. KOZ Boomed in: YOU MUST GET THERE BEFORE THE THOUGHT LEAVES YOUR MIND. We got to the end of a hundred plus door hallway and came to an open end. I stopped and looked out and saw what I can only describe as a neural cobweb structure. I was pushed out and started a freefall thru this neural web. As I hit each string of this web I felt a rush of an informational infusion. Thousands no hundreds of thousands even maybe millions of thoughts flashed thru me in a split second of this neural thread falling. I was coming to a white wall and it was coming fast. I fell through the wall and could swear that I had fallen thru a jungle of hair and headed for another white wall. As I got closer the white wall I could see lines on it and I saw my hand, with pen in hand writing. My hand was on autopilot. This is what it had written: TOUCHING THE ENTRENCHED MIND LOOPING OF ANOTHER. KNOWING WHAT IS IN THEIR MIND AND GOING DOWN THAT NEURAL PATHWAY CREATES AN INSTANT BONDING OF MINDS THAT IS A HIGHER LEVEL OF SCANNING OF ANOTHER'S LOWER MIND. This was the second time during this writing of this book that I had felt that Koz had stepped in and taken over. But this time it was very different it seemed more intense and more internally controlling. Where in the past I felt that he had put thoughts into my head that appeared in my typing. This time he had taken control of my physical body and was pushing it around at his will like a small toy car. I feel like that he is manifesting his presents now in a physical way that may be a start of an inner metamorphsis. Even though I had eaten and paid for my bill I was still sitting there. I was not drinking I was just sitting there soaking in and incubating in my mind what had just happened. I was queued to leave when my friend left. My friend jumped into his tricked out to the nines Mustang as I jumped into my 84 Ford Festiva. I told him that at one time that I had a Chevy SS 454 that was about as nice as his and the same color. That I did not like driving it to a bar because I was worried that some jealous person would key it or something. He nodded his head in agreement and we drove off. I got home to my camper and saw that Miss Talley the owner was still up. I told her that I had looked at the wall damage in the bathroom of cabin five and it didn't look like that big of a project that I knew a few tricks and short cuts that would save her some money. She handed me a check that she had written earlier and thanked me for my help. Again things just seem to go my way I know that I am on the path of the Giving Greater Known. This is where I had stopped writing in my morning session but was pushed by Koz to write more this evening. I was having trouble with my word processing and Miss Talley the owner of the park that I was staying at was able to talk me through my problems. That evening at ten o'clock I had solved my problem of not being able to transform my single spaced typed document into a double spaced one. Was it only by luck that I had picked not only a lady that owned a big house and cabins in need of repair but also taught computer classes at night at the local college. When I had gone into my future building thought session I did not ask for someone that could help me with my computer skills. My Lower Mind had stepped in and added this little tidbit on its own with out my Middle Minds instruction to do so. I went falling thru the neural cobwebs of two different people in one day and had been of a different mind ever since. Things seemed to be falling into place using this type of neural butterfly catching. I used F.O.R.M. (asking about Family, Occupation, Recreation, Money) process of finding a similar neural path as mine in someone else's neural soup.. KOZ: TRANSFORMING YOUR MIND INTO A MIND TRAVELER OF OTHER PEOPLES LOWER MIND WILL PUT POWERS IN YOUR MIND AND HANDS THAT WILL LEAPFROG OVER TRADITIONAL PATHS OF PROGRESS. BE A COLLECTOR OF MINDS AND OF THEIR HARD FOUGHT FOR KNOWLEDGE. I feel that my transformation has advanced to a level that has put me on a plane of aloneness. I truly hope that I will be able to have other people join me on this journey into the COSMIC GIVING GREATER KNOWN. I hope you will stay with me and continue the journey with me. Without you I am truly alone.

***

THE KEY TO KNOWLEDGE
OF THE GIVING GREATER KNOWN

I knew that I was on the path of the Giving Greater Known. My brain had developed an inner seek out and act mode. I could be standing anywhere and it would kick in. In the past I had to push myself into action, now it is an automatic function that by-passed my middle walk around self and taps into a fixed action pattern of my Lower Mind. Every time that I reached out with my Mind Energy and had given it to someone else good things came my way. To my Lower Mind it was like finding buried treasure. But I have found out that as you travel down the path of the Giving Greater Know and are a true member of the Greater Cosmic Family there comes about an intensifying process. This new process pulls in power from all you're past giving. The more Mind Energy that you give away the more receiving comes your way. There is a level that one can reach that can bring about a trance effect on the receiver of your Mind Energy. As you approach this person who you're giving a transfusion of Mind Energy to, they will fall into a trance state and start doing as you ask. When you are truly on the path of the Giving Greater Known your brain and your body sends out a higher level of communication. This higher level by-passes the Middle Mind and sends a message to the Lower Mind of the receiver. This state I have named the State of Sister and Brotherhood. Your Middle Mind is pushed to the side as you two become as one. The giver is asking Pure Questions and the receiver is giving to the giver what is needed without question. There is a feeling of a true team effort a team of two. But there is a bigger force at hand, bigger than just the two of you. The State of Sister and Brotherhood is the key to the knowledge bank of the Giving Greater Known. As your Lower Mind and theirs turns on at the same time magical things happen. All of their past giving and all of your past giving start to call in help through a cosmic communication system. Everyone that you have helped in the past wants to join in on this giving process. If they are true givers they know of what wonders will come their way. There will be a melding of minds, a reading of minds and a flow of physical action that will take no words. This pocket of interaction will be at a higher level than the spoken word alone. Even after the problem has been solved it will bleed over into a ; I don't want to let you go session. There will be the offering of money, food, or drink and sometimes all three. At this point the giver of Mind Energy must be sure that he dose not over ask for or over receive. The receiver of Mind Energy is in a trance and could be led into giving more than they would feel comfortable with. They may be surprised as to what they gave when he or she returns to his Middle Mind and leaves the Sister and Brotherhood connection behind.

  I want you to go along with me as I tell you of a time that I was in the state of Sister and Brotherhood. I was in Nice Ca. at the Harbor bar; I wanted to use the phone. My Aunt and cousin and her husband were going to take me out to eat and I wanted to let them know that I would meet them there at the Harbor bar. There was someone already on the phone I was going to have to wait. She talked for a while and then passed it off to a man that was having car problems. I was near enough that I heard what he had to say. When he was done I called my Aunt. I was in the Haze and there was no stopping me. I found the man with the car problems and started to ask the Pure Questions needed to be able to transfuse Mind Energy into the problem at hand. I heard that you are having car problems lets go look at it. We left our drinks behind and took off. His car was at the closed down Bartlet Springs water bottling Co. When we got there he asked me if I had any tools? I said no but that I could look at it and tell him what his problem was. I had him try to start it but after a few cranks had him stop. It's not your timing belt your bottom pulley is turning over. I pulled the coil wire and jumped it with a screwdriver to the engine block as he turned the motor again. "Nope nope stop you do not have any spark you have a problem in the control circuit of your ignition system." If I had a piece of wire I could hot-wire it from the battery to the coil and you could get it home. I was headed to a fence and he said that he had a wire cutter. With a few snips I had a chunk of wire and he was on the road again. When he got to the bar I instructed him to disconnect the wire until he was ready to go home so it would not run his battery down. In the bar he said that he would buy me a drink, I said that he owed me two because they took the one that I had left behind. He bought me a drink and a drink chip and gave me ten dollars. I thanked him not for the money or the drinks but for the chance to give. I told him that it was another person with car problems that had sent my life into a whirlwind and told him the story.

I told him that the reason that I helped him was that he

was on a giving path and I could sense it. He assured me that he was a giver and we went our own ways as my Aunt and cousin showed up for lunch. KOZ: THE STACKING OF LOWER MINDS THAT ARE BOTH ON THE PATH OF THE GIVING GREATER KNOWN IS THE PASSAGE WAY INTO THE KNOWLEDGE BANK OF THE COSMIC GIVING GREATER KNOWN. SEEK OUT THESE PORTALS AND YOUR MIND WILL LEAP OFF THE EARTH AND JOIN A COLLECTIVE COSMIC FAMILY. I can feel a building pressure inside me of Mind Energy. This pressure is of two types, amount and potency. I have been given more chances to give and my effectiveness has been enhanced. I feel as though I am part of a growing process that is moving faster and faster, exponentially. You too will reach this state if you stay on the path of the Giving Greater Know and join a larger Cosmic Family governed only by Cosmic Law.

***

Fasting

Even that I know that I am on the path of the Giving Greater known I must be on guard. The Lower Mind will slip into the state of nothingness its happy state. It will be at its happiest when there is nothing new to contend with. The Middle Mind must take control and use the body as a whip to keep the Lower Mind active. Without an active Lower Mind you loose the connection with the Higher Mind. The Higher Mind and only the Higher Mind has the power to tap into the universal knowledge source of the Giving Greater Known. You must have this connection with the Giving Greater Known to become a true member of the larger Cosmic Family.

One day I was day dreaming and KOZ enlightened me.

I was taken to Reach One. I can remember looking for what color my shirt was but was escorted by two men, at a high rate of speed. At a much faster than walking, than running, than a car or jet plain could go. We came to a very large door like the ones that I had seen on airplane hangers when I was in the Air Force. The light was very dim inside this room. I saw forever in all directions people, on their knees all facing the same direction. Above a large window I saw the words Winter Sun Solstice and then it changed to some writing that I did not understand and then to a pictograph that showed a sun inside a mans head. I saw everyone bowing as they were kneeling but they were still looking forward. The room was getting brighter and brighter. Then at the bottom of the window the sun came up. As this happened they all raised their hands and stared until the sun was full. They then stood up and started beating themselves with a cat of nine tails on their backs until they were bleeding. As I sat there back on earth my eyes opened all I could see was red. Slowly it turned to orange and then white. It was a very clear cold day the twenty-first of December. I watched the sunrise wearing a welder's helmet. When it was full I trusted my hands into a snow bank and held them their until they felt great pain and then felt no pain then I removed them. As they warmed, I felt pain again and then the pain in time was gone. KOZ: THE LOWER MIND CAN BE PUSHED OUT OF A STATE OF NOTHINGNESS USING PAIN AND FASTING. A MENTAL STACKING OF THESE TWO IS A VERY POWERFUL TOOL.

    As I am now staying in the south for the winter I have been using cold water instead of snow. My fast starts the 21st of Dec and runs till the first of February. A fast does not have to be abstaining from food only; it could be anything that the Lower Mind believes that it owns or that it is its right to do. For my fast it is no alcohol, chocolate, or caffeine for forty days.

This time frame from 21 DEC to 1 Feb is the worst or the best time to do this fast. It is very hard to stay away from these habits during this time because of the Holidays. What, no chocolate at Christmas time or no alcohol at New Years or caffeine either? If you can stay this course you will have developed a true tool of the mind to impress your Lower Mind as to who is in control. After breaking the fast I have found out that I have reduce the amount of consumption of these things drastically. When you are confronted by the hordes of no brain human-noids as to why you are doing this, (and you will be); just tell them that you are cutting back or that you don't drink in the month of Jan. If you try explaining to them what you are doing they will unleash their Lower Mind anti- new idea anti-body horde on you with all kinds of cute and dumb comments that you don't need fouling up your plan.

Through out the year I do mini-fasts to jolt my Lower Mind into action. This self-imposed punishment of the Lower Mind has only been mastered by a few. Those that have this tool are true masters of their inner self. Your Lower Mind and the Lower Minds of others stand in awe of any Middle Mind that has developed such powers. They know their own weak will and see you as a person of a higher thinking level. I have seen in the past some that would try a fast (not eating) too quickly and fail. This failure gives the power to the Lower Mind and makes any such attempts of fasting in the future even harder. A person must be very careful in his actions in pushing the Lower Mind. At the beginning you should start very small and build on your successes. This is an internal battle that must be won at all costs. You must pull in all the tools given to you by Cosmic Law.

KOZ has given us a chance to reinvent ourselves and become part of a Greater Cosmic Family. The first step is the identification of what the Lower Mind holds dear and use this against it to push it off it's path that it is used to going down. The fast must not use the thing that you are trying to change as the fasting tool. If you are trying to stop smoking do not fast from smoking. You must get the message to your Lower Mind underneath the anti-new way radar of the Lower Mind. I was not able to do the forty-day Lower Mind fast in the beginning. I started with the not until noon fast and then the one day fast and then the two day fast… until now I am on an open ended fast. An Open Ended Lower Mind Fast is one that dose not stop until you feel that you have impressed upon your Lower Mind that it has accepted the new path you have set down. This type of fast is not, (NOT) recommended at this time. This will become a lifetime's work in progress. As the Lower Mind catches on to what you are doing you will have to keep raising the level at which it will be impressed by. KOZ: THE LOWER MIND HAS POWERS THAT CAN ONLY BE OBTAINED IF IT IS TRAINED BY A TRAINED MIDDLE MIND. A FLOWING LOWER MIND IS IN CONSTANT TOUCH WITH THE UNIVERSAL KNOWLEDGE OF THE GIVING GREATER KNOWN. I hope that this cosmic message from KOZ and by now your tapings into the Giving Greater Known has impacted your life. If you were to stop now your brain would surely be stirred to an extent of bewilderment and ache with the not knowing.

***

BRAIN STALLING

I was sitting feeding the ducks and seagulls and watching the sunlight dance on the water. My brain not knowing which spot of light to look at or where the next one was going to show up I fell into the Haze. This happens to a lot of people, they call it a lackadaisical daydreaming. I was on Reach One there was no one to meet me I was wearing a brown shirt. I started walking down a long hallway looking for a brown door. I came to one and tried to open it. It would not open, I could see that it was a few shades darker than my shirt and went looking for another one. I came to another one but it also did not open it was a few shades lighter than my shirt. Now I was standing in front of a door with my shirt-tail pulled out making sure I had a match. This time the door opened and I went in. All of a sudden I was very thirsty. Standing in front of me was a drinking fountain. Above the drinking fountain was a sign that read "Out of Order". It also read that a part was on the way and it should be fixed any time now and that there was another drinking fountain thirty-two doors down to your left. My throat was so dry I was unable to speak. I headed out to my left as I got to the spot where the next water fountain was suppose to be I saw only two holes in the wall where one had been. Above the holes was a sign the same as the last one. Now my throat felt like it had been glued together. I set out to my left one more time this time at a more quickened pace. I was stopped by two men they asked me what I was doing there that I was in a restricted area. I did kind of remember a red and white striped line going across the floor and up the walls and across the ceiling. I tried to explain to them about the water fountains but they were not buying it. I said that I would turn around and go the other way. They grabbed me by the arms saying that it was not that easy that I had violated entry procedure and that this was a very serious offense and that I was going to have to face charges. They led me away down hallway after hallway door after door. We finally came to a door that had the same red and white stripe around the door. We went in and I was put in a holding room. This room was a padded room with only one chair and three lights on the wall. I had not been there long when in came a man caring a briefcase and a folding chair. He sat down and said to me that everything was going to be OK; I just had to answer a few questions. After about six questions the red light started to blink and a horn was blaring. He grabbed me and was saying that there had been a hull breach and that we were going to have to move to another section. We stepped out into the hall the last I saw of the briefcase and the man he said that he would take care of the security breach problem and not to worry about it. I could see down the hall and there were thousands of people standing in the hallway. All of a sudden they all sat down and so did I. Then there was a forward movement of the whole hallway the doors were moving past at a greater and greater speed until they were just a blur.

There was a duck pulling at one of my shoelaces, I had stopped feeding and it wanted more. I sat there a while trying to make any sense of this last trip to Reach One. I sure hoped that the hull breach was not serious and they got it fixed. I went on my way to Quail Run, a work out gym. I had finished my work out and was sitting in the hot tub. Next to me was a man we had said nothing so I broke the ice and asked what he thought of our spy plane that had been downed by the Chinese? He said that he felt that the whole thing was a set-up and that for some reason we wanted the Chinese to have that technology. That they did not get all that they needed through their spies and we had no other way to give it to them. He said that the government wanted to change the focus of the national thought, away from tax rebates onto something else. And that this spy plane problem will be replaced with something else. That this was a new way of governing he called it (it's in the works don't worry about it). Hey what happened to campaign funding reform anyway?

As I was getting dressed I was thinking about how I was not thinking about the water fountains that were out of order on Reach One. My brain had stalled and had moved on to the next problem. I wondered how many times in the past was this tool of brain stalling used against me and I didn't even realize it. What in my past had not been done because my brain had been stalled? And by the time that I did remember that there was something that needed to be done that it was too late. The statutes of limitations had run out or they said I had acquiesced and it was my fault for taking so long to do something about it. There is an automatic function in the brain that kicks in called the (IT'S TO LATE TO DO ANYTHING ABOUT IT NOW) function. This function will kick in and truly stall the brain. KOZ: BRAINS WITH SHALLOW SEEDED LOWER MINDS WILL BE BLOWN AROUND BY THE BRAIN STALLERS. There are many tools to come they will turn your brain into a neural fighting machine. At this point of this instruction manual you will have to start using you higher function of your brain in a more consistent pattern. We have come a long way together but the journey has just started.

***

LOST AND RE-FOUND

I was looking for a small piece of paper. It was not just any piece of paper this one had a persons name and number written on it. I just saw it within the last week and had put it somewhere so I would not lose it again and now I cannot find it. I know it's here somewhere. I find myself looking in the same places two or three times not remembering if I really gave it a good look. My brain was in a stir I fell into the Haze.

I found myself on Reach One. I did not want to be there I wanted to keep looking for the piece of paper with my friends' name and phone number on it. I was in a dark room the only thing I could see was a spot of light. I started moving towards the light, it got bigger and bigger. As I got closer I could see other people walking towards the light. At first I could only see an outline of the person. As we got closer to the light I could make out what their faces looked like. As we got closer we joined hands in a circle. The light had turned into a ball and was getting higher over our heads. I stepped into a hole and the people holding my hands helped me regain my feet. This happened many times I was so glad that they were there. I came to a large hole and I lost my grip on their hands and fell out of their sight. I was able to climb out of the hole. When I got out there was nobody in sight. I was walking very slowly and missing the people that I was holding hands with. A new ring of people caught up with me and I became part of this circle. This time we were joined at the elbows. My hands had locked on to my wrists and so had theirs. This was a much tighter formation that gave more stability. I was very happy to be linked up again.

I had not stopped looking for the piece of paper. I did find it and I put it a very special place as not to lose it again. Now having it again made it more special to me than in the past.

I can remember in my past when I had had a fight with someone and they became a close friend. This friend would become a foe again and then a friend again. At each rejoining the friendship got stronger and stronger. We would still argue but are friendship was so strong that we would stay friends. KOZ: TURMOIL AND LOSS WILL QUICKEN THE TRANFORMATION OF THE LOWER MIND. PRO-ACTIVE STRESS AND LOSS WELL PLANNED WILL BIND TOGETHER TWO LOWER MINDS TO A DEEPER LEVEL. I had to think about this one for sometime before I could make sense of it. When I thought I knew what it meant I tried to put it into my own words. It seemed to be saying that turmoil and loss was a binding tool of Lower Minds. As I was trying to make sense of it all, the trip to Reach One and what Koz had to say I heard a loud snap in my head and then Koz boomed in. KOZ: DON'T WAIT FOR TURMOIL OR LOSS PLAN AND STRUCTURE IT TO DEVELOP LOWER MIND TO LOWER MIND BONDING. I had never looked at problems as a tool. I had never thought about making problems, it seemed that there were enough as it was. Now I set up problems all the time knowing from the on set how I was going to solve them and how it would strengthen Lower Mind to Lower Mind bonding.

I want you to go into your movie picture mind and see a story of a self-made problem. I was having a hard time making a strong Lower Mind to Lower Mind bond. The person that I had picked was an alcohol induced mood swinger. I first had to find something that this person knew of that could help me solve a problem. He had a food management background and now was working as a handyman. He just got off a big roof job, maybe there was something he could help me with along that line. Let's see I want to make it more than just an information supply problem. I want it to be a hands' on show me problem. I know a lot about roofing so it will have to be a made up problem that is not really a problem. I'm going to put a three-tab shingle into my car and ask him where a person should be nailing them. I know it should be left and right above the slit. After he shows me I will give him a handshake and a small gift. I know that he will think that I am dumb about roofing but I must suck that up inside me and think about the bigger picture and what I am trying to accomplish. The thing that matters is a tighter Lower Mind to Lower Mind bonding. This process when well applied will transform the incubation time line and develop a short cut to Lower Mind bonding. A person must set aside his own ego and focus on the bonding. At times you will make yourself out to be a less informed person and this may rub you the wrong way. Rise above your comfort zone and learn a higher level of thought process. Be on guard as to not let the loose lips of the Middle Mind step in at the wrong time and spoil the process. This higher level of Lower Mind bonding will become a strong tool in your mental toolbox. Use it often and make it part of your automatic function mode of thinking. This tool can make the lost into the found along a cosmic link to another's Lower Mind. What powers this will put in your grasp. The power to find a linkage to a Lower Mind that was once lost. To lose even one Lower Mind bonding is surely a loss. There would not be any way to measure your true loss. Who could calculate what amount of Mind Energy that you missed out on. And what you may have lost in that persons tapping into the Giving Greater Known. KOZ: GATHER AS MANY LOWER MINDS AS YOU HAVE MIND ENERGY TO DO SO. GARTHERED LOWER MINDS ARE THE FUEL OF THE GREATER COSMIC LAW. The I that is not me and the you that is not you must transform thinking apart from ourselves. Don't let your Middle Mind with all its gathered mud puddle neural soup step in and spoil the process. Say to yourself many times in a chanting form. I am thinking at a higher level, I am thinking at a higher level. In saying this it puts your Middle Mind on notice to stay away. Your progress thus far has been of the type I would call filling the mental toolbox. Soon we will be using these tools on a grand cosmic adventure. Use your tools often and keep them well-honed and oiled. Be ready to jump into the realm of the Giving Greater Known. Our stacked Lower Minds will move us into a higher level of thinking that will pull us into a larger Cosmic Collective Family. Don't be left behind continue the transformation.

* * *

Replication

Many times in the past I can remember when I was outnumbered. Sometimes it would be a physical body count and I would have to run away or hide. Other times it would be that the collective thought was different and there was a brain neural imbalance towards their favor. I want you to go into your movie picture mind and take a little mind trip with me.

I was sitting in the dayroom of the barracks I was watching TV. Two of the troops came in one was showing that he had gotten one of his front teeth knocked out. He had come back to base to round up some of his buddies. They were going to a small town called Belt in Montana. We will show them not to mess with one of ours, let's go. There was about eighteen of us in three cars. We all wanted revenge, we had become a pack of dogs looking to take a bite out of somebody. The town of Belt, Montana was about a population of two or three hundred. Our group of eighteen was only surpassed in size when there was a street dance or a football game in town. We went bar to bar looking for the person that had knocked out our buddy's tooth. We never did find the guy but we did give everyone along the way a good verbal chewing on. We felt like that we were a team trying to correct an injustice. This type of feeling of having a support system behind you made us feel powerful.

Now I want you to come along with me still in your movie picture mind and see and feel the flipside of these types of feelings. I was living in a military housing area in Bad Kreknach, Germany. I was in grammar school I was just learning about the being out-numbered game of life. There was a smaller boy than me that was always running his mouth, pushing and hitting and getting away with it. One day he shoved on me and I shoved back. There was no fight he was being protected by some other kids. I wondered why they were protecting him they all had suffered from his physical trespasses. Then the behind the seen story came out. I was new to this area I did not have a good handle on who was who and what was what. As this smaller boy walked away I heard him say I'll meet you after school. A kid standing next to me said you are going to get your butt kicked now. I told him that I was not afraid of him. He replied Oh; you didn't know that he had four older brothers going to this school. After school I slipped out a back door and took the long long way home.

    I have given these mind picture stories hoping that you would be able to tune into your own life stories along these lines. I want you to boil these stories down until only the feelings are left. I want you to go back in your past and walk yourself through a similar mind picture story. Stay with it until you can feel the feelings again. I want you to feel both sides. The power side and the run and hide side of these feelings. Then I want you to let the run and hide feeling flow over your body. I want you to feel the fear the anxiety and the hopelessness. Do this until you can feel the anger build up inside you. When it comes to a boiling point I want you to see your hand reach down in through the top of your head and grab onto these feelings as if you were pulling a wet rag out of a bucket of water. See yourself taking this rag and throwing it into a deep blue green crevasse in a glacier. Now I want you to feel the feelings of the power side of having the numbers on your side in your favor. I want you to do this until you feel ten feet tall and can whip the world. See yourself reaching down into the top of your head and pulling this feeling out as if you were pulling a red-hot piece of steel from a blacksmiths forge. Take it over to a large anvil and start pounding on it. And every time you hit it I want you to say the words, (replication means power). Keep hitting this steel until you see it turn into a bright shinny sword.

See written on the side of this sword the word REPLACTOR. Open your mental toolbox and see that there was always a spot for it. This spot has a molded recessed place that your replicator sword fits into perfectly. Look to the right of your replicator sword there is another one just like it. It was always there you just did not know to look for it. Above it is written the word money. Look to your right and you can see a long line of swords each having a different word written above it. See yourself looking at each of these swords and feel a feeling of self-empowerment. These mental tools are your cosmic law ownership right. They have always been there and they are guided by pure cosmic truth and law. These tools will work for you every time without failure they can't there is no other way. As you put your repliacator tools to work they then take on a life of their own and infuses power into you. If you are feeling that you are not getting to where you would like to be in this stage of human reality start replicating. You only have to look around you and you can see that the more successful people are good repliacators. How well would the banker do with only one loan on the books. How well would the food market do that only sold one item? How well would a football team do with only one player.

Are you a team of one that keeps losing or have you replicated yourself many times over. Is there money out there working for you? Are there people out there working for you? Are there cows out there chewing their cud and working for you? Are there bees gathering you honey as you are watching TV. Is your mind collecting new and better ways to replicate yourself? How many vending machines are working for you? Have you set up any franchises that are bringing you in a monthly fee? If you are like 97% of the walk around Middle Minds that are trying to get ahead you have answered most if not to all these questions (NO). KOZ: COSMIC LAW

SHINES FAVORABLY ON GOOD REPLICATORS. THE STRONGEST IN NUMBER NOT STRENGTH SHALL INCREASE THEIR CHANCE TO JOIN THE COLECTIVE OF THE GIVIGING GREATER KNOWN. Read this book daily it will start the brain replicating process. Stay with me and you will become the new you that is more than one by using the power of one. When you feel the power of replication you will wonder why you had never been shown this path before. Stay on the path of the Giving Greater Known and you will never be alone again. Stay with me, through me and me through you we will build a future grander than one alone.

* * *

COPYCAT

When did it start or when did it end, was it wrong or was it right. I was leaning over the crib saying (da-da) talking baby talk. I was trying to get my son to copy what I was saying. At sometime this came to pass and I showed him a lot of other things by me showing him how I did it and then have him try doing it. I fed him until he started feeding himself. I tied his shoes instructing him to watch. I would even do it when he was sitting on my lap so that he could see a straight on frontal view. I watch my young son start learning from other kids in sandbox play. This is where the brain-bind started and would never end for the majority of people. After I had showed my son how to do something I would let him take over and try it. This little process played out hundreds of times before he was introduced to the interaction of the sandbox. The first time that I set him in the sandbox he just sat there watching the other children. I went into my "show him and let him try it" mode. He was so fascinated watching the other children play that he was not even looking at what I was doing. I stepped back and the fight began. There my little angel of a boy was pulling a toy out of one child's hand after another. And when that child hit him he started to cry and then hit back. What kind of monster had I raised what had I done wrong. The big word that hit the seen was SHARE this was a new concept for my son. Along with that came no HITTING, BITTING, or HAIR PULLING. The biggest brain stir that had to be dealt with was COPYCAT-ING. He's coping what I'm doing he's nothing but a copycat. This young mind had been led down the neural path of do what I did, for all of his life. Now a new rule was being pushed at him that would stir the brain forever more. I would tell him stop trying to reinvent the wheel. Meaning if there is a proven way to get something done use it, do it that way. Then came the word plagiarism. And then the word cheating and the idea that you could steal another person's ideas.

I want you to go into your movie picture mind. Now think of your past and feel the feelings that the words, COPY-CAT, PLAGIARISM, CHEATING, AND STEALING boils up in your mind. I want you to see yourself back in a space and time when somebody said these words to you. I want you to think of how old you were. Where you were when it happened. Also I want you to see the face of the person that said any of these words about you. When you have the full picture I want you to tune into your feelings. Let your feelings fill your thoughts and flow through your whole body. See the place and time melt away as you hold onto the feelings. See the persons face fade away into a fog bank, but hold on to the feelings. I want you to re-live these feelings to the point where you are expressing yourself out loud and with feeling. Think of how unfair it seemed to you at the time and how they were changing the rules in the middle of the game. I want you to see these words and rules flow out of the top of your head and fall to the floor. Watch them as they become transformed into a set of iron shackles. See these shackles around your legs and wrists. See you're past mind pictures that you saw about these words come out the top of your head. As these pictures start to drop in front of your eyes I want you to see them transform into a sleep time blindfold. See this covering your eyes and totally blinding your eyes in seeing anything that is new that could be copied.

Come along with me as I tell you a story of my copycat experience. I told my son that we were going to have to build some fences to keep the sheep in. I had never built a woven wire fence before. I got in my car and started looking at other people's fences around where I lived out in the country. I was out stealing others people's ideas I was making sketches, drawings and notes. When my son and I started working on the fence it seemed as if I was a wizard of fence building. I still had a deeply ingrained feeling that I was cheating somehow. I had to take my son around and show him what I had done, the copying of my neighbors fences. Later that day my son said that it was pretty tricky what I had done referring to getting information on fence building. I was alone, thinking about how that my son and I were in a mind-bind that stemmed back to childhood. I was sitting looking out the window seeing my fence that somehow in my mind was not my fence because I had stolen its conception from somebody else's fence. I thought how that my mind was put into a pretzel knot. First it was told to copy than not to copy and than that copying was OK. I saw my reflection off the window and could see myself in a daze. I fell into the Haze I was on Reach ONE.

I was standing in front of a door that had the number 1 written on it. It opened by itself and I went through it. I walked down a hall and I came to another door that had a number 2 written on it. This happened until I got to the door that was numbered 22. After entering this door the next door I came to had the number 1 written on it. I felt mind stirred and I felt that I was going in circles. I looked to my right and there was another door that had written on it, MINDS MIND MINDS. I went through this door and there was a room of doors. Written on the floor was, MAKE YOUR MIND MAKE A CHOICE.

    I was back looking at my fence. I looked at my watch I was going to have to get going if I was going to get to the mall before it closed. As I was driving down 12th street my mind started to pick up on things that were the same. Lets see, yes this stop sign is the same as the last one, there's coping. Look at this burger joint it's the same concept as the last three that I passed. Look here another used car sales lot. And really all the cars are the same with just a few adjustments. KOZ: THE COSMIC TEST OF THE GENIAL CODE IS SO VAST THAT NO ONE BRAIN WILL START AND FINISH IT. A COLLECTIVE LOWER MIND FORCE WILL BE NEEDED. GATHER AT WILL ALL THAT IS NEEDED FOR THE TEST IS LONG AND HARD. I will forever more not let the mind minders cement my actions with mere words. I from now on will be playing on a level playing field. My past mind set about copying has been written down and thrown into the blue green crevasse. I will now see what I want and copy how someone else got it. I will talk to as many people as I need to, to see my dreams become reality. I feel an empowerment I feel like I have been given a true path to follow thank you KOZ. Now I want you to go forth and copy, copy, copy. I want you to become a copy master. Take this cosmic mental short cut with me and we too will join the collective family of the Giving Greater Know.

* * *

MORE THAN ONE

Since the beginning of man the cry has been, "give me sons". I want sons that will be of like mind. I want my sons to have brothers so they will have like minds. Let them grow and fight together and develop a bonding that they may work as a team of one mind. These family Lower Mind Stacking Structures became so strong that that governments had a hard time governing them. They would keep the father's name and only add the second or jr. to it. This would make it easy to work in somebody else's place. If one of the weaker brothers got into trouble you could send a stronger brother in his place to the work camp. Mike Jones step forward let us see your identification papers. Lets see here yes Mike Jones OK, one year hard labor. Three months would pass and there would be a different guard at the gate. Every morning you would bring a brother along with you waiting for such a chance. The switch is at hand, in goes a different brother. Lets see yes Mike Jones good, OK. The powers to be did not like this type of power that the family unit had. So they tattooed numbers on people or gave them a number so they would know if they had the right person.

To this date we have the body or person number. The Social Security number is the watchdog mark. Even today the power of the stacking of Lower Minds is working the system over. I want you to go into your movie picture mind and come along with me. I want you to see and hear a story of system bending.

He was a young man he was only 65. It was his birthday it was a special day at work. All his workmates had planned a surprise party for him. Mike Jones did not want anybody to know that he was turning 65. He had heard stories from friends how when you reached that age that they turned you out to pasture. He liked his job at the packinghouse; it took him thirty-two years to get to a Forman's slot and pay. He had started work at eighteen and had been working there for forty-seven years. It had only been the last fifteen years that he had a mind job and was getting top pay. He went through his regular routine. Into the locker room he went. He changed into his work clothes and put his lunch in his locker. Just as he stepped in to his work section it started. FOR he's a jolly good fellow which nobody can deny. Small gifts came out and a plaque and yes a gold pocket watch. This was a big strong man, a man's man. He had been in and stepped in and broken up many fights. He had seen fingers and arms lost at this job. There were even lives that were lost. He had gone thru this and had not shed one tear. This day he would shed many tears, more inside than out. He was not shedding tears because of his age but because of the loss, of being a part of something.

  The party stopped as fast as it had started they were off to work. He turned to walk to his little cubbyhole office he had some work schedules to finish. Before he reached the office door he felt a tug at his coat. An office supervisor was telling him that before he did anything else he had to report to personal, in fact I'm suppose to escort you there company policy. As he walked towards the personal office a rush of thoughts went through his head. He had been called to the office before and none of them were good times. This time was different, in the past he had some kind of idea what was going on. This time he didn't have a clue. As he entered the office a mini party of hand shaking took place and then he was led to the personnel supervisor's office. Hi Mike this is a big day for you I bet that you have been looking forward to this day for a long time. Here is a certificate of appreciation along with your paycheck and a bonus separation check. I personally would like to thank you for a job well done. Oh! Jim in the security office would like to talk to you, see you later good luck. Mike was showed the door picking up his office supervisor escort he was walked over to the security section. Hi, Mike I will have to ask you for your gate badge and your keys. We took the liberty of cleaning out your locker and your desk its in the box on the table over there Sam will make sure you get to the front gate OK. As Mike Jones got to his car he couldn't believe what just happened. He checked out the contents of the cardboard box funny it was a lard shipping box. He thought of how that he too had been processed and now was leaving in a lard-shipping box. He looked inside and the first thing he saw was his paddle lock they had cut it off with a bolt cutter. He started to cry. Why did they have to do that those #*#*#*? That little padlock had been with him from the first day on the job. It was more than a paddle lock it had become a good trusted friend that had never failed him. Why couldn't they have asked me for the key, he felt he had failed his friend, his paddle lock for forty-seven years.

When he got home he would set the box aside not looking into again until the lunch started to stink. The paddle lock he put on his nightstand where he saw it in the morning when he awoke and in the evening when he went to bed. It became his symbol of hatred towards the system that he would take to his death. He was a simple man and asked for not many things but he asked to have his friend the paddle lock buried with him in his last will and testament.

Mike Jones became a bitter man when it came to anything that had to do with the government or as he called it "The Damn System". One day he thought of a grand plan. If he were to work under his sons Social Security number it would not show on his record. He could be working again and not lose any of his Social Security benefits. This little trick on the system is just what he needed. He found a night job because his son was working days part time and going to the University. When he took the job he showed his drivers license and his sons Social Security card. Not even his son knew about it he had said that he would have to have his Social Security card for some insurance purpose because he was still in school and qualified as a dependent. Sure enough this little scheme of his worked fine he got his full paycheck and his full Social Security check all the while earning quarters of work for his sons retirement under his sons Social Security number. His secret would follow him to his grave along with his trusted friend the paddle lock. Only years later when his son went to retire would it come to light.

    I want you to come back to your Middle Mind and look around you for your brothers of like mind. I want you to start thinking of the stacking of Lower Minds. Start building a team of people to work magic with. I want you to become more than one. I want you to have the power of the many that multiplies exponentially. This is where one and one equals any number you would like it to be. It all depends on whether you are breeding horses or rabbits. Weather you are one minded or are on the path of the Giving Greater Known. KOZ: NO ONE MIND CAN REACH A HIGHER LEVEL OF THINKING ON IT'S OWN. THE STACKING OF LOWER MINDS IS THE PASSAGE WAY INTO THE KNOWLEDGE OF THE GIVING GREATER KNOWN AND THE ONLY WAY TO JOIN THE COSMIC FAMILY THAT FOLLOWS THE PATH OF THE GIVING GREATER KNOWN. I do hope that you are starting to feel the power as I do. I feel it as a full feeling around my heart. It aches with loneliness for it wants to fill the world with empowerment. Why should I be the only one? Come with me on this grand journey of the inner to master the outer.

***

Saturation Points

I want you to go into your movie picture mind and let me tell you a story that will fill your mind and body. I was sitting in the barracks there were six or eight of us playing poker. We had skipped the chow hall dinner and were going to eat pizza and drink beer. The food was only a phone call away it would be delivered. I'd been playing poker for six hours and getting tired of it. I wondered how could I be getting tired of playing poker, poker was what I would like to be doing over anything else, well almost. I got up the food was here and I was hungry. I got some grumbling from the other players because I was a big winner and they wanted a chance to get their money back or maybe even some of mine. I was not going to be able to eat pizza and play cards at the same time. Greasy fingers and cards don't mix; I assured them when I got done eating I would be back to take the rest of their money. As I was eating pizza I looked over to the candy bar vending machine. I saw that there was only one Butterfinger candy bar left. I thought of how nice it would be to top off my pizza with my favorite candy bar and how when I got finished eating my pizza I would buy it. There was a big pot of money up for grabs in the poker game. This pot was the biggest I had seen for weeks. Damn it all why would I have to be out of the game eating pizza. I decided to do half and half. I would stand and eat pizza and watch the card game too. A guy we called Little Weasel won the pot I kept my eyes on him he owed me money from last weeks poker session. I went to go set back down where I was eating but someone had taken my seat. I looked for my Coke but it was gone. I looked over at the vending machine and my Butterfinger candy bar was gone. As I looked for a replacement candy bar the glare and reflections caught my eye, I was in the Haze.

 I was daydreaming about a way that I could have been eating and playing cards too. Into my mind popped a cartoon from many years back. The cartoon showed a pig strapped into a chair and he was being force-fed one pie after another until he blew up. The pig woke up it was only a dream. I was on Reach One I was in a room that had chests of gold and silver. I could see men trying to fill their pockets and their carry cases to the brim. They would walk over to a weigh in station and a big sign would come on blinking the word (OVER). I could see them go over to a table and start to throw things out of their carry-ons. I could see men looking at what some one else had thrown away and pick it up and add it to their collection. Time and time again they were over weight and getting no were fast.

    I looked over to the card game it was over. Little Weasel had gotten away again. I thought about what I had seen on Reach One and how it related to any thing that I was doing? What I got out of it was that there were limits to every thing or saturation points. As my head got saturated with poker playing it drifted to eating. As I was eating I was not playing poker and as I became full of food I thought about the candy bar. Seeing that I was missing out on a good money pot in the poker game I drifted away from eating and lost my seat and my pop and the candy bar. These saturation points were leading me down paths as the needing to change was felt. In doing so I was missing out on opportunities and getting no were fast. My body was shifting gears then my mind was shifting gears on its own. I didn't feel like I was in control. I felt that saturation points were blowing my neurons around with out a thought process behind it that I had anything to do with. I started to see how this could be turned inside out and be made to work in my favor.

    I started to think of the saturation points that were inherent to the human species. There was the amount of food I could consume in one setting. I could only be in one place at a time. I could only wear so many clothes at one time. I could only read or watch TV. I could only drive one car at a time. If I was doing one I could not be doing the other. I could see how

I could use this to sneak underneath the protective radar of the established Lower Mind. I would not let it know that I wanted to change something I would just give it less time to do something in.

    I would recognize what it was that I was doing that I would like to change. Then set out looking for something that I would rather be doing or could be doing that would chew into its time frame. I could see why the rich got richer and richer. If they had more money than was necessary to saturate their needs the money that was left over would turn over into earning more money. All I would have to do is manage my saturation points. If I was out drinking it would be hard to drink too much if I filled my stomach with water before bellying up to the bar. If I would eat a couple of bagels before going out to eat I would be satisfied with a dinner salad instead of a full-blown steak dinner. I found out that I was saving money and my Lower Mind didn't feel like it was being attacked. KOZ: NATURAL COSMIC LAW WILL OVERRIDE LOWER MIND DESIRES. MASTERING ONES SATURATIONS POINTS CAN AT WILL PUSH THE LOWER MIND INTO NEW DIRECTIONS. Do not let your walk around Middle Mind push this new tool to the side. If you catch it saying I knew that or so what, lock it down. Don't let your Middle Minds unknowing brain step in and ruin your progress. As you have a chance to use this tool many times over you will feel its true power to shape your future. Stay with this message from KOZ and you will take a grand voyage that will put you on the path of the GIVING GREATER KNOWN.

***

GENERATION JUMPING
(A DREAM)

It was a hot summer day it was a very special day. They had come from eleven different states and three countries. All eyes were on Great Great Great Grandfather and Great Great Great Grandson. Food was everywhere and the wine was flowing non-stop. There was no one there outside of the family. The Zambeno family now numbered 126, the 126th was a very special boy child. This child was conceived of mentally many years back. Great Great Great Grandfather Joe Zambeno had his first child at the old age of 16. He was 33 when his first grandson was born. He was 50 when his first Great Grandson was born and 68 when his Great Great Grandson was born. Now at age 86 his Great Great Great Grandson has been born. After all the eating, drinking and dancing got done the family business was attended to. Off by it's self was a set of five tables all in a row. The head of the inner unit families would make the transition to these tables. The process started with the close whisper, mouth touching ear. All that was said was, it's time. All the niceties and games were left behind along with the woman and the children. The order of business was the changing of the will. Zambeno after Zambeno came to the business table. There was Joe Zambeno, Joe Zambeno Jr., Joe Zambeno the 3rd, Joe Zambeno the 4th, 5th... I had been sitting in the car along with the Zambeno family attorney. I was looking for the sign in my rear view mirror when to get out and open the door for the family attorney in the back seat. After some small talk and getting the seating arranged to reflect the family power structure the business got under way. The family business manager stood up and looked towards our car. The family attorney nodded his head and I opened his door and let him out. I did not hear what went on in the meeting but I was told later that it was tax structured will signing. I sat in the car watching but not watching. I had twisted the rearview mirror so I could see when things were done and I could get out and open the door. I had went and done it again I'd fallen into the Haze.

I was on Reach One I came to a door with the words on it, THE BRIDGE TO FOREVER. I opened the door and went in. I could see as far as the eye could see men carrying a large stone on their backs. They were heading for a body of water that I couldn't see the other side of. Wave after wave of men would come to the waters edge drop their rock and walk into the water to be seen no more. To my left I could see a long line of men they were doing things differently. They would get to the waters edge and leap to a stack of rocks, and to another stack of rocks and to another and then throw their rock into the water building the next stack of rocks, and then disappearing into the water never to be seen again. I looked further to my left and I saw a line of men doing things differently. They where passing there rocks forward to the next man in line until it got to the end. The man on the end was building a stone bridge, placing stone after stone. This man would not walk into the water he would walk back down the bridge. Along the way he was greeted and thanked for his lifetime of building the family BRIDGE TO FOREVER. He would be taken care of by the women of the family and play out his life playing with the kids.

The next thing I herd was a tapping on the window the attorney had returned and he was a bit miffed that I had fallen to sleep. That was my last day on that job he let me go. It was many years later that I would run into a man that would further enlighten me on the tax ramifications of the will signing. The practice was called Generation Skipping or Jumping. By the Great Great Great Grandfather willing his assets to his Great Great Great Grandson they would avoid paying inheritance taxes on three generations. This could easily add up into the millions of dollars. I sat and thought about how their family structure was so different than mine. The men in my family only carried one stone to the waters edge and built nothing. I in my life will change this and start the stacking of Lower Minds and build a BRIDGE TO FOREVER. Without this mental Lower Mind Stacking the human sprit feels that all it had done was for not.

    Are you a stacker of one stone or are you joined with many Lower Minds building a Bridge To Forever? Are you becoming more bitter as time goes on or is your heart singing with every beat because you know that you have put your all into pushing your genial code forward. If you are still sucking in a breath of air it is not too late to reach out and start building your Bridge To Forever. Take your walk around Middle Mind and lock it up for it will not understand your actions. Call that held at arms length loved one and pull them in closer and closer. Be damned with your Middle Mind pride. Let it go those thoughts are just eating you up inside. Recapture your spark in life by stopping the drain of Brain Energy from your body. Forgive even if it hurts, forgive even if you must eat your past words, forgive even if it will cost you money. Don't forgive for their sake but yours. See how you may be affecting the people around you with your bottled up hate.

    I want you to go into your movie picture mind and take a walk down a different path. See yourself pulling a heavy fishing net. Your hands are bleeding and your shoulders are worn raw with rope burns. Turn and look into the net it is full of the past, the second after the now. See yourself cutting holes in the net and watching your past float away. See yourself taking this net over to a blue green crevasses and throwing it in. Look at your hands and see them heal instantly. Look to your right to make sure that your Middle Mind is still locked up in the strong box. We don't need its lower level of thinking screwing things up. Feel your shoulders being healed instantly. See yourself standing up straight and feeling ten feet tall. I want you to see yourself showing off a loved one and feel the feelings of being proud boiling in your heart. KOZ: THERE MUST BE A FREE WILL STACKING OF LOWER MINDS TO REACH A HIGHER LEVEL OF THINKING. DO NOT LET YOUR MIDDLE MIND HOLD YOUR PROGRESS BACK. MENTALLY RISE ABOVE YOUR MIDDLE MINDS WEAK WAY OF THINKING. YOU MUST DO THIS WITH HONESTY AND WITH AN OPEN HEART YOU CAN'T FOOL YOUR LOWER MIND INTO ACTION. This is a milestone in your leap into a higher level of thinking. You must take time for all the parts of this book to come together as one. Reread all that KOZ has said. Read as much more as you feel necessary to bring this message into a tighter circle of understanding.

***

Mind Puzzle

I truly have become a different person. When meeting someone I always have my Lower Mind Butterfly net at the ready. Each mind has it's own unique path that it only has traveled. Because of this diversity of thought every thought that will be needed to reach a higher level of thinking has already been thought. These thoughts whisk in and out of our brains many times. If we don't stand at the ready with our Lower Mind Butterfly Net looking to capture somebody's else's Lower Mind Butterflies, how can we be ready to catch our own Lower Mind Butterflies or messages from the Giving Greater Know when they whisk through our brains at light speed or even faster. I was just last week that I caught this beautiful Lower Mind Butterfly from a friend. We were talking about how the spell check on the computer that it would not see a misspelled word if it formed a new word that was spelt correctly. We talked about how confusing the words, to, too, and two were. (Mind Puzzle) How would it be if those three words were in a sentence next to each other? The next day I ran into my friend again, he said "Thanks a lot I must of thought about how to put the words to, too, and two next to each other in a sentence for an hour or more after you left." I could have let this Lower Mind brain pusher whisk through my brain and thought nothing of it. Thank you my friend. I wish that I could have been at the ready with my Lower Mind Butterfly net as he was pondering over those three words. The brain goes into a different side looking mode when it is trying to solve a problem. The brain will look at the easiest way to solve the puzzle and when that doesn't work it shifts modes. The brain goes into a float mode where it travels at a speed greater than light through its brain neural leakage soup. When we are traveling down this non-path of neural leakage soup we are traveling next to the path of the Giving Greater Known. This puzzle-solving mode in our brain is a direct link to the Giving Greater Know. Our neural leakage soup acts like a net and caches in coming messages from other Lower Minds and the Giving Greater Known. Everybody's neural leakage soup is different and pulls in and attracts different incoming messages. The Giving Greater Known of other Lower Minds will not waist their Mind energy sending to a non- receiver.

    When you are using the Inner Eye That Glimpses The Future or Future Building you are in the Brain Puzzle mode searching through your neural soup. You have turned on your cosmic radar and are ready to receive all incoming messages. Where two or more come together with like minds following the path of the Giving Greater Known their neural soups will flow together to combine and build a larger and more tightly woven net.

Now I want you to go into your movie picture mind and see the things that KOZ has given to us, it is time to pull them together into a larger and tighter net. If you went back and read all that KOZ had given us as you were instructed this will come easy to you. If you did not go back and do it now or you will suffer from a whirlwind of brain stirring. I want you to see yourself as a glowing person amongst a field of dim wits walking around like zombies. You are carrying a bucket and on the side of it is written Instant Neural Soup Fluxing. You are going to one person after another and pour the bucket over their heads until you can see it flow over their feet. Your bucket never empties and you never tire. These people stand in a self determined time frame in a stupor and then begin using their bucket of Instant Neural Soup Fluxing. You see them doing the same thing that you were doing, pouring over head after head their bucket. Their buckets never empting and they never tire. I want you to watch them doing this and feel a feeling of joy in their works and see a wave of Mind Energy flowing out over the multitudes.

Come now and listen to a story of bucket pouring. I was sitting in the Moose Lodge bucket in hand. (Brain Puzzle) I asked Gene how long was it now that he had quit smoking? He told me five weeks now. I lifted my bucket and started pouring. Wow that's great I'm proud of you. Still pouring. I now see you in a different light I'm impressed with you. Still pouring. Wow! I can't believe it, must have been hard how did you do it? Gene now shifts to talking about the (Brain Puzzle) how he quit. I could feel and know that the Instant Neural Soup Fluxing had reached his feet. I went and sat at a table behind a man we called Buzz. Gene tell Buzz about your quitting smoking, (Challenging Someone to Challenge Someone Else). Buzz said "I know three weeks now". Gene raised his bucket of Instant Neural Soup Fluxing and poured it on Buzz. He said with emotion with a sense of pride and inner power hugh, "Its been five weeks now". I mentally sneaked up behind Buzz and poured another bucket of Instant Neural Soup Fluxing over his head; when is it your turn... (Challenge) I went back up to the bar I could see and know that the Instant Neural Soup Fluxing had flown over his feet when he bought some nicotine patches from Gene. I will have to see later if Buzz in turn will pour a buck of Instant Neural Soup Fluxing over someone else's head when he gets home.

I want you to go back into your movie picture mind and join me on a most wonderful little story. We were sitting close to each other, she was pouring her Instant Neural Soup Fluxing over me. I was taking it in and combining it with my Neural Soup then reaching down into it with my Neural Strainer and filling my bucket. I would pour my bucket over her and she would go through the same process I did and pour her bucket back over me. This process would go on for hours we were clicking. I want you to go back in your life and find that feeling of clicking with someone. That feeling is the feeling of having a burst and rush of Mind Energy flowing into you. As you receive Neural Soup from someone else your neural soup goes into a fill in the blanks system. It will read all that has been given it in a mode for your Middle Mind to transform the words into mind pictures before it melds with your Neural Soup. Then a splendid dance will be created where every step is stepped off in both Neural Soup Bowls simultaneously. And when you can get your buckets pouring on a constant dribble; then you have found your Lower Mind Cosmic Traveler that will make your journey back to the Collective Family Of The Giving Greater Know a pleasure. KOZ: PULL AS MANY MIND ENERGY POURS TO YOU AS YOU CAN. REACHING OUT TO A HIGHER LEVEL OF THOUGHT WILL TAKE LARGE AMOUNTS OF MIND ENERGY. POUR

FROM YOUR BUCKET OFTEN AND BUCKETS WILL BE POURED OVER YOU AND YOU WILL NEVER DEPLETE YOUR MIND ENERGY AND NEVER GROW TIRED. Now go forth and pour and pour some more. In pouring you will receive more in return than the Middle Mind can grasp. Don't be an island of taking come join with the Collective Family Of The Giving Greater Known.

* * *

THAT'S JUST LIKE

I'm not sure when it starts but I know that it is well established by the age of ten. I was trying to teach my son chess. This is where I think I first recognized the, (That's Just Like) mind shortcutting. My sons name is Oak. One day I said to him that I was going to teach him how to play chess. He said, "That's just like checkers isn't it." I sat there trying to think of a way to take him away from his deeply ingrained past neural paths. I did not want to shut his brain down by it feeling that I was attacking it. I said something like; "No checkers is not like chess". I had gone and done it now. From then on I would have to work around an entrenched Lower Mind. I got through how all the pieces moved and called it quits for the day. My son went to bed and I sat there looking at my reflection off of the dinning room window.

I fell into the Haze I was on Reach One. I was standing in front of a door that had written on it (Same Same No No). I went inside and was greeted by a large Black Lab dog. He was very friendly and was following me around. I saw a park bench and sat down. A lady came by walking a dog I said "Hi" and we started to talk. The two dogs were playing. She left and I got up and started walking, the dog at my heels. We past a park ranger and he greeted us with a good afternoon. I came to a wall with a door in it. Written on the door where the words (No No Same Same) I went inside. A large Black Lab attacks me. I ran over to the park bench and jumped up on it. A lady came by and her dog got in a fight with what she thought was my dog. She cussed me out and stomped off. A park ranger came over and wrote me a ticket for having a dog in the park and for standing on a freshly painted park bench.

    I was back still looking at the window trying to interpret this last trip to Reach One. My mind was on a sideways slip looking for anything in my Neural Soup Bowl that's like what I had seen on Reach One. I did remember the time that I was heading into a bar and I had stopped to pet a dog. He looked friendly enough to me so I put my hand in the window to pet him and he bit me. I found myself doing the same thing that I got bent out of shape over that my son had done, I was doing a (that's just like). I sat there letting the story from Reach One, the chess lesson and the (that's just like) fade away. Holding onto the feeling my mind was feeling when it was doing a (that's just like). My brain felt like it had found an old lost friend. It had found a match so this was a no-brainer. I felt proud and well informed and well versed on that subject. In fact it had a feeling of knowing all that was going to be needed to be known. In an instant it was up to speed using this tool called (that's just like). My brain was feeling a sense of relief that it was not going to have to try or think about anything new. I took these feelings and felt around in them until I could see them as a cherished part of my thinking process. I thought about my son and how he must of felt when I stomped on his feelings of (that's just like). In my mind I was trying to get a handle on the (THAT'S JUST LIKE TOOL). I saw this as a shortcut to my Lower Mind and to other peoples Lower Mind. Instead of saying, No checkers is not like chess. What I should of said was. Yes! That's right there are a lot of things about checkers that are the same as in chess. This wouldn't stomp on his (that's just like feelings). In fact it sends a rush of self-made endorphin over his brain-making it feel good. It would feel so good that it would like to stick around to see if it could get another hit of pleasure endorphin by finding more (that's just like feelings) and have me saying YES! That's great. This interaction smacks of something else. Here I go. This is just like the feeling of pouring a bucket of Instant Neural Soup Fluxing over this person. I want you to go into your mind and see a teacher teaching a class. I want you to see but not be seen. This teacher is of a class of teachers called brain chasers. Listen as the class is being taught. SSH! Just listen now. (TEACHER) "Is there anybody that knows the speed of light"? (STUDENT) It depends on what color it is if it is a red one it is zero, if it is green its as fast as you feel like. (TEACHER) "That's very good I liked that answer. But you left out as fast as your driver license and wallet can afford". The speed of light that I want to talk about is not related to traffic lights. It has more to do with distance....

Did you feel the feelings of this type of teaching? Could you feel how the student felt? I could and they both felt right and good. I want you to feel this feeling over and over and feel how it seems to grow. Get inside this feeling and really feel how it feels. Do this until it builds up inside of you until you feel like passing this newfound feeling to somebody else. Think of what type of student you would have been if you had a teacher that was a brain chaser. Slip back into your movie picture mind. See yourself reaching into your Lower Mind and pulling these feelings out with both hands. Feel these feelings they feel like clay. Mold this clay into a book and see written on it, Mind Chaser. Reach over and open your mental toolbox and open it. Look inside that's right there is a place predesigned for it to set in. Yes this tool was always yours you only had to reclaim it. KOZ: LOWER MIND TO LOWER MIND SHARING OF FEELINGS BUILDS MIND ENERGY IN AMOUNTS THAT THE MIDDLE MIND WILL NEVER GRASP. READING HOW A LOWER MIND FEELS IS A TRUE SHORT CUT TO ANOTHERS LOWER MIND. Go forth and be a reader and teacher of Lower Minds. Feel your feelings, feel their feelings and know the right path to take. Stop stomping on feelings and start seeing and feeling them.

* * *

OPPORTUNITY POSITIONING

There I was again forking out $2.35 cents for a quart of oil. I had bought a full case of oil at 89 cents a quart last month. This was my third time I had forgotten to check the oil before I drove off going to work. I was standing there pouring oil into my engine watching the trickle off of the gold liquid flowing from the bottle.

I had fallen into the Haze and was on Reach One. I was greeted by two men they whisked me off down a hallway in a frantic. They were telling me that I came just in time. There were big problems and I was just the person to solve them. We came to a side hallway the two men just pointed down the hallway. The two men stayed behind I soon came to a sign that read, (Quarantine Highly Contagious). I went through a door at the end of the hallway. It led to a small town the name of the town was OHWELL. I came to a lady she was standing along the road crying. She told me that she had not gotten any mail for months. I looked over at her mailbox and it was turned around backwards and leaning up against a tree. I grabbed the mail box, turned it around and stuck it in the ground along the side of the road. She gave me a look like so what good is that going to do. As I was walking away I looked back and saw the mailman putting mail in her box and the lady was waving at me a hand full of letters. I then came to a man that was standing at the end of his driveway crying. He told me that he wanted to sell his boat and he was not having any luck. I asked him where his boat was he said out back. I went around to the back of his house. There it was covered with a tarp. I pulled it out by the road and put a for sale sign on it. As I was walking down the road I looked back and could see him waving a hand full of money at me as somebody was towing his boat away. I came to a little girl she was looking for her dog. She told me that she could not remember to shut the gate and the dog gets out every day and makes her late for school. I saw a toy bone lying on the ground. I picked it up and tied a string around it and tied it to the gate so it dangled in front of the gate latch. I told her that from now on when she saw the bone that it would remind her of the dog and she would remember to close the gate.

As soon as the oil had all poured out I was back. I took the cap of the oil bottle and set it on my dash. When I got home that evening I saw the cap and went inside and put a quart of oil on the hood of my truck. The next morning I saw the oil bottle checked my oil and it was Ok and put the oil behind the seat of my truck. Thank you Reach One better yet thank you KOZ. The next day I pulled out a camper trailer that I wanted to sell for the last two months and set it next to the street and had it sold that week. I found myself using this tool given to me by KOZ many times. One day KOZ boomed in KOZ: POSITION YOURSELF FOR OPPORTUNITY. With in a month I had studied and taken the SAT scholastic aptitude test and was taking a college class.

I want you to go into your movie picture mind and see a little story of mine. I want you to see it and feel it and mind twist it. I want you to see this powerful tool in action and impress on your Lower Mind of its importance. I want you to go over to the freezer and pull out something cold such as a frozen bag of vegetables. I want you to put your left foot on this frozen bag of vegetables until you have finished reading this little story. Don't let your Middle Mind step in and say anything not even think anything. Hum Old Mc Donald had a farm or the pledge elegance to the flag while you are getting ready to read.

It was break time we all found a shady spot to sit to get out of the heat. We were on an oilrig move in North Dakota in the hottest summer that had been recorded. This was one of the big diesel electric rigs it was going to take 57 truckloads to get it moved. I looked over at the scale car. This man had it made sitting in his air-conditioned car. All he had to do was to weigh the trucks and fill out some paper work. I dreamed a little dream of how that could be me. I got up off the ground and walked over to the scale car. (If your foot is starting to hurt remove it for a bit and then put it back.) I said, "Hey how's it going? How would a guy get a job like yours?" He asked me if I was really interested. I said "you bet I am". He got out of his car and walked over to the truck pusher said something and came back. You are on loan to me for the day. I worked with him that day and was hired the next day. I looked back at my old work mates I could see them staring and wondering how I was able to get that plush job.

Take your foot off of the cold thing and let your foot fully warm up. I want you to set this book aside for exactly 12 minutes and then come back to it. I want you to read this little story again with your left foot on the cold item again. These are very important steps that you are now taking follow them to the letter. Don't let your unknowing Middle Mind get in the way. Things that will be happening and are happening now will not be understood by the Middle Mind and never will be not now or ever. KOZ: REMOVE YOURSELF FROM YOURSELF REMOVE YOUR MIDDLE MIND SO YOUR LOWER MIND CAN BE FULLY ENERGIZED WITH MIND ENERGY. YOUR MIDDLE MIND WILL STEAL MIND ENERGY FROM YOUR LOWER MIND IF YOU ARE NOT AWARE. YOUR LOWER MIND NEEDS LARGE AMOUNTS OF MIND ENERGY TO TAP INTO AND MELD WITH THE GIVING GREATER KNOWN. I want you to see yourself from now on as two different people. The person that you are now and the one that is positioning things, in space and time. See in your movie picture mind a person that is also you out in front of you clearing a path to your future. In real estate the saying is location location location. In your inner space and outer space the new saying is position position position. Go now and let your other self position things in your path that will shape your future, as you desire it. Go Forth And Multiply.

* * *

The Power OF Truth

There are powers that we have no control over, we must abide by their rule. I want you to go into your movie picture mind and listen to and see and feel my story of The Power of Truth. I want you to link this story to a past story that you have already lived. Your past story has the feelings in it that no amount of words can do justice to.

I was in Nice, Ca. volunteering my time working as a bartender for a Northshore private club. It was a Saturday night at seven thirty when everything broke loose. There was an argument over a dice game. I asked the gentleman to leave.

I was told by the district President that I was over-stepping my authority and that I should take my tips and leave. I said "That he also had too much to drink and that he should leave". After passing back and forth a few choice cuss words Buzz grabbed me by the collar and threatened to hit me with a balled up fist. Jaky pulled Buzz's hand off me and I said, " this bar is closed" as I pulled the money from the cash register. I'm asking you all to leave and if you don't I will call the cops. Buzz said "go ahead and call the cops," so I did. I stood my ground and invited any one of them to stay until the cops came if they thought they could pass a sobriety test. They all scattered like a bunch of rats from a sinking ship. The cops came and I pressed charges on Mr. Buzz for assault.

The next Monday I received a letter from Mr. Peck charging me with cussing, shutting a bar down improperly and insulting a lady of the Club. I felt that they were attacking my central core value system of being a giver and not a taker not even with my mouth. I would have to fight. I wrote letters to the regional district president and to Club International, no response. I tried to get another member of the Club, Willy to be a go between me and Buzz. He told me that he didn't want to be involved. I tried to get big Bill the Governor of the club involved he said that he was not going to choose sides and I would just have to wait until after the House Committee Meeting. I called Karla, Buzz's wife and tried to ask her help. She assured me that she didn't for one monument believe that I said anything about her and that she wished that the little boys of the Club would grow up. She said that she would always trust and believe in me that she knew that she was married to an alcoholic jealous husband.

One day she came to visit me at Talley's Family Resort. After talking for a while she said that she loved me and I said I loved her. She asked me if I really meant it and would I take her with me and some day marry her and I said yes. We had both had enough of the lies and being threatened by Buzz him saying that he was going to get his gun and kill us. The plan was in the works. Friday the 18th day of May 01 we set off to make a new life together.

 As I was looking at a set of keys and taking the one off to the car I was giving to Karen I fell into the haze.

 I was on Reach One. I was standing in front of a door on it was written Group Lower Mind Future Building. I opened the door and floated in. I saw a group of men standing in a circle. I could see one man whispering into another man's ear and this man was whispering into another man's ear until the last man in the circle of six was whispering into the first man's ear. From the tops of there heads came a pure light blue light. The light weaved and made a tornado above their heads. The tornado looped to the side and formed a blue screen, which the circle of men moved into.

 I was back on earth I must get going Karla was waiting for me I didn't even take the time to tell Karen that the car was there. I said good-bye to Miss Talley and gave her a hug and kiss. I was in such a hurry to start our new adventure that I had forgotten my laundry in a dryer and some food in a refrigerator. I was trying to drive and think at the same time about what I had seen on Reach One.

 Our first stop was at Sentry Market so that Karla could stop and say good-bye to her co-workers and her boss. I stayed in the truck and was thinking about my last trip to Reach One. I could not seem to get a grasp when KOZ bombed in: THE LOWER MIND DOES NOT HAVE THE POWER TO PUSH THE FUTURE ON A PATH OF NON-TRUTH. THAT A LOWER MIND FLUXING POOL WILL ONLY BE ABLE TO CHANGE THE FUTURE ON A COURSE THAT IS IN ACCORDANCE WITH PURE COSMIC LAW.

TRUTH PREVAILS OVER LIES EVERY TIME. Koz had done it again he had poured over my neural soup a fluxing catalyst that brought every thought in my mind into focus.

All I could do now is set in wonder and thank the men in the circle of Lower Mind Fluxing. They surely pushed my future into a beautiful state of happiness. Thank you Buss, Hap, Big Bill, Lynn and anybody else that bought into the story of how bad a guy I was. Thank you Buzz for laying down the law to Karla and threaten her with the idea that you would kill her if she ever saw me again. You pushed her to make a choice. Oh! How happy a man you have made me. KOZ: THOSE THAT TWIST AND TRY TO PUSH COSMIC TRUTH TO A FALSE PATH WILL HAVE THINGS TAKEN AWAY FROM THEM. THERE IS NOT AN EVEN SCALE OF GIVE AND TAKE ONLY GIVE AND TAKE. Oh! What powers the mind has to push cosmic energy around to build the future. The time factor that was needed to shape my future building was less than six months for now it is the 18th of May 01. I got all I asked for and as I predicted the Giving Greater Known added so much more. I am glad that I did not let my Middle Mind get in the way. I was very lucky that I had Koz to reinforce how powerful the tools were that he had given me. Stay with me we have such a long ways to go yet. Get to work putting these future building tools to work in your life and you will feel the power of change. Don't be one of the people that I left behind that are still mind looping in their small circle of existence. Lets see; oh I wonder what Bert (one of the club members) is doing on this Monday morning? Oh! I know he is cleaning the bar at the lodge poor little man stuck in his small mind loop just looking for another free drink. I will pray and try to send some Mind Energy his way even though I think it will be a waste of energy on him but it will regenerate me. I forgive you Bert.

***

Guess Link

I want you to come along with me on a trip that will never end. Oh but you are already on that trip if you have let your Lower Mind fall into the Guess Link Loop. Do you hear yourself saying well I thought that he was going to do this or that? Or that he was going to say this or that. Or that he was going to move this way or that. And that is why I was not expecting him to do what he did.

I was looking out over the waters watching the sun set. The waves from a long ways off were jumping up to kiss the sun. I fell into the Haze and was on Reach One. I was in a confused state I had looked to see what color my shirt was and it had many colors on it. It was a checkerboard pattern of many different colors. What color door was I looking for? I had no clue. I tried one after another, door after door. My hand and wrist was getting sore from twisting doorknobs and pushing. After pushing on over three hundred doors I came to a door that was a muliti -colored door that was an exact match to my shirt. I grabbed the doorknob and the door opened on its own. I walked in and was in a circular room that had many muliti-colored doors. I went in one of them and found myself walking through a glass tube I could see that it was going to loop back to one of the other doors in the circular room. I thought that this would be a waist of time so I turned around and went back through the door that I had just gone thru. I was still in a glass tube and I could see that it was going to another door in the circular room. I felt frustrated and did not know which way to turn.

I was back on earth hugging the lady that I love Karla.

I knew instantly what was meant by my latest trip to Reach One. That I was not going to guess what was going to happen anymore. I was going to rely on only what is happening at the time and what I had structured through Lower Mind Future Building. In my minds eye I saw myself write down the words, guess, bet, and maybe on a piece of paper and saw myself throw them into a blue-green crevasse. My life from that time on took on a very directional forward moving structure. I would reach out to many Lower Minds to find champions and tap into the Giving Greater Known through my Higher Mind. I must gather large amounts of Mind Energy the fuel that this process needs to run on. I feel so lucky to have Karla by my side for she through me and me through her we will be able to give and receive large amounts of Mind Energy. And as she wittiness my giving to others and I witness her giving to others it will grow in strength and take on a different form. There will be a glow between our eyes that will pass between us large amounts of cosmic understanding. This glow that is seen is pure Mind Energy that has gone through a double Lower Mind Fluxing and has folded over on itself many times and become a super charged flow of energy. If you have not found your Mind Energy Fluxing mate yet you must take action.

    I want you to find a place where you can take out the whip and make your Lower Mind pay attention. Whip your Lower Mind until you see it begging you to stop. You must change your Lower Minds path if you have been without a Mind Energy Fluxing Mate for longer than five years. Your lazy Lower Mind has said little lies to you to keep things simple and easy for it to work with. Have you heard yourself say any of these things that are a sure sign that the lazy Lower Mind needs to be whipped into a path change. (I don't think that I will ever get married again.) (Why do I need some in my life screwing things up?) (I'm too old to change my ways now.)

(Who would want me any way?) If any one of these have crossed your lips you are in a deep dark hole of Lower Mind stagnation. You must take action fast and swiftly or you will go into a downward spiral into depression and even suicidal tendencies.

It is time for you to reach into your mental toolbox and pull out the tools needed. Get busy living your dreams or you are just waiting for death to knock on your door. Come along with me as I dream a dream of change and see how it is done so you may do it too.

I see myself rising out of my body I am standing there with clipboard in hand. I'm watching myself going through its daily routines, eating up my life. I watch myself go through a compressed month of activities. Upon examining what I have been doing with my life I'm looking for looping patterns that take me through the same doors and on the same paths. I see myself putting big nails in the doors and tank barriers across the paths. I know that these doors and paths are looping back on each other and are holding me in a holding pattern in life. I now take out my whip. Oh! Do I have to say the J word (JAIL). With the mention of this word I see my Lower Mind snap to attention ready to receive my instructions. Now I replace the doors and paths with different ones. Instead of mowing the lawn on Sundays I'm going to hire someone to do it and I am going to church. Snap that whip and don't let your Middle Mind walk around self get in the way. See yourself making sure that your Middle Mind is in the strong box and locked and buried. Replace each and every life stealing looping doors or paths. Do this for thirty days whether you like it or not. And let your Lower Mind know that you are going to start taking things away from it if it dose not tow the line of change. KOZ: DO NOT LET YOUR LOWER MIND STEAL YOUR LIFE AWAY WITH IT LAZINESS. USE THE COSMIC TOOLS

GIVEN TO YOU TO MAKE COSMIC LAW WORK FOR YOU AND YOUR POWER OF CHANGE. As you change and as I change so the world will change. Stay with me and the collective Giving Greater Known and we will change this world together into a wonderess place to live.

* * *

Inner Small Talk

I was working on my Jeep. I was replacing a flywheel. It was done all but for putting it back together. I could not get the transmission and transfer case to line up with the engine. Every thing I tried seemed to fail. I was saying a lot of cuss words and saying negative things and thinking negative thoughts. I was saying things like I should of not even started working on this @#$#$ Jeep. I was thinking that I was going to have to have it towed in and have someone else put it together. My mouth never stopped my brain was in a stir and I was getting nowhere fast. Another drip of something dripped on my forehead. This drip was very different it felt like it had hit my head and kept on going. As it touched my brain Koz boomed in. This time was the first time that I really felt any pain when Koz tuned in. My head felt like some one had it in a vise and the pressure was being applied. KOZ: KEEP WORDS STILL FOR THEY IMPRESS THE LOWER MIND. WHILE THE LOWER MIND IS LISENING TO WHAT YOUR MIDDLE MIND IS SAYING IT IS NOT WORKING THROUGH THE HIGHER MIND AND PULLING IN ANWSERS FROM THE GIVING GREATER KNOW. KEEP YOUR MAN MADE WORDS SILENT OR THEY WILL FILL YOUR PRESENT AND AGAIN BECOME YOUR FUTURE. WORDS MEANT OR NOT MEANT STIR THE LOWER MIND

INTO NON-ACTION.

I was on Reach One I was standing in front of a long table of food and drink. Above the table was written the word in big letters GIFT. I saw some people rush over and fill a tray of food and walk away. There were other people that would look at the food and the other people taking it and shake their heads. The head shakers would not take any food they would just walk with their hands behind their backs shaking their heads. I walked over to one of the head shakers and asked him why he had not taken any food. He told me that it was poisoned. I ask another head shaker and he said the same thing. I asked him why he thought it was poisonous he pointed to the word GIFT on the wall and gave me a look of are you some kind of stupid or what. I stopped another head shaker and asked him about the word GIFT and what it meant to him and he said that he was from Germany and in the German language the word gift or giftig meant poisonous.

I was back on earth laying under my Jeep the drip had run down the side of my face and into my ear. I laid still thinking over my vision on Reach One. After a long spell of thinking Koz boomed in KOZ: WORDS ARE LIKE POSION TO THE LOWER MIND AND WILL MIND STIR IT INTO NON-ACTION. I laid their saying nothing about the whatever it was in my ear I was just looking letting the optical extension of my brain, work on the problem. Without words so that my Lower Mind could tap into my Higher Mind and have it gather answers from the Giving Greater Known. It did not take long I had come up with an answer that involved using a scissor jack and a come-a-long. One end attached to the end of the transmission and the other end attached to my front bumper. In a matter of minutes I had it put together.

I wondered and thought about how many times in the past I let the words and the body antics of throwing things or just throwing my hands up in the air and walking away control my life by brain stirring my Lower Mind. In my inner self I feel a conflict. On one side there are the words and on the other side there are no words. One side is saying how good it is to have many good and powerful words to use. On the other side it is saying that words are mind stirring. For me it is a easy choice for I am going to listen to what Koz has told me and leave the small mean nothing words behind and be a person of few words. On this path of few words coming from the mouth you will run into a lot of distracters. For without words they do not have a handle on who you are. They can't twist your words into their own agendas. They can't use them to look into your deep imbedded hard fought for thought patterns. They will try to pump you with probing questions. Are you feeling all right? You have not said much today you are awfully quite. Did I say something that was wrong that made you mad at me?

When I hear these type of probing questions I know that I am on the path of the Giving Greater Known and they do not have a clue as to where my mind is and it makes me fell powerful and alone all at the same time. KOZ: MAN MADE WORDS WILL HOLD YOU BACK. COSMIC LAW WILL SHOW THE WAY. LET YOUR GIFTS FROM ME FILL YOUR BRAIN AND IT WILL JOIN THE COLLECTIVE FAMILY OF THE GIVING GREATER KNOWN. Stay with me as Koz leads us down grander and grander paths of awareness. Stand with me with our cosmic butterfly nets at the ready and we together will shape the grand future to come. Listen to your mind and the Lower Mind will choose what needs to be reinforced. Re-read areas which your mind feels like it wants to refresh it's thoughts. Let your mind flow freely through these powerful truths of Cosmic Law and you will speed your way to joining the Collective Family of the Giving Greater Known.

* * *

Reticular Activating System

I was on my way to work. I could see that one of my tires was a little low. As I was putting air in I saw that on the inside of the tire it was wore down to the core threads. I changed it out with my spare, which did not look much better. I checked the oil I was two quarts low. As I was waiting for the oil to pour into the engine I checked the water level in the radiator. That's right it was low and needed some water and antifreeze. I got in and tried starting my car and it barely was turning over. I found the battery charger and hooked it up. I went over to my hunting truck and tried starting it, it was dead. I jerked the battery out of it and put it in the oven. I popped open the trunk I was looking for my jumper cables. Yup, they weren't there or any place else I looked. I took the battery charger off the car and hooked it to the battery in the oven. I had a fifteen-minute time frame to get the car started and still make it to work on time. The battery was so hot that I had to use a pair of gloves and a rag in both hands to pick it up. After installing it I tried starting the car it turned over like mad but would not start. I poured some gas down the carburetor and it started. Off to work I went. I looked at the gas gauge it was almost on empty. I got to Tammen Oil looked into my wallet and there was no money I put it on my gas card. During my frantic rush to get the car started I did not make a lunch and with no money I was going to have a hungry day.

As I was driving to work I was thinking about how was I able to let things get so out of working order. What was the problem why was everything falling apart. I got to the parking lot at work I looked at my watch. I held my watch out the window so the parking lot lights would shine on it so I could read it, that's right the dome light in the car was not working. As my breath turned to vapor and fogged over my watch and the lights danced over it I fell into the Haze.

I was on Reach One watching one person after another come up to me and say I forgot what I was going to ask you. They would turn away and I could see them loop back towards me and again say I forgot what I was going to ask you. Than a man with a list walked up to me and read off a list of things that he needed. I turned around and there on a shelf was everything that he needed. I saw him pushing his cart away and other people looking into it and talking to him. He was handing them his list and pointing to me.

I got to the time clock it was out of order so I could not swipe my card thru it to register my arrival time. I went to my shop and started to think about what I had seen on my last trip to Reach One. Koz Boomed in; KOZ: STOP TRYING TO ANALYZE YOUR TRIPS TO REACH ONE WITH YOUR MIDDLE MIND. YOUR MIDDLE MIND WILL NEVER GRASP THE IMPORTANCE, IT IS AT TO LOW OF A THOUGHT LEVEL. ALL FROM REACH ONE IS DIRECTED TO YOUR LOWER MIND IN A FORM THAT IT WILL READILY ABSORB. I stopped thinking about Reach One and started thinking about it again. And as soon as I started thinking about Reach One my temples and forehead would start aching and throbbing. Even now when I am just writing about it to tell you my head is throbbing.

When I got home even though I was very hungry the first thing I did was to make a checklist for the operation of my car that was done the night before. I find myself using checklist even to this day. My Lower Mind is indeed impressed by the spoken and written word and goes into action. As Karla and I are traveling we go through a morning checklist. The first thing is checking the engine oil. Un-plug the electric cord. Close all windows and hatches. Check to see that all side compartment doors are latched. Take off the back step and put it in the camper. This seems like a simple little list that I should not need a list. This is my proud Middle Mind stepping in trying to impress me that it can do just fine on its own that I need not bother the Lower Mind with such trivial things. I know the shortcomings of the Middle Mind so I going to stay with my checklists. KOZ: THE MIDDLE MIND IS A SUB-LEVEL THINKING SYSTEM THAT IS PROGRAMED TO KEEP THE BODY IN ORDER FOR A PLACE TO HOUSE THE LOWER AND HIGHER MINDS. IT HAS A NARROW RANGE THAT WILL FOCUS ONLY ON THE TASK AT HAND AND FILTERS THE REST THROUGH. It was many years later that I ran into the man made words that were trying to explain what Koz led me to understand. It was the Reticular Activating System, a process of the mind to skip over or not pay attention to anything that was not needed to complete the task at hand. I sometimes wonder why that the school systems or the government doesn't want me to know the truth about my own brain and how it works. Are they afraid of what powers a collective thought force would have? I think they want to keep us as gathering bees and not thinkers of how things could be. Thank you Koz for showing me another path. I just hope I don't let you down. I hope I will be able to finish this book of yours.

* * *

Moving Body Language

I was sitting in a restaurant in Upper Lake Ca. I could not take my eyes off of her. She was floating thru space and time with the grace of a ballerina. Her movement was a joy for the eye to see. She was dancing thru life with a feeling of effortlessness. Her whole body would move with a fluidity just to pick up a coffee cup and then again to gently lift the coffee pot and with a smooth flowing movement pour the coffee into the cup. She gracefully pirouetted away, which sent a feeling of please don't go away thru my whole body. I was done eating but I still sat there watching her. I sipped my coffee slowly. Why was I so captured by this delightful specimen of mankind? I ask for another cup of coffee just to watch her move. As I was stirring in the cream and sugar my eye was pulled into looking at the reflections off the surface of the coffee.

 I fell into the Haze I was on Reach One. I was standing in front of a door written on the door are the words, Movement Synchronizing. I walked in I was greeted buy three men we floated down a path. We came to a group of other men. One of the three men with me took off towards them. He kept his eyes glued to the path and in a marching style of walk went right past the group of men. The second man in my group headed towards them. He was walking with an ease of strolling thru a park. The men in the group were say things to him but he didn't answer. The second man of my group got by. The third man walked slowly as he was looking at a map. He was approached by three men from the group and was lead off behind a wall. I was being asked if I would like anything else. As I am writing this I have a feeling of loss that she is in Ca. and I am in Montana now. Even though I knew that I could not have a relationship with her, my body intellect is attracted to her and does not want to let her go. I want to take your mind down a story path so that you can feel the feelings of Body Movement.

  It was a sad day for the king of lower Prussia what was he to do. All of his fields of wheat had burned and the grain bins were so low that his subjects were going to starve this winter. He had called in all of his smartest men to come up with some answers. Only those with an idea need show up. After listening to all the ideas there was not one that the king liked. In came the court jester dancing his way across the floor. The king was so outraged by this show of aloofness and foolishness that he announced off with his head. The Bishop and some of the other kings advisors asked mercy for the jester for he was only doing his job to make light of things. The King said my word as spoken stands. But I will allow the jester to choose the way that he shall die. The jester danced to the right then back to the left acting as only as he could even while looking death in the face. Bowed in front of the king and said you're Majesty I would like to die of old age. The king laughed and said so be it. The jester then asked the king to hear his suggestion. The King nodded that it would be Ok. I suggest that you make a contest of the problem. I want you to give five pieces of gold to the person that could harvest the most wild oats and put them into your grainery. The king did so and there was enough grain to last the winter. The jester had danced his way into and out of trouble.

    I want you to go into your movie picture mind and see and feel the feelings of body movement thru my eyes. I was with Karla we were at a bar eating and drinking. We were done and She went to the bathroom. We were in Polson, Montana we had driven in from Libby, Montana I had been setting all day. It felt good to be standing still and to be standing. I was shifting my weight from one side to the other slowly working out stiffness. Karla came out of the bathroom she was in a   different mood. She asked me was I ready to go? There's your coat and then she asked me why was I standing. She was trying to read how I was thinking by how my body was moving or positioned. She took it to mean that I was mad at her for taking so long in the restroom. These were the days that she was using the restroom to sneak a smoke. I had shifted her Lower Mind with my body movement. I wondered how many times in the past had I shifted somebody's way of thought with my body motions.

I have become a person that has become very tuned into how I move my body or don't move my body. I have found out that I can shift at will how some one thinks about me with body movements alone. When working all I had to do was just move ten percent faster than my fellow workers to look like I was doing things a lot faster then the rest. The fact that I was getting less done seemed not to matter. What mattered was the perception that I was moving faster and cared about a time factor of some kind in getting the job done. Listen real closely as I tell you these next words. (The mind makes itself feel good when it thinks that it can read another's persons thoughts by their body language). KOZ: THE MOVEMENT NOT THE WORD WILL PUSH THE LOWER MIND. THE MOVEMENT WILL ALWAYS OVER-RIDE THE WORD WHEN SHIFTING THE LOWER MIND. OLD SYSTEMS THAT HAVE BEEN INGRAINED PUSH THE NEW WORDS A SIDE. I wonder at times how much of my life I have just thrown away because I was just floating thru life without guidance. At times I curse this book as a burden that I would like to get done and over with. But most of the time I am so glad to have Koz in my corner leading the way. I have been told by Koz of things to come that the lower thought level of the mass majority would not believe to be possible. Stay with this transformation of the mind and you will along with me be able to partake in grand things to come.

* * *

WHEN THE WIND BLOWS

I was being mind bent and I did not understand why. I was throwing things and saying a lot of trashy words. It was a warm sunny day one of the ones you think about all winter long wishing they would come sooner. I was roofing and then I was not roofing. I found myself setting in a bar drinking and in a better mood. It was early; the after work crowd was not going to start trickling in for another hour and a half. When they did I was three or four drinks ahead of them. In they came one at a time or in small groups. There seemed to be an uneasiness in the air. They were finding a place to set and drink. They had a quietness that sent out a message of leave me alone. After a few drinks you could see this edge ware off and them loosening up. They would start to say small four or five word statements.

    I want you to go into your movie picture mind and see, smell, taste, and feel the goings on this day. Set down with me and have a few drinks of your choice even if it is water. Listen now to some of what is being said at the next table. Did you see that piece of metal fly? That thing went right by my head. Yhea! Did you see that aluminum latter blow over and hit the truck? Wow! If some one had been standing there they would have been hurt. There came a moment of silence and then it would start up again. Did you see how mad Jerry got when his hat got blown off his head for the fourth or fifth time? Then after a few drinks the mood shifted and the funny was lurking about. Did you see when Jack all most took a flying lesson off of the roof when the wind caught the tin he was carrying? If he didn't let go he would have went on a flying vacation to the hospital. The funny bone was struck and they started to laugh at what had happened. They had twisted in their minds the serious to the laughable. They had found a way to release the pressure of a dangerous windy day through laughter.

    The rub started when a new person came in from the other world and wanted no part of any kind of laughter or funning around. The beast was about and he wanted to come out and play. It did not take much and the fists were flying. The group that had shifted into the laugh it off mood had said something to a new person just in from the real world. It went something like, look at the hairdo on that one, looks like he got a dirt blow dry. I thought you, one of the inside mechanics would be all fancy cleaned up. That day all the shop bays were filled and Mike had to do a break job outside on two different flat bed trailers. He was not in the laugh it off mode and replied, do you think you can straighten my hair out as he walked over to the table with balled up fists. All it took was a tug on his arm and the fight was on. It was not my fight so I moved away taking my drink with me. I sat so I could see the goings on in a mirror. I had fallen into the Haze I was on Reach One.

    I was in a long hallway packed with people looking for the right color door. I looked at my shirt and it was a blue and white one. I could see a door with the same color so I started for it. The crowd was moving the other direction and I was not able to move towards the door. I saw another door my color that was down stream from the crowd's push and started heading in that direction. Just as I was going to reach out and grab the door knob a man pushed by me and I was now moving away from the door as the crowed shifted in the other direction. I was feeling frustration and anger. I saw another door my color and headed for it, my mood had shifted I was going to get to that door even if I had to do some pushing and shoving of my own. I was pushing and shoving and as I was right at the door I pushed a man aside and he fell to the floor. I saw him lying there holding his head. I looked around and saw everybody stop moving and then start moving away from me. Two men put handcuffs on me and led me away. I looked down into my drink and only saw the bottom of my glass. I looked into the mirror and saw two police officers. I found myself slipping out a back door.

Now come with me as I take you on a story that I lived. I was into my second day of my new life with Karla. We had driven from Ukiah, Ca. to Noya Bay. We were having Margaritas on the rocks with salt around the rim, waiting to be seated for lunch. We were at the Harbor restaurant right on the water. I had folded a heart out of a dollar bill and had given it to the bartender. We were shown our table it was perfect and worth waiting for. We ordered fish, mine was sole and was very good. The waitress said that she had seen the heart I had folded and said that she and the bar tender and the rest of the crew liked it very much. I asked if she would like me to fold her something. She whipped out a dollar bill saying please. I folded her a whale I could see her showing it to the other waitresses. I was thinking how I wanted to be done with this book and get on to my next. I wanted to write a book on origami for a dollar bill. I could see how people liked my origami and liked sharing them with others. The waitress came to our table with two drinks on the house saying how much they enjoyed my origami. She asked where we were from and where we were going. I said that I was writing a book and we were traveling up the coast. She asked me what the book was about. I said "Oh it's on how the brain works. I asked if she would like to be in my book and she declined.

Now I want you to stand with me with your Lower Mind Butterfly net at the ready. I want you to catch this next cosmic pearl and put it into your mental toolbox. The waitress said "That if I wanted something for my book I should write something about when the north wind blows." Hold your net at the ready here it comes. She then said, "That the wind blowing produces negative ions and makes people go into a crazy mode. Just ask the teachers or law enforcement officers." Did you catch it? KOZ: THOUGHT PRESSURE WILL SO PUSH THE LOWER MIND INTO A STATE OF MIND

STIRRING THAT IT WILL LAXEN THE GAURIDAN AT THE GATE AND THE BEAST WILL BE ABOUT. USE A MIND WEDGE TO CONTROL SUCH PRESSURES. I'm having a hard time seeing how this cosmic pearl that I just ran across was going to be shapened into a tool that I could put into my mental toolbox. KOZ: KNOWING THE KNOWLEGE AND SEEING THE PRESSURE IS THE TOOL. It hit me like a bolt of lighting this message from the beyond was pure and to the point. I saw in my mind's eye a book and written on the book was the words LOWER MIND PRESSURE. I see myself putting this book into my mental toolbox right in the spot already made for it. I realize that this tool was always mine I just had to re-awaken it. I am growing weary of writing this book and would like to get on with my life but I have been told that there is much more that needs to be done and time grows short.

* * *

MIND WEDGE

I'm having a tuff time staying tuned in and writing this book. My mind wants to wander in all types of directions that are taking time from my writing. I have come way to far to give up now. KOZ: FOCUS THE MIND WITH A DOUBLE MIND WEDGE. GO INSIDE AND BUILD A STRUCTURE OUT OF PURE MIND ENERGY. SEE A WEDGE ONE EDGE THE WIDTH OF YOUR BRAIN. THE OTHER EDGE AT THE POINT HAS A MUCH SMALLER WEDGE POINTING TOWARDS THE BRAIN. I sat for a long time just looking at nothingness wondering what to make of this last input from Koz. I sat looking past the edge of my computer screen into the dark. I ran my cursor down to the bottom of the screen to check the time. It was 3:44 am. I closed my eyes wondering why I was up so early writing. I fell into a deep sleep. When I awoke I again scrolled down to see what time it was 5:33. I could remember everything that took place in my dream. Koz had manifested an image of himself. I looked into his eyes and a flash of green blue light flowed from his eyes to mine. I had at an instant received a Mind Energy transfusion from Koz. What he showed me made a profound impression on my brain and set me down a new path at a higher level of thinking.

    I want you to go into a slumped down position and go into your movie picture mind and see my dream from Koz. I was walking down the dirt road that went past the front of my farm site in South Dakota. I was on an evening walk looking for prairie agates. I would walk to the west letting the suns angle help me spot agates. I was knocked to the ground. All I could think of was that there was going to be a lot of damage from an earthquake that could send a shock wave as strong as that one. I stood up I was now facing east. The wind had an eerie straight and even flow to it. It increased to a point that I was being pushed backwards. The ground at my feet felt like Jell-O. A wave of earth was coming my way the last thing I saw was the neighbor's farm house that was three quarters of a mile down the road above me about two hundred feet in the air. In the next split second I thought of how that the only survivors may be who ever was in orbit at that moment. I thought of all things done by mankind and hoped that there was a record of these some were out there in space safe from this our last day. Even though my body was gone the dream went on. I was led by the hand by Koz over to a window. I looked out the window and this is what I saw. I saw earth and it was not round it was shaped like a jelly donut. Out of the center was squirting a large mass of cream. This formed into a column that made it look like a mushroom. This column receded and I could see a like column push out the backside of the planet. The whole earth was then covered with a chocolate blanket cloud. I was led away we went through a door. I saw a mass of people standing and crying. A man appeared and went over to a grease pencil board and picked up an eraser and whipped the words off the board. I could hear the people saying as they faded away how could of this happen we were so close what went wrong. KOZ: THEY FOUGHT OVER A ROCK THAT WAS NEVER MENT TO BE THEIRS. THE ROCK WAS THEIR BIRTH MOTHER ONLY A SEED POD. THEY WOULD NOT HAVE ANOTHER CHANCE IN A BILLION BILLION YEARS. I was led to a room that had only one table in it in the center of the room. Lying on the table was a brain a wedge and a book. In from a side door came a group of four men. They were pushing a bed on wheels you see in a hospital and some other medical equipment. I was laid on the table. I floated out of my body and stood there as an observer. They took out my brain and put the one on the table in and I saw myself get up and walk away. I could see a foggy cone wedge shape along side of my head and it was pointing to a book. I saw written above a door the words LAST CHANCE FOR MANKIND. I was pushed out the door and I was standing in front of a crowd they were all standing and clapping. I turned to my left and as plainly as I could see my own hands I saw a beautiful black lady holding my book high and saying thank you. I stood and cried and she was crying too. The crowed stood and clapped and I could see them also crying. I saw a blue light flow over them and saw them looking at each other and shaking hands and hugging each other. I felt inside of me a rush of relief as though a heavy weight was lifted off of my shoulders. This seen faded away and again I saw myself walking down my dirt road looking for stones. I saw myself stop and return to the house. I sat on a chair and closed my eyes. I saw myself in my mental workshop making a Mind Wedge. I saw a working model and how to use it. All that need be done is to point the Brain Wedge at what ever the task is at hand. It will let into your brain what it was focused on through the small wedge and the larger wedge will divert all other distractions around the brain. I saw a pure blue light going straight into the brain and a flow of white light flowing around the brain. I saw myself opening my mental toolbox and placing it into a preformed spot made for it. It went through my mind that this tool was always mine I just had to reawaken it inside me. KOZ: THE MIND WEDGE I GIVE TO YOU NOW TO FINISH THIS BOOK. THE WHOLE PROCESS OF MANKIND JOINING THE COLECTIVE FAMILY OF THE GIVING GREATER KNOWN NEEDS THIS BOOK. I know now the importance of getting this book done. I will use my mind Wedge tool to keep focused. Now no matter what wind blows I can keep my mind focused. Thank you Koz for this new tool that you have added to my mental toolbox. Stay with me as we awaken many more tools and add them to our mental toolboxes.

* * *

LETTING HABITS RULE

She was a tall girl for her age I a tall boy. We met in 1960 or 61. We were both the same age but she was a grade ahead of me. We had fallen in love in Zwiebruken Germany on a military instillation. Her father was a sergeant in the Army and I was a son of an Air Force sergeant. We were very young both of us twelve years old. We would stand apart at school only winking at each other and at times we were bolder blowing kisses when there was nobody looking. After school we would meet down stairs in the basement of her housing unit where the storage and maid's rooms were. We would stand or sit on the steps and kiss until she heard her mother or father come home. At times she would tell me to wait. I could hear her say, "Hi dad I'm home I'm outside playing". I heard her father say Ok. She was soon again by my side. She would melt into my arms and me into hers. Her folks would call her in for super and I would head for home. This lasted this secret meeting in the basement for about three weeks. One day I suggested that we meet at a tree that the kids called Old Zwei. It was a Saturday it was a warm summer day the meeting time was set for 1:00 O'clock pm. All week long the week before we would plan our secret meeting. If one of us had not showed up by 1:30 something had happened with our parents wanting to go some place or wanting us to do something. Friday the day before the big meeting everything was a go. As I was walking home after meeting Ruth Montgomery all I could think of was how good it was going to be. Maybe we would lie in the grass and kiss and who knows what all might happen. I was sure some feeling around and exploratory kisses for sure. I was there early and she showed up a little after 1:00 O'clock. We were not too sure of what was going to happen. We were going through some warm up kissing and feeling around. I had her backed up to Old Zwei kissing her. We heard a rustle coming through the bushes. They went past us two of my school chums. As they past one of them said that he had a pack of his fathers cigarettes. I was off with them not even saying a word to Ruth. After I had my fill of smoking I remembered my dear Ruth I went to pick up where we had left off. She did not wait for me. She was gone in fact she was gone forever. I tried many times in the next week to say that I was sorry she was having nothing to do with me. Wherever you are Ruth Montgomery I want you to know that even now at the age of fifty-two I still think of you my first true love. I was just a foolish boy that let a habit rule my world.

I have sat many times thinking of my stupid actions that day. All I can do is now think of what might have of happened on that fine summer day. My mind now thinks more of the why it happened. How were mere cigarettes able to push my life around? I know now that it was not the cigarettes it was the habit that pushed me around. I had a choice either a person or another hit of nicotine. My body addiction won out and I lost out. I used this feeling of loss when it came time for me to quit smoking in 1970 ten years later. Thank you Ruth Montgomery I owe you a lot maybe my life. Oh! How I wish I could see you one more time and tell you how sorry I still feel, fifty years later, forgive me. I am now on the receiving end of your feelings and I now know how you felt. I know now why you sent me on my way if I thought a habit as dirty as smoking was more important than you were. Good for you Ruth Montgomery you were right I didn't deserve having you as a girlfriend. In the past I thought that love would win out and I lost. I was setting one day thinking of past loves and old baggage and habits. I was staring off over my woodland property watching the gold colored leaves flicker in the wind. I fell into the Haze.

I was on Reach One standing in line in front of a window. Over the window were the words Pay Window. The line was not moving. I stepped to one side to look down the line and I could see that the window was closed and there was a note taped to the window. I left my spot in line knowing that I would loose my spot. When I read the note it said that the pay office has moved to room 16 three doors to the left. I went three doors to my left and got paid. I went past the line at the old pay office and there was still a line. I walked over to one man standing in line and showed him my money and told him about the new pay office. Listen very closely to what he said. "I have always gotten my pay from this window and I 'm not changing now, you just want my spot in line." I told him about the note on the window but he would not believe me. The next payday came and they were still there waiting. I saw one lady with her two kids trying to pull her husband out of line but he was not going to be moved. She finally gave up and I saw her walk away with another man that had come from the new pay window.

    I was back on earth, my son had driven up the driveway. I told him that it was not going to work out between me and Gail that I was going to have to ask her to leave. Her smoking and drinking habits were more important to her than I was and she could have them and leave me behind. I thought she would stay but the habits won out and I was left heart broken. I swore that I would not put myself into that position again. KOZ: YOUR HABITS ARE OVERRIDING YOUR THOUGHTS AND PUSHING YOU AROUND. HABITS COME IN MANY FORMS AND INTENSITY LEVELS. ONE CAN BE BLINDED BY A HABIT SO AS NOT TO SEE A HABIT OR TO THINK THAT IT WILL BE EASILY CHANGED. BECOME A HABIT AVOIDER NOT A HABIT COLLECTOR. YOUR HABITS ARE HARD ENOUGH TO DEAL WITH DON'T CHOOSE SOMEONE WITH HABITS THAT ARE DEEPLY INGRAINED. MOST PEOPLE DON'T THINK AT A HIGH ENOUGH LEVEL TO GET RID OF HABITS.

    I want you to go into your past and pull out the feelings of being hurt by somebody's habits. Think about the feelings and let the habit fade away. Feel these feelings until you feel the hurt and the mad flow over you. I want you to make sure that your Middle Mind is locked up and buried. See yourself reaching down through the top of your head and pulling these feelings out the top of your head. See yourself taking these feeling and laying them on a table in front of you. Reach out and touch these feelings. See and feel your hand being burnt.

Watch this glob of feelings turn into a tool that looks like a small chalkboard. See written on the chalkboard a list of habits that you will not put up with. Open your mental toolbox and put your newfound tool in the place made for it. Say these words in your mind ten times. HABITS ARE HABITS I CAN DO WITHOUT! Then say it out loud ten times. Use this tool or you will be burnt again. I do hope that I will heed this message from the great beyond. Thank you Koz.

* * *

Gathering Of Male Hormones

The betting would start and then it would stop and the fight would start. It was man on man a fight to the death. From the time that a person woke up to the time of the kill, the brain was anticipating an up welling of male hormones. The air would be buzzing with chat of the up coming fight. This was not fight day this was the pre-inspection and buying day. They would go to look at the new group of gladiators hoping to find one that would kill. They would be wined and dined and brought to a point where the brain had been pushed aside and the animal gut feelings were in control. The owner of these slaves turned into gladiators knew all the tricks to get past the rational mind and put the animal mind in control. It would start with mind movie games that built up grand visions of owning a champion. The process really started years ago at the end of a whip in a slave galley. A man who was a slave in a slave galley would be glad to do anything to get out even kill. A whisper went out among the slaves there is a buyer aboard he is looking for some gladiators. This is my chance to get out of this hellhole and do something other than die. There were stories of how men that did well in the arena were given their freedom. It was the bite of the whip that brought these men to this point in their lives where life meant all and nothing all in the same thought. They were led from their sleeping bunks into the rowing gallery and chained in. Their performance at the oar would some times mean life or death to them. If they did not perform well in a battle they would go down with the ship being chained to it. They must perform well or they could be killed by the whip. It was not the whip that killed it was the infection in an opened cut made by the whip that would kill you. You had seen it many times a strong man becoming weak and being whipped. Days passed and the infection would take its course and the man would grow weak with fever. The whip would find him again and again until he would go into shock and die. After seeing this happen to someone next to you that you thought was a better man than you the will to get out of there boiled on high heat.

    The whip snapped and the drumbeat started. A richly dressed man stepped onto the viewing and inspection platform, it was show time. Most of the time it was just another day that you must survive through. Today there was a chance to be bought and have a chance of a better life or even a chance of escape to freedom. The chain rattling and the oar thrusting started, anything to bring attention to you so as to be looked at and may be chosen. The finger pointing and the head shaking would let you know which way they were looking and who they were looking at. The drumbeat was sped up to see who would survive this endurance test. The buyer was looking for sprit and endurance and the ability to withstand pain and even ignore it. He after narrowing his selection down would ask to have one of them whipped. He was doing this to test that mans will power and to see if he could ignore pain, to win being bought. Three were bought that day and their lives would be changed. They would be trained for two years in the art of killing their fellow man.

These slaves had traded one taskmaster for another and are now looking to trade again by being bought and owned by a man of money that some day could grant their freedom. This was another day that the slave would have to show his will to fight. Three men were bought that day and they would be sent to a finishing school of killing. Their new taskmaster was one of their own kind. He had done well in the arena and now was training others as a free man. He would use this carrot of freedom daily to get the work outs that he wanted from these men. The games as they were called were only three weeks away there was not much time and the training at times made you wish that you were back on the galley.

I want you to let this story flow over you and I want you to feel the boiling up of the male hormones and pheromones. I want you to let the story and the words fade away only holding onto the feelings. Feel inside yourself this rising level of male hormones and how that it builds a pleasure site in your brain. I want you to linger in this pleasure site and get a good feel of it. I want you to only feel the pleasure that your brain apart from you is feeling. The brain is addicted to this feeling of pleasure and will do anything for another journey to this pleasure site. KOZ: THE CONTROL OF THE MALE HORMONE PLEASURE SITE WILL PUT THE BEAST IN CHAINS. THIS WILL DEVELOP A HIGHER LEVEL PLEASURE SITE AT A HIGHER LEVEL OF THINKING. THIS NEW AND PURER PLEASURE SITE WILL BRING YOU INTO THE FAMILY OF THE GIVING GREATER KNOWN.

I want you to turn your attention away from these goings on and show you a side story to this story. Look to your right and you can see the ladies talking amongst themselves. Focus on what they are saying, come and listen with me. Oh! How strong he looks I wish I had the money to buy that one and put him in my bedroom training camp. I would like to lick the sweat off his armpits and rub my body all over his. I will be bidding high on his vile of scrapings. Come into the back room and see through these words the process at hand. I want you to go into your movie picture mind and really see these happenings letting the words paint a picture in your brain. After the fight to the death is over and the victor returns to his dressing room this little known process takes place. Come with me as we peek thru a crack in the wall. I see them undressing the champion and leading him over to a bench. He sits motionless and says nothing. Cup after cup of water is poured over hot rocks heating up the room. Look at the sweat running of the champion. In come two men caring a basket of odd looking sticks. Look into this basket with me and really look at these sticks. They are about twelve inches long and have a small tube at one end that acts like a cup. Watch real closely to what they are doing. They are using these sticks to scrape the sweat and dirt off of the champion. They hold the stick against the skin at an angle so that the sweat will follow the stick's edge and flow in to the tube at the end of the stick. When the tube is full it is passed on to the second man and he pours these but few drops into a vile. This process goes on until the total first body scraping is finished. The sticks are wiped clean with small pieces of cloth and the clothes are put into bottles. The first scraping done and the process starts over again. They will do five scrapings of this man not caring about his well being or discomfort. From the first whip bite to this moment all was calculated to be able to harvest this body syrup that contains the male hormone and pheromone that is the true prize and value being sought after. The price will be very high indeed for these scrapings. With the brain rolling around in its male hormone pleasure site and the smell of and the applying of this body alisequre your body intelligence is fooled into a state of self-accomplishment.

I have even heard the drinking of these scrapings after they had held it in their mouths for a few minutes. Even the small wiping rages fetched a good price and were worn next to the skin.

I was on Reach One I was not standing their long when I heard a voice calling me," over this way". I looked in the direction that the voice had come from but saw no one. I went in the direction that I had heard the voice come from. I went around a corner and saw a long line of people. They passed by me every one of them shaking my hand. They would walk away from me backwards not taking their eyes off me they would then stop and stare. The room was getting full I felt a tug at my shirt. Then the pushing and grabbing started. I soon found myself standing there with no clothes on and they were pulling at my hair. I was pulled into a side room and given a new set of clothes. I saw one man after another come in behind me with a blank bewilderment look on their face as they were handed their new clothes. KOZ: THE HORMONE COLLECTORS ARE ALL ABOUT YOU IN MANY TYPES OF DRESS. THE THING BEING DONE IS NOT THE THING BEING SOUGHT AFTER ONLY THE MEANS AND THE VEHICLE TO EXTRACT YOUR HORMONES FOR THEIR BENEFIT. SEEK OUT AND PULL IN HORMONES THAT WILL INCREASE YOUR BODY INTELLIGENCES AND LET YOUR BODY PERFORM IN A STATE OF WELL BEING. I sat and wondered a long time about what Koz had me write. I thought of how much some of this reminded me of the military and their games and wondered about what was really going on. It meant for me another tool for my mental toolbox. I want you to see the gathering of hormones and pheromones behind the seen. See all that is being done to reach this end goal of raising their own hormone levels. This awareness is your new tool. See this awareness flow out the top of your head and from into a magnifying glass that has written on the handle " follow the trail of male hormones". Look into your mental toolbox yes there is a spot just made for it. From now on you will be able to stop trying to make sense out of what the boss is doing you will be able to see with this new tool the trail of male hormones. Thank you Koz things sure seem clearer to me now and I am able to do things ignoring the pain of what is being done wrong.

* * *

PUSHERS

I want you to come along with me on a trip-story. I want you to feel the outside pushing me around. I want you to see and feel the power of slipping through the Pushers. Go into your movie picture mind and see a movie from these words. I was on Reach One looking for the right door that would match my shirt. I saw one and I went inside. I was in a long hall way with no doors except one at the end. As I moved towards it seemed to move away from me as fast as I was going towards it. I stopped and it stopped I turned around and started moving back to the door that I had come in. As I walked towards the entrance, it too was moving away from me. I stopped and started to walk backwards the door was following me keeping the same distance. I stopped abruptly when I backed into the door at the end of the hall. I did not turn around I reached behind me, opened the door, and went inside. I turned around and I saw a man standing in front of me. I went to talk to him but he moved away from me as fast as I went towards him. I stopped I looked to my right and their was a table with a collection of magazines and books on it. I walked over to the books and I could see out of the side of my eye that man that I saw was now moving closer. I did not look at him directly but I was watching his every move. I picked up a book and opened it, all the pages were blank. I set the book down and picked up a pamphlet it was blank. I started to fold a bird out of the pamphlet. I could see that the man was close enough that I could reach out and touch him. Behind the man came a woman and she talked to the man and then talked to me. She asked what I was making. I talked through her with words that were for the man. I said some fine words that drew him in closer. " There are not to many men that can fold as I do" I saw the man picking up a piece of paper and trying to copy what I was doing. I was talking to him but not to him. The first step is that I must start out with a square piece of paper. Then I have to fold it corner to corner and crease it well. I reached not for the man but his piece of paper he did not move away. I showed him these folds and we started talking and working together folding a bird. I want you to see the man fade away. I want you to see the woman fade away. Watch as the Pile of books and table melt and flow into the cracks in the floor and disappear. I want you to look around, see nothing, and feel only the process of drawing in not pushing. Reach out into the nothing and grab onto these feelings of drawing things in. Bring these feelings with you as you read these selected words.

  I was getting up out of bed I wanted to talk to my son before he went to work. Yesterday I had been pushing my son away with my words and body movement language. Today I was going to use what I had learnt on Reach One to pull him closer to me not to push him away. The day before he was talking about how that he felt, it would be nice if he could become a residential house electrician. I keyed into this road sign of where his brain was going. I asked him if it would, be all right, if I would look into what classes they offered, at Southeast a local vocational training school. He said some fine words that made my heart sing. I would like to go back to school. I stood there in wonder what had I done so differently this time, that I had not done before in the past. Why was I able to pull in close and really feel like he was listening? All I could think of was thank you Koz for this new tool.

Come along with me as we work together on this production. We are looking at a person and we see into the inside workings of his thoughts. I want you to make sure that your walk around, self, is buried. The Lower Mind easily sees the things I ask you to see. Stay with me as we see things that the eye will never see, but we will see them by using the Lower Minds Inward Looking Eye. I want you to tune-in your Lower Mind Butterfly Net. I want you to see in your minds eye that the holes are getting smaller and smaller in the net. The holes have become so small that you cannot see them and the net looks like a fine piece of silk. Hold your net in one hand and look over to your Mental Toolbox. Open your Mental Toolbox and pull out the magnifying glass that has written on the handle Follow the Path of Male Hormones. Reach out with a third hand grab on to the Challenge tool. Reach out with a fourth hand pull out the Secret Tool. Look into your Mental Toolbox now with your fifth hand and pull out your Neural Soup Strainer. See yourself standing in front of this person at the ready with all these tools in your five hands. Say these words to the letter. "I think that I could help you help yourself if that would be alright with you". Don't say another word stand at the ready with your Lower Mind Butterfly net tuned in. When you hear any kind of words that sound like they are giving you the green light, interrupt them and say these words to the letter. " If I am going to help you must work with me and keep this just between me and you until things come together can you handle that?" You hit him with a mental one two punch the Secret and the Challenge. Now do some mental pumping to establish in his minds eye this thought path. Look through your magnifying glass that has written on the handle Follow the Path of the Male Hormones. See now what I see when I looking through my magnifying glass. See him getting out of his new work truck and saying that he is an electrician. See how that is making him feel all pumped up and full of pride. Now hear what I said to my son. "Yeah; it sure would be nice to jump out of a new truck and be able to say I am an electrician." Know that he saw this picture in his mind. See this mind picture as a chemical electron jumping the gap in a nerve chain in his brain. See this electron getting larger and larger. See it become so large that it is bigger than the brain or the person. I want you to see it change into a locomotive that is moving down a set of tracks. I want you to see which direction it is going in and see yourself in another locomotive in front of it. Look down the tracks be on the look out for anything that might stop you or the train behind you. Think what is there that I could do to keep the thought path clear and do it. KOZ: STOP BEING A PUSHER OF MINDS AND BECOME A NEURAL PATH BLAZER. DRAW THEM IN CLOSE AND BECOME THEIR MENTAL SNOW PLOW. BY DOING THIS YOU WILL BRING IN LARGE AMOUNTS OF MIND ENERGY AND BRING YOURSELF INTO THE FAMILY OF THE GIVING GREATER KNOW. I at times wonder why was I not shown these tools earlier in my life and where I could have been now. KOZ: YOUR BRAIN IS READY ONLY AS IT REACHES HIGHER LEVELS OF THINKING. DO NOT QUESTION THE PROCESS IT IS PURE COSMIC LAW WITHOUT QUESTION. JAIL.

    This was the first time that Koz had used the word that started with the letter J and I felt it burn through my body. I knew that I had let the Middle Mind in and it was messing around where it had no business doing so. I want you to say these words along with me out load. MY MIDDLE MIND WILL NEVER THINK AT A HIGHER LEVEL DO NOT EVEN LET IT TRY.

* * *

HOW WORDS FEEL

I was in trouble, I had totally forgoten about a geography test. The thing that was going to be hard is I only had an hour and a half to study. I was not going to be able to do the Repetitive Exposure on a Non- Scheduled Interval process because there was not enough time. I was really starting to feel a feeling of anxiety flow over me. If it were any other type of a problem, I would just turn it over to a Champion and let them take care of it. KOZ: WHEN THE WORD CHAIN FEELS GOOD AS IT FLOWS OUT OF YOUR MOUTH IT WILL EASILY SLIP INTO THE LOWER MIND AND OUT AGAIN THROUGH THE MIDDLE MIND. USE SOUNDS THAT VIBRATE THE MOUTH CAVITY AND GENTLY MASSAGE THE BRAIN. Koz was now coming to me in a wholly different mode. He was taking direct readings of my want list that I wanted the Higher Mind to go out and gather for me. He was now just as much a part of me as any other thinking process. Out of my mouth came these sounds Bee Daa Faa Gee Laa Mmm Naa Peee Soo Uoo Vee Zeee. I found myself mouthing these sounds repeatedly. I stopped abruptly and I sat in a stupor as now Koz took over my body. I could hear what was being said but not with my ears but thru a brain link. I was sitting chanting at a high rate of speed drawing people my direction. I want you to listen closely as we listen to Koz come from my mouth. Bee Faa Naa, Gee Soo Maa, Bee Naa Laa, Pee Uoo Daa. I sat streaming these sounds as fast as my lips could go and then as if my lips fell off these sounds were only going through my brain. How they feel in your mouth was only a tool, to pick the sounds that the Lower Mind would accept easily. As I was no longer mouthing these sounds other students paid no attention and passed by with out even a look. The thinking speed was now ten to twenty fold of the speaking speed and thirty to fifty times faster than the reading speed. I stood up I only had four minutes to get to class. I sat down, finished the test with a large time differential sooner than anybody else, and had aced it. Every thing that I needed to know was on the tip of my brain. Buffalo, NY was there and so was Jackson, Miss., Baton Rouge, Louisiana, Pierre, SD. I left the classroom drained I found the next bench to sit on and as I was watching the grass fold in the wind I was in the Haze.

 We were floating along at a faster and faster speed. My body, feet first floated in a lying position. I was turned so that I was moving head first in my direction of movement. My body started to roll at a slow speed. I could tell I was rolling but it did not make me sick or uncomfortable. I was being held on high. The only thing that was touching me of these five men was there hands and forearms. All of a sudden, they threw me like a javelin and the rush of speed went through my body. I first felt a touch, than a flowing through me sensation and then I saw the cobwebs passing by. They were of many colors, sizes, and patterns. I was shot through those cobwebs for a long time and then into a mass of Jell-O like substance that slowed me down. I fell into the hands of my five escorts and then was stood up right. I was led over to a chair and a hood with a screen in it was placed over my head. The screen started to show me pictures and then movement until it was a film. The film sped up until there was only a flutter than just a white screen and the hood was taken off. I could see around me other people some with their hoods on and others with them off and others just having them removed. When the last hood was removed, their chairs started to move to form a circle. Looking across the circle I could see that the people across from me had a blue light coming from their eyes. Then I could see a tunnel of light blue almost white light in front of me. This tunnel of light would go to the middle of the circle and then go straight up and back down forming a dome. The ends of these tunnels of light would loop back to the tops of the heads of the people sitting in the circle. Then the dome of light started to rotate in a clockwise direction. At first, the rotation of these tubes of light moved slowly. They went faster and faster until they were a blur and formed a dome of Pure Mind Energy. I felt a tingling rush moving in from the top of my head and out my eyes. I could see people being removed from the circle. As soon as they stood up, they were replaced with a new person. The new persons eyes would in a short period start sending out a light blue tunnel of light and he was now a fully integrated part of the dome of light. Now I want you to really listen to what I have to say next. I am going to set it apart from the rest of the text so you will be able to return easily and reread it.

    I saw a man being sat down to replace a man getting up. He would not sit still and was looking side to side. He was talking and asking questions about what was going on. He was removed and I could see that he was escorted to a side door. Another man took his place in the circle of light.

    (I in turn was replaced and was brought to a room of people that were mingling and talking. I could see their eyes glowing and a blue tunnel of light flowing out of their eyes, meeting with another's, and forming a double arch. When other people would stand and listen the blue light would flow over them as well. I looked to the edge of the room and saw a man not mingling. This man was soon asked to leave and escorted out.)

I was again looking at the grass watching it move with a pattern of non-pattern knowing that I had fallen into the Haze. I wanted to go back the blue light felt so good, how could I get back? KOZ: SEEK OUT AND BECOME A MEMBER OF A BLUE LIGHT CIRCLE. LET THE MIND ENERGY OF THE MANY FLOW INTO YOU. WITHOUT THIS DAILY TRANSFUSION YOU WILL BE MIND STIRRED AND TURN INWARD AND DROP IN A DARK CREVASSE OF THE MIND. USE THE WORD SOUNDS THAT FEEL GOOD COMING OVER THE LIPS. THESE SOUNDS ARE A KEY TO REJOINING A CIRCLE OF BLUE LIGHT. BEING PART OF A MIND ENERGY BLUE LIGHT DOME WILL PUT YOU CLOSER TO JOINING THE COLLECTIVE FAMILY OF THE GIVING GREATER KNOWN. In the past I can only think of a handful of times that I was in the blue light. At the time that I was in the blue light, I did not know that I was and had in the past left the circle of light. I would find myself feeling in the dumps until I would find another circle of blue light. KOZ: THERE ARE MANY CIRCLES OF BLUE LIGHT. BECOME A READER OF BLUE LIGHT DOMES TO CHOOSE A MIND ENERGY FLOW THAT WILL BUILD UP INSIDE YOU. BEWARE OF BLUE LIGHT DOMES THAT ARE DRAINING DOMES AND ARE STEALING YOUR MIND ENERGY AND GIVING NONE IN RETURN. Join with me as I seek out and find, and move from blue light dome to blue light dome. I want you to be a seeker of blue light domes that will fill you with Mind Energy. See yourself as a vessel that fills only so that it can in turn give it away. I want you to go into your past and feel the feelings of being part of a Mind Energy Blue Light Dome. Think about what you were doing and then stop thinking of what you were doing. Let the doing fade away until only the feelings are left behind. See yourself reaching down through the top of your head and pulling those feelings out of the top of your head. See yourself holding these feelings in your arms as if you were carrying a baby. See yourself carrying this bundle of feelings over to your mental toolbox. Look inside you will see a place for it labeled Blue Light Mind Energy Dome. Place your bundle of feelings into this pre-made spot. Think of how this was always there you just had to dust it off and put it into action. I want you to feel the new feelings of how words feel as they pass through your lips. Know that these feelings are a key to entering your next Blue Light Mind Energy Dome. See these feelings come out of your mouth and form a key. Take this key over to your mental toolbox and see that there is a spot for it next to Blue Light Mind Energy Dome.

* * *

SMELL PUSHING

I wished for many years as a young man that I could buy 496 Hewitt St. Santa Rosa Ca. I thought it sure would be nice if I could own the place where I had so many good times. I could push my Lower Mind into a state of relaxation just by being there. The last year that property was owned by my grandparents was 1968-69.

I want you to slip into your movie picture mind, come along, and smell a little story with me. 469 Hewitt St. had many smells to it that made me feel like I was in a place of comfort, protection and relaxation. The one smell that in the late spring and summer that wafts over you're every move is the smell of roses. For me the smell of roses brings me back to happy times. The smell of roses will make me cry inside wanting to go back to my youth when things were so simple and I was so naive.

I was sitting folding roses out of bar napkins, handing

them out to the women. One of the women said that it sure would be nice if I had some rose smelling perfume to put on them. The next day I found myself standing in front of a rack of scented oils looking for a rose scent. I cracked the cap and took a whiff. I found myself looking around the store to see if anybody saw what I had did and if they could see me as me or as a young boy. I say this because that is the way I felt as I smelt the rose oil. I looked back down at the rack of small shinny little bottles and fell into the Haze.

    I was on Reach One standing in a long line which I could not see the end of, in ether direction. Written on a road sign were the words (THE WAY HOME). Along side of a line of people were other people with trays of small bottles. I could see person after person standing in line look at the tray of bottles and shake their head no. I saw one-man point to a bottle and it was handed to him. He opened it and smelled it. In front of my eyes I saw him transform into a different person. I was not seeing this transformation in the physical but in the actions of this man. First, he looked up and down the line of people as he was shaking his head in disbelief. Then he looked around as if he was looking for a guard or teacher that was going to tell him to stay in line. I saw him take a baby step out of line and then get back into line. He took another whiff of his little bottle. He then looked around again and then left the line all together. The line closed up behind him as the people in line gave him a look of you lost your spot what were you thinking. I watched this man being led away and taken out a side door. I too took a smell and was being led out a side door. Written over the door were the words, (SHORT-CUT HOME). Inside this door was my boyhood Grandparent's house with roses in full bloom. I was there only a few minutes and I was looking back at the line of people waiting in line. I looked at these poor people standing in line for something that at any time they could have instantly. I even saw a man pass on and he was taken away on a stretcher. I followed I wanted to see where they were taking him. They went thru a door that had written on it (ROOM OF UNFILLED DREAMS).

"Can I help you with something"? " Yes; I will take this one" handing her my selection of rose oil. There was no way that I was going to leave this secret to my short cut home in the rack. From that day on, I have used smells to push my Lower Mind into a slump down regeneration mode.

I want you to set my story aside. I want you to see it fade away and I want you to put your own story of a peaceful place with its smells in its place. Think of a place of yours and then let it fad away all except the smell of it. Smell this smell with your mind's nose as you remember your blissful past. See yourself standing in front of a rack of scented oils and buying the choice that brings back a rush of good feelings. See the good feelings flow from the top of your head into your selected scent bottle. See yourself walking over to your mental toolbox and opening it up. Look inside it there it is a pre-made spot for your scented oil that has your feelings in it. Add this tool to your mental toolbox and use it often when you need to regenerate. KOZ: MIND STORED THOUGHTS LINKED TO SMELLS ARE A VERY POWERFUL TOOL TO PUSH YOUR LOWER MIND INTO A REGENERATION SEQUENCE. THIS TOOL I GIVE TO YOU IS A TOOL WITH TWO SIDES. YOU MUST NOT LET THIS TOOL BUILD A PLEASURE SITE IN THE BRAIN THAT WILL DRAW YOU DOWN A DARK PATH THAT WILL PULL YOU INTO A STATE OF NOTHINGNESS. USE IT AS A TOOL, NOT AS A PLAY THING. Every time that I want to get a quick regeneration I will stack the smell tool and my place with a large body of homogeneous mass together. The feeling that we have in our youth of lazy days filled with carefree moments is what we are trying to put together in the present. Our mental toolboxes grow heavier, soon they will be full, and this grand journey will leap forward into the realm of the Collective Family of the Giving Greater Known. Stay with me our thought provoking journey has just started.

***

DREAM READINESS

I want to take you to a higher level of brain processing. After thinking of your dream, what you would like to see happen in your future, and the best possible outcome I want you to write it down on a three by five index card. Read this card every night before you go to bed. Go into the Inward Looking Eye That Glimpses the future. After your adjusting or replacing.

I want you to go into your Movie Picture Mind and see in your mind's eye what you have written down on your dream card. I want you to fall asleep seeing these dream pictures move across your Movie Picture Mind. After the first, second and third time that you go thru your mind movies I want you to look for a Dream Pusher. I want you to think of how your future building dream is matching up with your reality. I want you to think about a linkage site for this dream to become part of your life.

I want you to come along with me as I tell you of a dream that was pushed into reality. I want you to feel this process so you can adopt it into your Future Building. I want to show you how to build a dream vacuum. There was a young man that was twenty-five that was looking for a good working mate to build his life with. He sat and only wished and hoped that someone would show up some day. I told him about dream future building and dream vacuums. He dreamed his dream and started to adjust his reality to build a receptor site for his future mate. He saw a problem in the type of car he was driving and upgraded. He also started to keep a neater house. He went as far as even putting stakes in the ground to show where some day that he would like to build a new house and three car garage. He even drew up house plans that had five different floor plans. Now he was on the right path, but there was a lot more to be done. He built up a time line for his education betterment. He was the same person but now his direction in life had a new pushing force behind it. He now had a dream that could capture another persons dream inside of it. He had built a dream vacuum.

 I want you to leave this dream story behind but take the process with you. I want you to use these processes in your own dream future building processes. Come with me now as I tell you of a story of future building crushing. She had just turned fifty and life was not happy. She had left her husband for what she thought was the man of her dreams. She had dreamed this dream many times in the past but did not get ready for the dream. There were so many lose ends that she had doubts of whether or not this new adventure was going to work. She kept a daily journal and wrote in it the happenings and her feelings. She was trying to change her reality on the fly. Some of the things that she was trying to change were habits deeply imbedded into her Lower Mind. She would write about how she could not believe that she was actually living her dream. Now I want you to read and feel the impact of this next thing that she wrote. (I sure hope that I will be able to change fast enough so that I will not push my dream lover away.) She had used the written word, the tool that impresses the Lower Mind into action. With in a month she had pushed herself out of her new dream life and was back to square one starting over again.

 I was looking into the night sky watching the fire works

go off 4 July 2001. I had fallen into the Haze and was on Reach One. I looked to see what color shirt I was wearing. I was not wearing a shirt I was not wearing anything. There were people walking past me but they were not seeing me. I saw them stopping and talking to each other and sometimes going off arm in arm or holding hands. I wanted to get closer so that I could hear what they were saying; as I moved towards them, they moved away. I could see this spacing all around me. It was as if I had a contagious disorder of some sort. A siren blared and a group of five men came and floated me off. We arrived in front of a door that had written on it Dream Works. I went to open the door but it opened on its own. There were people sitting on the floor, in chairs and on couches. They would be setting with their eyes closed and open their eyes and write something down. Some were standing reading a card. I looked to my right and there was a door and on the door were the words Dream Classroom. I went inside and took a seat. There was a screen with a man teaching a class on dreams. Come and sit with me and listen to what he had to say. I want you to judge for yourself what is being said. Now stand at the ready with your Cosmic Butterfly Net to catch some Lower Mind butterflies. Let what you hear go straight into the Lower Mind. Make sure that your Middle Mind is locked up. Now listen to what was being said.

The Lower Mind communicates in mind pictures a system vastly superior to the spoken or written word. If you do not have a mind movie or a dream for the Lower Mind to follow, it grows stagnant and is stuck in a mind looping processes. I want you to find a quite place to sit and start seeing in mind pictures, where you are. I want you to see in pictures inside your mind how your daily routine is going. I want you then to see yourself as a director of a movie with total powers to change this mind movie at will. Start slowly and go over where you are many times. I want you to see your System Lifestyle Circle that you have fallen into. Go around and around in this circle until you find an interaction site that you feel that needs to be exchanged with something that will open up and expand your possibilities and change your life. See in your movie picture mind yourself standing there with a scissors cutting out the segment that you want to change. See this segment fall to the floor. Then I want you to see yourself standing there with your eyes closed dreaming in mind movies the new segment that will replace the one you snipped. See yourself reaching down thru the top of your head, pulling your newly dreamed segment out, and splicing it into your System Lifestyle Circle. Now go around and around in your new System Lifestyle Circle in your mind's eye. See and feel the changes and how this has truly changed your life. KOZ: WHEN YOU CAN AT WILL READ YOUR SYSTEM LIFESTYLE CIRCLE AND MAKE CHANGES THEN YOU WILL HAVE MASTERED THE POWER OF INNER CHANGE. THIS PROCESS WILL SO IMPRESS THE LOWER MIND THAT IT WILL KNOW THAT YOU HAVE GONE INTO A HIGHER THINKING PROCESS AND WILL NOT INTERFERE. YOUR LOWER MIND WILL STAND IN AWE AND NOT TRY TO PUSH YOUR LIFE AROUND BY WANTING TO HOLD ONTO DEEPLY INGRAINED THOUGHT PATTERNS. I myself feel so much more in control over my life and what direction that it is going in. The real power comes from knowing; that because I have mastered the tool of inner change that what ever I changed can also be changed if it is not working for me. When you have reached this level a glow will flow over you and you will be perceived as a person in control of their destiny. I want you to see yourself folding up your director's chair and placing it into your mental toolbox. This tool was always yours. See a ready-made spot for it and how well it fits. See that it is linked to the tool (Change) by a small piece of string. Koz has told me that we have only a few new tools to be reclaimed. We together are at a place of transition. Stay with me as we take this next step into this journey into the great beyond.

* * *

Group Lower Mind Pool

I was blind-sided. I did not know what had hit me. I had let my Lower Minds' deeply ingrained patterns out and tried making my son see them. I was talking about ideas such as owning versus renting a house. I talked about the idea of having a carrier that some day a person could retire from and just not a string of jobs. That life is an on-going building process. That we build our education and our savings in a long drawn out process. This process comes in as little pieces, jerks, and sputters. The parts are so small that they seem unimportant at the time.

I was way off base. I did not recognize the real driving force behind my son's process of life. No amount of words would pull him from a Group Lower Mind Pool that had its own deeply ingrained thought patterns. My words would be like a foreign language not being understood. That all he could hear was I was telling him that he was doing it all wrong. He grew tired of my words and stayed away. He wanted to be swimming in his group pool of how life is to be lived. This Group Lower Mind Pool has such a pull on one's Lower Mind that it is sucked in even when things do not even make sense.

I want you to think about such a process. I want you to feel the pull of the Group Lower Mind Pool and feel the vacuum. I can hear them as I am now writing. They are about a half-mile away. They are going east on highway I-90. I live a quarter mile north of I-90 just about twenty miles west of Sioux Falls, SD. There are the loners and the groups. They are all being sucked into a Group Lower Mind Pool. Listen as this Doctor, Lawyer, Construction Worker expounds on why he is going for hundreds of miles on a motorcycle and spending hundreds of dollars. Listen to a conversation that is based on the pulling of a Group Lower Mind Pool.

Honey you are not going to Sturgis this year are you? We could really use that money that you spend on Mark's braces or paying down our credit card bill. You know that I have planed my vacation and saved two thousand dollars for this trip. I wish that you would get off my ass; you know that I am going to Sturgis. No amount of words that his loving wife could say would change his mind. She tries again. If you could just stay home this year and go next year it would sure ease our money problems. I worked all year for these next two weeks. I give you fifty weeks of my life and you begrudge me taking two for myself. Can you see that this conversation is getting no where. The Group Lower Mind Pool has become an identity of its own. He has been pulled into this vacuum for more years then they have been married.

If she could really see the goings on at this coming together, she would understand its drawing power. The rush starts to build the moment the brain starts thinking of heading that direction. As all the planning falls together and the bike takes you to another world. You start out on your own and then the one becomes the few and then the many. You leave your name and your past life behind and become a different person as soon as you turn the corner of the block that your house sits on. You are known as only Chain Brain and you only know of others by their street name. This using of an alias is a shot of pleasure to the brain on its own. That what ever I do as Chain Brain is apart from who I really am. You hit the local gas mart and things start to fall into place or out of place. You are a very conscientious about your health type of person fifty weeks of the year but anything goes for these two weeks. You are a non-smoker and you don't drink that much not even pop. The helmet was strapped to the sissy bar and your bandanna goes on. Your gas bill is only half of the cost as you load up with a Coke a hand full of candy bars and a box of those Swisher Sweets cigars. You drive many miles by yourself and then it starts. You hit a main route headed for Sturgis. As you pull into a gas station, your every thought is being supported. You see them and they see you as a part of the Group Lower Mind Pool. The small talk starts. How many trips does this make and where do you stay. How and which way do you go and how many miles do you do a day and what is your next stop. Then it comes the link-up. You find a group of people going down the same brain path as you and things start to click. You start acting as a pack member. There are rules of the open road that are as none back in your past reality. Leaders are made by followers and given powers granted to them at the whims of the group. Your rank is that you have no rank. People who like the feelings of (king-making) gave your power to you. In addition, now they can do things at the order of a boss of their own selection. Moreover, at any time you do not like this pack you can peel off in another direction. All you have to say is that your bike is acting funny or that you are going to look up a friend in the next town. You may be picked up by another group or wait to join the mother of all the groups Sturgis. The goings on there can only be experienced. It will be different every time for everyone, only the feelings of being apart from the real world will be the same. Go at the risk of being a slave to a Group Lower Mind Pool that will pull you in without any rhyme or reason.

Let this story of mine melt away, only hold onto the

feelings, see, and feel the pull of the Group Lower Mind Pool. KOZ: GROUP LOWER MIND POOLS CAN ONLY BE PULLED AWAY FROM BY ANOTHER GROUP LOWER MIND POOL THAT HAS A HIGHER VACUUM. DO NOT WASTE YOUR TIME TRYING TO PULL A LOWER MIND AWAY FROM A GROUP LOWER MIND POOL WITH YOUR MIDDLE MIND. BUILD A VACUUM OF ANOTHER GROUP LOWER MIND POOL TO PULL THEM AWAY. I want you to set this story of words aside and only feel the frustration that one feels when you are trying to pull someone away from a Group Lower Mind Pool. Feel this as a fight that you cannot win person to person and see the answer Koz has given to us. Take the feelings and feel them repeatedly in a story from your past. See how people flowed from one vacuum to another. Take these feelings and see yourself reaching into your heart and pulling them out. First take a hand full with your left hand and then take a hand full with your right hand. See these two handfuls of these feelings turn into a paddle lock and a key. Neither one of them any good by themselves. See yourself opening up your mental toolbox and seeing the spot made for them, labeled Group Lower Mind Pools. This tool has always been there now you can use it as you see fit. KOZ: USE IT ONLY FOR GOOD AND BEWARE OF THE DARK SIDE OF GROUP LOWER MIND POOLS.

* * *

Taste Lower Mind Pushing

Taste is a body intelligence that is linked into brain intelligence by trial and error. We have to teach our taste buds to like some tastes and other tastes come in as an immediate, wow that tastes good. Let me take you back in my past and tell you a story of taste that pushed the Lower Mind.

We did not live that far away. We were within stroller pushing distance of the ice cream shop. This was my son's first trip to the ice cream shop. He was so young that words had not come into the picture to spoil his reactions. I could have told him that he was in for a treat and he would have not understood and would not have built up any preconceived ideas. In the first spoon of ice cream went. At first it was the cold sensation that took him and shifted his thoughts. Then as the ice cream melted the taste took over. As soon as the taste was out of his mouth, he was like a little bird looking around for the next spoon full. He was not even willing to let my wife take a bite in between his. When the ice cream was gone and it was time to go home all hell broke loose. We had a little monster on our hands. Taste had twisted his mind and made him into a screaming thrashing force that wanted more of that taste, whatever it was called. At that point in time, if he were the fittest he would have been unstoppable. I thought of a story that my father told me about a bear in Yellowstone Park that got a whiff of some jam in a man's new 1930 Buick Road Master Convertible.

The jam was in the trunk safely locked away. The bear hit the trunk with his paw and it sprung open. The bear proceeded to crawl in and as he did, the trunk lid came down, hit him on the rump, and scared him. He trusted forward and pushed the back seat in and now he was inside the car. He felt trapped, went into a scratch, and bite anything in his way mode. By the time, that he had ripped a hole in the top and was on his way, the car was a total loss. It looked like someone had built a giant eggbeater out of razor blades and turned it loose on the in side of the car.

I was back thinking about my son and what he would of done if he had the strength of a bear. All I could of done was stand and watch as he tore away from us and went through that ice cream shop no holds barred. There would be no way that you could stop his taste drive short of shooting him. Moreover, who's fault was it anyway presenting such a power taste to a beast such as a child or bear.

 Let me take you to the other side of the world and the other side of taste. I had been down town Tokyo antique shopping with my friend Tony, an American service man that had decided to become a national after his tour of duty in the military. He told me that there was a volunteer firefighter's feed going on and it was time for us to head that direction. When we got there they were still pounding rice with large wooden mallets into a gum ball glob of dough. They would grab this ball of rice dough and break it down into chucks that were about five mouthfuls. On went the spices and it was put into a Styrofoam box then handed out to someone with a polite bow. I received one and the woman seeing that I was a foreigner handed me a fork. I took a bite and was immediately looking for a place to spit it out. I felt like I was Tom Hanks in the movie Big trying to spit out the fish eggs or caviar. At that moment I could understand why the president I think it, was Bush got sick trying to eat some food in Beijing home of the famous Peking duck. I was going to eat this rice ball no matter the taste. In went the second fork full and out it came and I found a trash can and with a big smile and bow got rid of it.

 I am now sitting with my camper in a KOA campground typing this. It is 8:38 am Sun. July 22, 2001, and the sun is up and flickering on my laptop screen. I fell into the Haze and was on Reach One. I was a tail wag counter. They had a line of dogs strapped into a wooden frame. A man would give them something to eat, which I could not see and then I would count the dogs tail wages as he was eating it. The feeder called out a number and I wrote it down next to the tail wag count. I was led by a man and was shown to a seat. I was sitting in front of a large monitor screen. I saw a large cat that had three rats backed up into a corner. These rats were not going anywhere they were frozen with fear of the cat. A buzzer sounded and a glob of gook was placed in behind the cat. I want you to see and feel what I saw as a total picture. The noses of the rats went up in the air and things changed. They moved as if they could no longer see the cat. As the cat batted at them, they were all teeth and claws scratching. They went over to the food glob and started to eat with their backs to the cat. The cat was now in the corner frozen with fear of these super rats.

    This reminded me of my youth, remember the boys grabbing for the ice cream bars. I was thinking of not thinking of what I had seen on Reach One when my elbows got stiff and these words flowed out of my mouth. TASTE WILL PUSH THE LOWER MIND, PAST ANY BUILT UP DEEPLY INGRAINED LEARNED PATTERNS. This was the first time that Koz had manifested himself through me in a physical state. It scared me and I wanted to stop writing altogether. I sat for a long time before I started writing. My head felt like it was in a vice. My temples felt like they were burning. KOZ: I WILL FROM NOW ON COME TO YOU IN TWO FORMS THOUGHT AND THE DRIVEN SPOKEN WORD. I was about ready to dump my laptop into the trash dumpster and turn myself over to the physic ward at the V.A. hospital. I no sooner thought those thoughts and these words came out of my mouth. THERE ARE TWO TYPES OF TASTES ONE OF THE TOUNGE AND ONE OF THE BRAIN. YOUR BRAIN HAS TASTED THE POWER OF THE COSMIC LAW MESSAGE FROM KOZ AND NOW IT WILL NOT BE ABLE TO TURN BACK. I sat and thought Koz was right I could not stop now even if I wanted to. My Middle Mind was powerless in the face of such great wisdom.

I want you to think in the present and the past about some tastes that you are letting push your Lower Minds' deeply ingrained thought patterns around. I want you to bring into the present these feelings and how these feelings felt when you were driven to your next hit of beer, cigarettes, or your choice of soda pop. Feel these feelings build up inside your stomach and start to drive you down those paths again. Let the things and tastes fade away and only hold onto the feelings. Feel the feelings of frustration. Now reach into your stomach with both hands and pull these feeling out and see it from into an ice cream cone. See yourself opening your mental toolbox and seeing the spot made for it. Understand that it was a tool that was always yours. This is a very powerful tool if used right. Come with me and watch me use this tool to change my reality by pushing the Lower Mind off center.

I have told myself that I would not be fed if I did not do a writing session for the day. Moreover, if I did my writing, I was allowed go to town and eat whatever I wanted to. What in your life is so important that you can go with out your favorite taste until you have done as much on it as you could that day? Twist this around in your mind until it forms into a self-made game plan to push your Lower Mind into action. I stand in awe of this another great tool that Koz has brought to us. Thank you Koz. Stay with me, are first level of training is almost complete and our journey into the great cosmic beyond will start. We that have chosen this path laid out before us by Koz and have come this far are true members of the Collective Family of the Giving Greater Known.

* * *

Power-Sudo-Power

There he was a small man with a big mouth. In real life, he had always been a step and fetch it person. He retired from the food industry doing grocery store work. This type of work was a task that any young man out of high school could do. After many years of cleaning and stocking, he fell into a management slot just because of time and the lack of anybody else to fill the position. This was his first feel of power and he would become addicted to it. His next area which he could feel power was the controlling of a woman. He was a master of controlling a woman; just ask him, he had been through five wives. The next point of power was being able to push around and brow beat his kids to a point that they will have nothing to do with him.

He is the type of man that boasts of his sexual conquests and how often he was king of the bedroom. The true story is that he has drunk and smoked his manly hood into non-performance. His last three wives had been caught by him in bed with another man or had run away with one. He is not able to work for someone else for any amount of time or have anybody work with him. He started his own clean up fixit business that gave him a position in his own mind of supreme power. If this were, the good old days he would have been ran out of town. Nevertheless, now there are support groups that are looking for such men that love power. They call themselves brotherhoods and are named after some kind of animal. His choice was a large four legged one with big flat horns that is a bottom feeder in swamp bogs and lily ponds.

He was a member in good standing now for the third time; he had quit three times before. He was a good candidate for office for he would spend large amounts of time and money for the taste of power. His past membership record and his ability to spot others looking for power were pluses. The origination got new blood and if they wanted to get rid of the   Buzzard all they would have to do is make some demands down the road that he would not like and he would quit and be out of their hair. Oh yes, this is the type of man I would like in my family??? Orientated futurity. Good with pushing woman and young children around and brow beating anybody else that did not see it his way. In fact, he should be placed in high office for other men to look up to as a leader among men. Ha!

The real shame is the people that support such a boob and are no better themselves in doing so. They are the ones that give him his power and the ones that could take it away. Their giving of their Mind Energy, build such a monster every one of them that pays lip service to him, and pay their dues. KOZ: BE CAREFUL WHOM YOU SUPPORT WITH MIND ENERGY THEY MAY BECOME AN UNWANTED TAKER OF YOUR MIND ENERGY. DO NOT GIVE WITH SMILE OR THE SHAKE OF HAND TO THOSE THAT ARE NOT GIVERS. LOOK BENEATH THE COAT INTO THE HEART TO SEE THEIR BLACKNESS. BRUSH THEIR WORDS ASIDE AS IF CHASING A FLY AWAY FOR THEY ARE HOLLOW AND FALSE. LOOK FOR THE TRUE STORY NOT HIS WORDS THAT LEED YOU ASTRAY.

I will track and follow this man's path through life to see if these words are true. Whom else will he use up to a point that they have lost touch with reality? Who will be his next ex-wife who he is looking for right now? I want you to leave my story behind and search your past for a like story. I want you to feel how you felt being a victim of such a man. I want you to let your story fade away and only hold onto the feelings. Let these feelings build up inside of you until you feel like you would like to punch that person. See yourself reaching into the frontal portion of your brain were it is now aching and pull these feelings out. See them form into a small carpet. Look into your mental toolbox and place this new tool in the spot made for it labeled Carpet Pulling. The next time you run into such a person you will pull your carpet of Mind Energy out from under him before he craps on it.

I was on Reach One I went through a blue door. I saw a man standing on a carpet. He reached down and pulled the carpet out from underneath himself one time after another. Around this man were people winding up balls of string. The string was coming from the carpet the man was standing on. Soon the carpet was gone and he was off looking for another carpet. When he found his new carpet, he would start pulling it out from underneath himself again. Soon a group of people would start to wind up balls of string from his newly found carpet.

Let this trip and its meaning flow past your Middle Mind and let it settle into your Lower Mind. Your Lower Mind will see the meaning and actions will follow without thought. When your Lower Mind starts to see other Lower Minds winding up string it will too. This process is a natural one that is based on cosmic law. The carpet pullers can't stand behind falsehoods, truth will prevail. As the string winders wind the carpet gets smaller and smaller and it is easer for the false person to pull it out from under himself and go into an I quit mode.

See yourself as a string winder and you with the many will pull down false leaders. I again thank Koz for showing me this new very powerful tool. KOZ: THIS TOOL MUST ONLY BE USED IN TRUTH. THE UNRAVELING OF A TRUE MAN'S CARPET WILL TAKE MIND ENERGY FROM YOU AND SHRINK THE SIZE OF YOUR CARPET ON WHICH YOU STAND.

I have seen many times these types of men that are power hungry. When I have a run in with them, I need not take any action. All I need to do is to stand aside and watch them self-destruct. I have seen them lose their jobs; wives and some have gone to prison. I have even seen the final quit when they committed suicide. Stand with Koz and me and watch the carpet pullers pull their life out of themselves.

***

Mobious Strip Cutting

I have brought you to a place that is no where out there. The place that I have brought you to is an inner place. This journey has been an inner space journey bringing things to light. Now step to the other side of the inner. I want you to see how much that there is yet to go of this journey. The exercise that I am now taking you through will enlighten you. I want you to see the testing as a self-testing and an understanding of what is not understood. I want you to see the limits of even the great brain that you have. I only do this to stretch your thinking. To let you know from within what is not there. I need you to look for a one dimensional plain that is flexible and of the same color on the other side. I will be doing this test along with you. Follow my lead and do as I do. I am going to stop writing to find a sheet of notebook or typing paper, ink pen, scissors and some Scotch tape. I want you to stop reading now and get these things. Without these things, you will not be able to follow me into the next stage of this journey.

Take the paper and fold it in half lengthwise. Crease it many times folding it first one way then the opposite way. Now tear the sheet in half along this crease. Do this procedure again until you have a strip of paper one forth the width and a full length of the sheet. Lay this piece of paper in front of you on a flat surface. I want you to look as if you had never seen a piece a paper before. See how thin it is and so flat. I want you to see that it takes up hardly any space at all. Place the paper length wise up and down in front of you. Move your eyes to the thin top edge. I want you to think of how the paper ended there. I want you to pick this piece of paper up, lift it over your head, and drop it behind your back. Retrieve the piece of paper and set it in front of you again on the flat surface. Which end of this piece of paper were you looking at before? With out some kind of a mark you would be lost. Now take the ink pen and mark the top edge with the letter A. Now look to the bottom edge and see that it also stops. Since this edge is in the same dimensional plain I want you to also mark it with the letter A. Now turn the paper over and mark the top and bottom edges with the letter B. hold the paper up in front of you the (A) side facing you. I want you to think in your mind how the bottom letter will end up if you were to push it backwards until it met the top edge making a circle. After doing this you can see that, both (As) are up side right one on top of the other. Turn this circle of paper to the side and you can see in the inside that the B's are stacked one on top of the other. Hold the bottom A in place and turn the top A around until you see the B on the other side above the A. Slip the A over on top of the B thus lapping the edges a half inch. Take some Scotch tape and tape both the inside and outside edges. You have just created a mobious strip. Look at it, see how now that it fills space and has a form. I want you to look for the B's and see that they have disappeared and have now become part of the A plane that is no longer one dimensional. Take your ink pen and draw aline in the center of the strip under the A the full length of the strip. You will notice that you come to the second A and must keep on going to get back to the first A. This will let you see that the B plane did merge with the A plane and there was no loss in their surface areas except for the overlap.

I want you to think of how this form would change if you were to cut along the line that you just drew. Would it become two linked together or one large one. Write down what your mind has come up with. Take your time and think this out before cutting. Now cut it. Was your mind right, did it know that it was going to become a larger double looped mobious strip or did it have no clue? Now do it again. Mark down the center of the strip and cut it. Before doing this again think of what will be its next form. Did your mind foresee what you would come up with two double looped strips linked together or did it not have a clue? Cut both of these double looped strips again. Did your mind come up with that you would now have four all looped into each other. In addition, did your mind ask why did the first time we cut it, it got larger and the next two times they were doubled. Bring your four inter-locked loops with you on this journey they will be a key to unlocking your mind in the future. KOZ: YOUR MIND DOES NOT HAVE ON ITS OWN WHAT IT TAKES TO JOIN THE COLLECTIVE FAMILY OF THE GIVING GREATER KNOWN. YOU MUST GET TO REACH TWO. I looked at my multi looping mobious strip and fell into the Haze I was on REACH TWO. I hope that you will join me there. Our journey has just started. Do not be left behind make this leap with KOZ and me into a higher level of thinking.

SEE YOU ON REACH TWO
THE BEGINNING

INDEX

A Place to Regenerate	156
Banana Food	119
Best Outcome	226
Body Language	43
Brain Wave Control	174
Brain Future Building Tool	195
Brain Stalling	242
Brain Stirring	87
Challenge	22
Champions	29
Change Inside	178
Change	126
Choice Directing	47
Circles of Influence	99
Collective Lower Mind Pressure	66
Copan	11
Copy Cat	252
Cosmic Seeding	217
Cosmic Oceans	223
Cosmic Shortcut	21
Cosmic Lookout	41
Dislodging An Entrenched Lower Mind	64
Dream Readinesses	318
Dream Within A Dream-Mind Energy Stacking	27
Fasting	239
Fear Of The Watchers	91
Fishing Trip	13
Fist Push	149
Focus Inward	113
Gap of Change	140
Gathering of Male Hormones	302
Generation Jumping	263
Group Lower Mind Pool	322
Guardian At The Gate	20

Guess Link	280
Have No Conflicts	18
Head Pounding	110
Hose Draining	209
How Words Feel	311
Hurt Time Factor	188
Inner Small Talk	283
Inner Stray Voltage	143
In The Beginning	1
Internal Brain Shift	23
Internal Body Knowledge	39
Inward Looking Eye	20
Judgment	37
Laughter	32
Leakage Soup	49
Left Brain Right Brain Shift	30
Letting Habits Rule	298
Lost And Re-Found	245
Lower Mind To Lower Mind Communication	55
Lower Mind Pumping	69
Lower Mind Focusing	60
Lower Mind Butterfly Catching	160
Lower Mind Transfusion	56
M.O.R.T.	136
McCross Boys Ranch	185
Mall Window Looking	167
Melding Of Ideas	12
Mind Energy	24
Mind Take Over	170
Mind Number Blowing	206
Mind Puzzle	266
Mind Wedge	295
Mirror	164
Mobious Strip Cutting	333
Money Looping	106

More Than One	256
Movies	34
Moving Body Language	289
Music	33
Neural Cobwebs	232
New Car Project	198
Not Alone	17
Opportunity Positioning	273
Outside Change	102
People Needing Help	2
Power Of Oneness	28
Power-Sudo-Power	330
Preaching and Teaching	26
Pure Question	45
Pushers	307
Putting Yourself Last	10
Reality Within A Reality	213
Repetitive Exposure	154
Replication	249
Reticular Activating System	286
Reunion	77
Rock The Rock	75
S.O.L.E.	219
Saturation Points	260
Scared	19
Secret	23
Seeing The Not And Nothing	192
Self Asking Question	25
Self-Made Rules	182
Shift To Non-Reality	133
Slow Lower Mind Shifting	53
Smell Pushing	315
Speck Of Pepper	8
State Of Nothingness	36
Stopping	15
Suspend Fear	152

Sycophant Looping	80
Taste Lower Mind Pushing	326
Ten Feet Tall	5
That's Just Like	270
The Key To Knowledge Of The Giving Greater Known	236
The Nothing As Something	229
The Power Of Truth	276
The Wrong Bus	11
The Giving	14
The Future Reunion	84
The Shield	96
Thinking Bad Or Negative	10
Thumb Pinch	129
Time Line	123
Triad The Power Of Three	71
What I Have Quit Doing	9
When The Wind Blows	292
Word	16
Yes-No Rebound	17